0

introduction to phonology

introduction to phonology

CLARENCE SLOAT
SHARON HENDERSON TAYLOR
JAMES E. HOARD

/ *University of Oregon*

PRENTICE-HALL, INC., *Englewood Cliffs, N.J.* 07632

Library of Congress Cataloging in Publication Data

SLOAT, CLARENCE
    Introduction to phonology.

    Bibliography: p. 189
    Includes index.
    1. Grammar, Comparative and general—Phonology.
I. Taylor, Sharon Henderson   joint author.
II. Hoard, James E.   joint author.
III. Title.
P217.S57   414   77–23100
ISBN 0–13–492207–7

© 1978 by Prentice-Hall, Inc., *Englewood Cliffs, N.J.*   07632

Printed in the United States of America

10   9   8   7   6   5   4   3   2   1

Prentice-Hall International, Inc., *London*
Prentice-Hall of Australia Pty. Limited, *Sydney*
Prentice-Hall of Canada, Ltd., *Toronto*
Prentice-Hall of India Private Limited, *New Delhi*
Prentice-Hall of Japan, Inc., *Tokyo*
Prentice-Hall of Southeast Asia Pte. Ltd., *Singapore*
Whitehall Books Limited, *Wellinto 1 , New Zealand*

contents

3 PHONETICS: CONSONANTS   27

4 SYLLABLES   56

5 PROSODIC ELEMENTS   70

6 DISTINCTIVE FEATURES AND NATURAL CLASSES   82

7 NATURALNESS 99

8 NATURAL PROCESSES 112

9 MORPHOLOGY AND PHONOLOGY 125

10 PHONOLOGICAL RULES 141

11 PHONOLOGICAL METHOD 167

preface

This is a book intended for beginners. It is also a book on a very complex subject—phonology. Our primary aim in writing it has been to make the facts, assumptions, and issues of phonology accessible to those with limited experience in the area. Because it is an introductory text, it focuses on fundamental matters. It does not purport to take its readers to the frontiers of research: even well-charted terrain can seem rough and rocky to those unfamiliar with it.

To show that the principles of modern phonology can be generally applied, we have provided examples and problems from a wide range of languages. The examples from the Northwest Indian languages Coeur d'Alene, Quileute, and Puget Salish (Nisqually and Skagit dialects), given without reference, are from the field notes of the authors. For the remaining examples, we are grateful to those scholars whose works are cited throughout the text.

Chapters 1 to 5 introduce the basic phonetic concepts necessary for the study of phonology. Because we wish this work to be a practical guide for the beginning phonologist, we have spent a good deal of time on articulatory phonetics, a subject basic to all aspects of phonology. We have not, however, taken up acoustic phonetics. It is too large and technical a subject to be treated in the limited amount of space we could have afforded it.

Chapters 6 through 11 build on the phonetic concepts of the first five chapters and provide an introduction to modern phonological theory and analysis. The basic premises of modern phonological theory derive especially from the work of Morris Halle and Noam Chomsky. Many phonologists have extended Chomsky and Halle's work in a variety of ways. We have not adopted any one of these extensions in the text and have tried to avoid taking controversial stands wherever possible. Where we have taken theoretical positions, they are in the spirit of modern generative phonology. However, by far the greater part of the book presents information essential to phonological investigation regardless of one's theoretical stance.

There has been no attempt to introduce the reader to the full range of possible applications of phonology. We feel that one-chapter treatments of sociolinguistics or historical phonology are not a profitable use of space in an introductory text. This space can be used better to concentrate on the bases of phonology. In lieu of such discussions, we have provided a list of suggested readings in various areas, through which students can pursue their particular interests.

In all, we have attempted to write a book which will enable the beginning phonologist to read the phonological literature, to undertake competent phonological analysis, and to understand the analyses of others.

We wish to thank the University of Oregon for its generous assistance in the preparation of the manuscript; and we extend special thanks to Joan Swanson and Arlene Rose for their excellent work in typing it. Additional thanks goes to Arlene Rose for her work in preparing the index. We are indebted also to the many students who gave thoughtful comments on various versions of this work. We have profited from their suggestions.

introduction to phonology

1 the study of phonology

1.1 INTRODUCTION

Phonology is the science of speech sounds and sound patterns. Each language of the world—English, German, Chinese, Navaho, Swahili, or any other—has its own sound pattern. By a sound pattern we mean (1) the set of sounds that occur in a given language, (2) the permissible arrangements of these sounds in words, and (3) the processes for adding, deleting, or changing sounds.

Although all languages share certain basic properties, it is highly unlikely that any two languages have exactly the same sound pattern. Sound patterns may differ in three ways: (1) the sound inventories may be dissimilar, (2) the sounds may occur in different orders, and (3) the rules or processes that affect sounds may be different.

The sound patterns of German and English, for example, are distinct in all of these ways. German has vowel sounds written with the letters *ü* and *ö*, as in *fünf* 'five' and *können* 'to be able to', that do not ordinarily occur in English. On the other hand, English has consonant sounds spelled with *th*, as in *thin* and *this*, that do not occur in German. Clearly, then, the speech sound inventories of English and German are not the same.

The permissible combinations of speech sounds in English and German are also different. German has initial consonant clusters of *kn*, as in *Knabe* 'boy' and *Knie* 'knee', that are pronounced as they are written. English does not have the initial sound sequence *kn*. (The English words *knave* and *knee* are spelled with *kn* but the initial *k* is not pronounced.) On the other hand, English has initial clusters that do not normally occur in German: the initial *st* and *sp* clusters of *stop* and *spot* are examples. (German words like *Stadt* and *spielen* are pronounced as if they began with *sht* and *shp*.)

Finally, the sound processes of English and German are different. German words written with final *b*, *d*, and *g* are pronounced as if they ended with *p*, *t*, and *k*. For example, *Dieb* 'thief' is pronounced as if it ended with a *p*. Similarly, *Hund* 'dog' is pronounced with a final *t* and *Tag* 'day' with a final *k*. However, if an ending is added to each of these basic words, the *b*, *d*, and *g* are pronounced as spelled. English, of course, does not substitute the sounds *p* for *b*, *t* for *d*, and *k* for *g* in final position, as the words *bib*, *bid* and *big* illustrate.

We have so far noted several of the many ways that the patterned interaction of German sounds differs from that of English sounds. A comparison of any two of the world's languages will reveal such differences. However, the sound patterns of English and German also share many characteristics, as indeed do the sound patterns of all languages. For example, all languages have as part of their sound inventories both vowels and consonants; in all languages these vowels and consonants are arranged into syllables; and all languages have syllables at least some of which consist of a single consonant followed by a vowel (as in English *to* and *tea* and German *da* 'then, there' and *See* 'lake, sea').

Characteristics such as these, which are common to all languages, are called **true linguistic universals**. Features found in almost all languages of the world are called **near universals**. For example, nearly all languages have the sound that is represented in English by the letter *n* (as in *noon*), although a few languages (for instance the American Indian languages Quileute and Puget Salish) do not.

Sometimes the presence in a language of one feature implies the presence of another. For instance, if a language has the sound represented by the *d* in the English word *deer*, it will almost certainly have the sound represented by the *t* in *steer*. The situation in which the presence of one feature in a language implies the presence of another is called an **implicational universal**.

Linguistic universals of all three types reflect certain principles that determine the general nature of language. Phonologists are just as concerned with understanding these general principles as with providing descriptions of the phonological systems of particular languages.

1.2 THE PHONETIC BASIS OF
PHONOLOGICAL DESCRIPTIONS

In the German example above, the sounds represented by the letters *p*, *t*, *k*, *b*, *d*, and *g* are not a random collection. All are made by interrupting the airstream completely. Technically, sounds made in this way are called **stops**. The stops in the German example are made by stopping the airflow at one of three places in the mouth: *p* and *b* are made by closing the lips; *t* and *d* by pressing the tip of the tongue against the gum ridge; and *k* and *g* by pressing the back of the tongue against the soft palate.

Further, in the production of *b*, *d*, and *g* the vocal cords vibrate, whereas in the production of *p*, *t*, and *k*, they do not. Sounds made with accompanying vocal cord vibration are called **voiced** sounds; those without are said to be **voiceless**. Terms such as *voiced, voiceless,* and *stop* come from the branch of linguistics called articulatory phonetics. **Articulatory phonetics** is concerned with defining and classifying speech sounds according to how they are produced. Using phonetic terminology, we can now say that *b*, *d*, and *g* are voiced stops and that *p*, *t*, and *k* are voiceless stops.

As you can see, phonetics points up facts about how sounds are made and gives names to these facts. By using the terminology phonetics provides, we can describe how sounds are distinguished from one another and class together sounds sharing a particular mode of production. Phonetic classes are relevant to the statement of phonological rules. For instance, the pronunciation of the final stops in the German examples *Dieb, Hund,* and *Tag* of section 1.1 can be simply described by means of a general rule using phonetic classes: as the last sound of a word, a voiced stop becomes the voiceless stop made in the same place in the mouth.

Because the groups of sounds that enter into rules are not random, we can state rules in terms of phonetic properties. A random group of sounds, say *a*, *t*, and *f*, is not expected to enter into a rule precisely because such a group of sounds will not share appropriate phonetic properties. We do not simply list the sounds that take part in a process but specify the phonetic class the sounds comprise. In the German case we noted that *b*, *d*, and *g* are voiced stops (a nonrandom group of sounds), and that when final they are pronounced as the corresponding nonrandom group of voiceless stops *p*, *t*, and *k*.

1.3 THE PSYCHOLOGICAL BASIS OF PHONOLOGY

In the preceding section we discussed the phonetic (or physical) aspect of phonological descriptions. Phonology also has a psycholoigcal aspect. Even though phonetics can identify many properties of speech sounds, only certain of these properties play a role in phonology.

For instance, with appropriate instruments, precise values for the length, loudness, and pitch of sounds can be measured. We speak of these values as measurements of absolute length, absolute loudness, and absolute pitch. However, within rather wide limits, these absolute values seem to play no role in phonology. Speaking at a rate of x words per minute conveys the same message as speaking at, say, $x+10$ words per minute or at $x-10$ words per minute.

Absolute loudness is also irrelevant to the study of phonology. So far as understanding speech is concerned, it generally makes no difference where the volume level is set on a radio or television as long as the volume is high enough to be audible but not so high as to be annoying or painful. Neither does absolute pitch play a role in phonology. Men's voices are typically pitched lower than women's voices. However, the meaning of a word or sentence does not show any systematic change if spoken first by a man and then by a woman, despite the fact that the absolute pitch at which the word or sentence is uttered will usually be quite different in each case.

Although the absolute values of length, loudness, and pitch are not important in phonology, the relative values of these properties play a significant role. By a relative value, we mean a comparison of absolute values. We speak of sounds as being longer (or shorter) than other sounds, as being louder (or softer) than other sounds, or as being higher (or lower) in pitch than other sounds. Relative values can be expressed as ratios: half as long, twice as loud, an octave higher, and so forth.

Relative length, relative loudness, and relative pitch play a role in English. Contrast the noun *rébel* with the verb *rebél*. The first syllable of the noun *rebel* is longer, louder, and higher in pitch than its second syllable. The situation is reversed for the verb *rebel*, where the second syllable is more prominent than the first. The differences in relative length, loudness, and pitch play a part in distinguishing the noun and verb forms of *rebel*. Similar differences in syllable prominence (that is, differences in relative length, loudness, and pitch) serve to distinguish the nouns *insult* and *insert* from their corresponding verbs.

The fact that the relative values of length, loudness, and pitch play a significant role in language while their absolute values do not, indicates that the mind is disposed to consider some aspects of sound as more significant linguistically than others. Within the range of sounds that are linguistically significant, this disposition seems to constrain quite narrowly both the kinds of sounds that can occur in human language and their arrangement in words. Moreover, this disposition narrowly limits the kind of phonological processes that can occur in languages. If there were no such dispositions, a much wider range of processes would logically be expected to occur than is actually observed. We are thus led to conclude that human beings are genetically programmed to accept certain sounds and processes as relevant to language and to reject all others. This psychological bias on the part of speakers accounts for the remarkable similarities to be found in the phonological systems of culturally diverse and unrelated languages.

The mind's predisposition toward certain sounds and rule types is part of the subject matter of phonology. Just as physically based phonetics has a role in phonology, so does the psychologically based preference for certain sounds and certain processes. By investigating a variety of languages and the rules they contain, it is possible to determine which sounds and processes are most basic and natural to language. In Chapters 7 and 8 we will discuss naturalness in some detail with respect to both sounds and processes.

1.4 GENERAL PRINCIPLES OF PHONOLOGY

Since naturalness is part of the subject matter of phonology, it follows that phonology has two main goals: the first is to set forth the general principles which characterize all languages, and the second is to write adequate descriptions of the sound patterns of particular languages. By formulating phonological principles we can explain the limitations on phonological inventories, on the order of sounds, and on the processes which are observed in the world's languages.

As we noted in section 1.1, language inventories are limited in various ways. For example, both the set of consonants and the set of vowels in a language must include certain types of sounds. The set of consonants seems always to include at least two voiceless stops. This means that a language ordinarily will not have voiced stops, like *b* and *d*, without having voiceless stops, like *p* and *t*. Similarly, the set of vowels almost always includes the *a* of *father* or *spa*. Nearly all languages also have the sounds written with *i* in *machine* and *u* in *Hindu*. Moreover, languages apparently do not have the vowel of *grey* unless they also have the *i* of *machine*. From what we have just noted about sets of consonants and vowels, we can say that large sound inventories are orderly expansions of smaller inventories. We saw in section 1.2 that phonological rules involve nonrandom phonetic classes of sounds. We can now add that sound inventories are not random collections of sounds but are made up of well-defined subsets of phonetic elements. These subsets are defined on phonetic and psychological bases. The psychological bases, however, are not nearly as well understood as the phonetic ones.

In addition to restrictions on inventories of sounds, there are restrictions on the orders in which sounds can occur in a given language. The permissible orders are generally quite limited. The simplest and most natural arrangement is the alternation of consonants and vowels in the pattern consonant-vowel-consonant-vowel . . ., so that every syllable (and every word) begins with a single consonant and ends with a vowel. This arrangement is the only one permissible in Hawaiian (at least for words said in isolation).

Less natural, but still very common, is the situation in languages such as English. English has many words with the pattern consonant-vowel-consonant, as in the words *dog, cat, man, top, pan,* and *nut,* and many others containing consonant clusters, as in *stream, glimpse, ask, splint,* and *shred.* English consonant clusters are quite limited in the sounds they may contain, however. For example, no more than three consonants may occur at the beginning of a word. Further, when three initial consonants do occur, the first must be *s.* Initial clusters such as *fts, zdl, mtr,* and the like are not permissible in English. Apparently they are less natural than clusters such as *str* and *spl.* Languages that permit consonant clusters of more than three members are rather uncommon. One such language is the American Indian language Coeur d'Alene, which has initial consonant clusters of up to five members.

The arrangement of sounds in words is often limited in other ways as well. Another common limitation is that every word must contain at least one vowel-like segment. In English, only interjections like *pst!* and *sh!* consist entirely of consonants. The American Indian language Bella Coola has a fairly large number of words that consist only of consonants. But this is an extreme case; and even in Bella Coola most words have at least one vowel, and there are no words consisting entirely of stop consonants. In English, there are limitations on the co-occurrence of certain vowels with certain consonants in the same syllable. The vowel of *house,* for example, does not occur before a final *b, p, m, f,* or *v.* There is thus no word like German *Raum* 'room' in English. In Proto-Indo-European (a prehistoric language which has been reconstructed by linguists) there was a limitation on the co-occurrence of consonants. No monosyllabic word could contain two voiced stops. There were, then, no words like English *bud* and *dig* which begin and end with voiced stops.

The phonological processes that occur in languages are also quite limited. Apparently no language has a rule that completely reverses the order of sounds in a word or a rule that inserts some sound, say *b,* between each two adjacent sounds of a word. On the other hand, the German rule which changes voiced stops to voiceless stops in final position is quite natural, since the silence or pause which can occur after the last sound of a word has been uttered is characterizable as voiceless. This means that final stops in German become more like the voiceless pauses that sometimes follow them.

The inverse rule—that is, a rule whereby voiceless stops become voiced stops before a pause—is apparently impossible. The use of the word *impossible* here is not to be understood in purely physical terms, nor is there anything illogical about the inverse of the German rule. Rather, the inverse of the German rule is apparently excluded as a possible phonological process on psychological grounds, since such a rule would violate the basic design of languge.

One of the important goals of linguistic research, then, is to discover the general principles which limit phonological inventories, orders of sounds, and processes. Through the detailed investigation of many languages it should ultimately be possible to state these principles precisely and with some confidence. Even from our present vantage point it is clear that all phonological systems are highly organized and highly constrained.

Phonologies of particular languages are explained, rather than merely described, only if they can be related to general phonological principles. Consider this analogy from physics. One can easily describe a man leaping from a boat toward a dock without securing the boat. A typical result is that the boat moves rapidly away from the dock and the man falls in the water. Such descriptions are interesting and can assume many forms. In physics, however, the event has a prescribed description as an instance of a general principle. The principle is, of course, that each action has an equal and opposite reaction. The general principle provides an explanation for the event described. It also provides a basis for the recognition of further instances of the phenomenon. In other words, it provides us with a means of explaining and interpreting events. In just the same way a description of the phonology of a language can be viewed as an instance of general principles.

Another way of viewing general scientific principles, in both physics and linguistics, is to say that they have predictive power. In physics, given the principle of equal and opposite reaction, we can predict what will happen in appropriate circumstances (as in our example of the man in the boat). Given general principles of phonology, we can predict a great many things about the sound systems of languages not previously observed or described by linguists.

1.5 APPLICATIONS OF PHONOLOGY

Information gained in the investigation of phonology, besides being interesting in its own right, has many possible applications. Because the phonology of a language constitutes a highly organized system of knowledge, the study of phonology provides information to those interested in the psychology of cognition and in epistemology. Both cognitive psychologists and epistemologists are interested in explaining how a learner can acquire such a system. They are also interested in the nature of the system itself, particularly as it relates to other systems of knowledge, belief, and expectation. In its search for the general principles which explain phonological systems, then, linguistics forges a strong link to psychology and philosophy.

A further, very important application of phonology is in the teaching of foreign languages. Here both descriptions of particular languages and general properties of phonology are pertinent. Clearly, an insightful description of the phonological system of a language can be valuable to a teacher of that language. In addition, the general theory of phonology may help instructors by allowing them to take certain aspects of phonology for granted in any language. Also, good phonological descriptions of the native language and of the target language (the language to be learned) can enable teachers to study the two languages contrastively, thus providing a blueprint for the development of an effective pedagogy. Such a blueprint can tell the teacher which aspects of the target language differ from and which are the same as those of the native language. The teacher can then have students concentrate on mastering the dissimilar aspects.

1.6 SUMMARY

Each language has its own unique sound system. Individual sound systems may differ from one another in three main ways: (1) in their sound inventories, (2) in the sound sequences they permit, and (3) in their phonological processes. One goal of phonology is to describe these differences. But phonology has another goal as well: that of stating the general principles which determine the characteristics of all sound systems.

Phonology has both a physical and a psychological aspect. The physical aspect is dealt with in the study of phonetics; the psychological in the study of naturalness.

The information gained from phonology has applications in a number of areas, both practical and theoretical. Among these are applications to psychology, philosophy, and the teaching of foreign languages.

2 phonetics: vowels

2.1 INTRODUCTION

The science of phonetics provides descriptions and classifications of speech sounds. Phonology employs these descriptions and classifications to describe sound systems and explain sound processes. Traditionally, speech sounds have been described and classified in terms of their articulation. In this chapter we will be concerned primarily with the articulation of vowels.

2.2 THE ORGANS OF ARTICULATION

Most speech sounds (and all of those in English) are normally made with outgoing breath which exits the lungs and passes through the vocal tract. The **vocal tract** comprises the larynx, the pharynx, and the oral and nasal cavities, as shown in Figure 2.1. Toward the back of the oral cavity is the soft palate or **velum**. The back portion of the velum can be moved up and down. Sounds produced by raising the velum, thus closing off the nasal cavity and directing all of the airstream into the oral cavity, are called **oral** sounds. When the velum is lowered, all or some of the airstream is

9

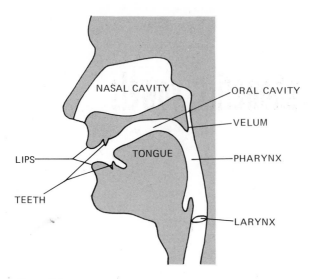

Figure 2.1
The Vocal Tract

diverted through the nasal passages and resonates in the nasal and sinus cavities to produce **nasal** and **nasalized** sounds.

Of all the various components of the vocal tract the tongue is the most mobile. It is possible for the tongue to assume a number of shapes and positions within the vocal tract. These shapes and positions are of paramount importance in the production of vowels.

2.3 BASIC VOWELS

Vowels are speech sounds made by shaping the oral cavity while allowing free passage of air from the lungs. The primary criteria for the classification of vowels are: (1) the distance between the top of the tongue and the roof of the mouth and (2) the retraction or extension of the tongue.

The first of these criteria is defined in terms of the relative openness of the oral cavity. Closeness and openness generally correspond to lesser and greater jaw opening respectively, as well as to the relative height of the tongue. Those vowels that are articulated with the top of the tongue relatively near the roof of the mouth, and with a narrow jaw opening, are called **close vowels**. Those made with the top of the tongue relatively far from the roof of the mouth and with a wide jaw opening are called **open vowels**. You can get the feel of the distinction open/close by pronouncing the vowels of *bah* (as in *Bah! Humbug!*) and *bee*. Say only the vowel sounds, omitting the consonant. Notice how much more open the mouth is for *ah* than for *ee*. The vowels with the most open articulation are called **low vowels**; those with the closest articulation are called **high vowels**. The vowel of *bah* is low whereas that of *bee* is high.

Tongue retraction and extension also play a role in vowel production. Imagine the tongue to be divided into three parts from front to back. The anterior part, which is not attached to the floor of the oral cavity, is called the **front** or **blade**. The posterior part is called the **back** or **dorsum**. The main or central part of the tongue is called the tongue **body**. Retracting the tongue body causes a concentration of the tongue's mass in the dorsal region. Extending the tongue body distributes its mass more uniformly. Vowels with tongue body retraction are called **back vowels**. The vowel of *boo* is a back vowel since it has considerable tongue retraction. Contrast this vowel with the vowel of *bee*, which lacks tongue retraction and has the tongue extended forward. Vowels made with the tongue body extended toward the front of the oral cavity are **front vowels**.

The parameters high/low and front/back intersect to produce four vowel classes: high front, low front, high back, and low back. The extreme high front vowel is symbolized [i]. The extreme low front vowel is symbolized [æ]; this symbol is called **digraph-a** or **ash**. The extreme high back vowel is symbolized by [u]; and the extreme low back vowel by [ɑ], called **script-a**.

These symbols represent part of a special orthography called a **phonetic alphabet**. When they are used to indicate—more technically, to **transcribe**—a pronunciation, they are enclosed in square brackets. Letters used as phonetic symbols do not necessarily indicate the pronunciations usually associated with them in the orthographies of various languages. Rather, they represent precisely the articulations described by phonetic parameters such as high and back.

A secondary criterion in the classification of vowels is the rounding of the lips. Of the four vowel symbols above, only [u] implies lip rounding. High back vowels are assumed to be rounded unless specially noted not to be.

To illustrate the relationship between the symbols [ɑ, i, u, æ] and the articulations they represent, we will use the symbols to transcribe the vowel sounds of some English words. This is not without its hazards because English has many dialects, and the vowels in many words tend to vary according to dialect. Thus the pronunciations represented here may not be your own, but you should recognize each transcription as a possible pronunciation of the word in question.

The vowel of *heat* is pronounced [i] in most of the northern United States. *Hoot* has the vowel [u] in many northern dialects. The vowel [æ] is the vowel of *hat* in most parts of the country. *Car* is pronounced with an [ɑ] in many areas; but this is not the pronunciation heard in much of the northeastern United States (see section 2.6). *Hot* also is pronounced with an [ɑ] in many areas of the country.

2.4 MID VOWELS

There are many more vowels in the languages of the world than those classified above. In order to describe the pronunciation of these additional vowels, we intersect other parameters with high/low and front/back to provide more classes. One of these parameters is mid.

The vowels [e] and [o] in Figure 2.2 are mid front and mid back, respectively. The **mid vowels** are articulated with less tongue height and greater jaw opening than for [i] and [u], but with more tongue height and less jaw opening than for [æ] and [ɑ]. The back mid vowel [o], like [u], is rounded. The vowels [e] and [o] occur in *bait* and *boat*. In Spanish, [e] is heard in *mesa* 'table' and [o] in *coco* 'coconut'.

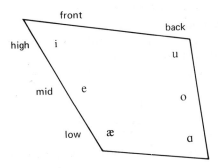

Figure 2.2
High, Low, and Mid Vowels

Figure 2.2 shows the positions of the vowels we have described thus far. The quadrilateral represents the area of the oral cavity in which vowels are articulated. We use a quadrilateral figure to represent the positions of the vowels because the area of the mouth in which vowels are made is approximately of this shape. The distance between front and back is greater for high vowels than for low, and the distance between high and low is greater for front vowels than for back.

2.5 LAX VOWELS

The vowels discussed thus far are called **tense vowels** because their production involves tension of the muscles of the vocal tract, especially the tongue. Vowels articulated with little muscular tension are called **lax vowels**.

The lax counterparts of the vowels [i] and [u] are symbolized [ɪ] (**iota**) and [ʊ] (**upsilon**). The mid vowels [e] and [o], which are tense, also have lax counterparts. The front lax mid vowel is [ɛ] (**epsilon**), and the back lax mid vowel is [ɔ] (**open-o**). The four lax vowels [ɪ, ʊ, ɛ, ɔ] are displayed in Figure 2.4. Like [u] and [o], [ʊ] and [ɔ] are rounded.

The vowels [ɛ] and [ɔ] are those most widely heard in pronunciations of the words *bet* and *corn*. The vowel [ɪ] is generally the vowel of *pit*; its back counterpart [ʊ] is often heard in *put*.

2.6 CENTRAL VOWELS

Central vowels are those articulated with the body of the tongue neither extended nor retracted. Central vowels, then, are neither front nor back. The primary central vowels are shown in Figure 2.3. **Barred-i** [ɨ] is the high central vowel often heard in the second syllable of *basket*. The mid central vowel [ə], called **schwa**, ordinarily occurs at the end of *sofa*. The [ɐ], **inverted printed-a**, is the lax low central vowel in some pronunciations of *cow*. The tense counterpart of [ɐ] is [a], **printed-a**, the vowel of British English *grass*. This vowel is also heard as the vowel of *car* in much of the northeastern United States (for example, Boston). In the phonetic alphabet used here, [ɑ] and [a] must be carefully distinguished because they symbolize quite different sounds.

All the central vowels are naturally unrounded and, with the exception of [a], all are lax.

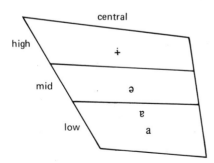

Figure 2.3
Primary Central Vowels

2.7 SECONDARY VOWELS

The vowels discussed thus far are called **primary vowels**. The high

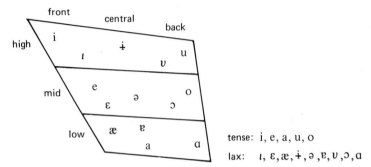

Figure 2.4
Primary Vowels

and mid back vowels in Figure 2.4, [u, ʊ, o, ɔ], are naturally rounded. All the remaining primary vowels are naturally unrounded.

Another set of vowels may be produced in most of the vowel positions associated with primary vowels; but unlike the primary vowels, these vowels are unrounded in the high and mid back positions and rounded elsewhere. Vowels with rounding opposite to that of the primary vowels are called **secondary vowels**. The secondary vowels are given in Figure 2.5.

The extreme high front secondary vowel is [ü] (**umlaut-u**). Its lax counterpart is [ü] (**umlaut-upsilon**). The rounded counterpart of [e] is symbolized [ö] (**umlaut-o**). The rounded counterpart of [ɛ] is [œ]

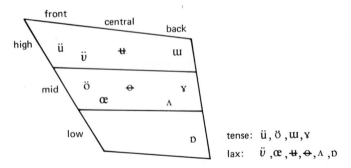

Figure 2.5
Secondary Vowels

(**digraph-o**). There is no extreme low front rounded vowel. The rounded counterpart of [ɑ] is written [ɒ] (**inverted script-a**). The [ɒ] is an extreme low back rounded vowel.

The primary back vowel [u] has an unrounded counterpart, [ɯ] (**inverted-m**). The primary vowel [ɔ] has the unrounded counterpart [ʌ] (**caret**). The tense counterpart of [ʌ] is [ɤ] (**small gamma**). Among the central vowels only [ɨ] and [ə] have rounded counterparts. These are symbolized [ʉ] (**barred-u**) and [ɵ] (**barred-o**), respectively.

The secondary vowels [ʌ] and [ɒ] are common in English. *Cut* usually has [ʌ]. And [ɒ] is the vowel of *hall* in many dialects. German has all four of the front rounded vowels: [ü] in *fühlen* 'feel', [ü] in *Hütte* 'cottage', [ö] in *Söhne* 'sons', and [œ] in *können* 'be able'. Some French dialects have [œ] in the first syllable and [ö] in the second of *heureux* 'happy'. Norwegian has the mid central rounded vowel [ɵ] in *hund* 'dog' and the high central rounded vowel [ʉ] in *hus* 'house'. The back secondary vowel [ɯ] occurs in Turkish, Mandarin, and Korean; [ɤ] (small gamma) occurs in Mandarin and Thai.

2.8 NASALIZED VOWELS

The primary and secondary vowels discussed above are all articulated with the velum raised. If the velum is lowered during the production of a

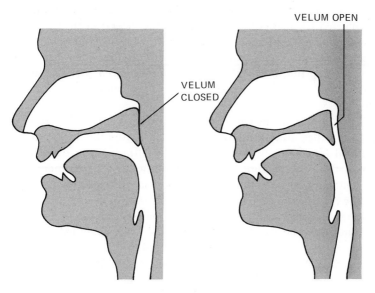

Figure 2.6
Position of the Speech Organs for [æ]

Figure 2.7
Position of the Speech Organs for [æ̃]

vowel, permitting part of the airstream to exit through the nasal cavity, the result is a **nasalized vowel**. The symbol for nasalization of a vowel is a superscribed **tilde** [˜]. Thus, [ɑ̃] is a nasalized [ɑ] and [õ] is a nasalized [o]. Compare the articulation of the vowel [æ] of *cat* shown in Figure 2.6 and the nasalized [æ̃] of *can't* shown in Figure 2.7. Notice particularly the position of the velum in each articulation. Nasalized vowels are common in French: [õ] in *bon* 'good', [ɛ̃] in *cinq* 'five', [ã] in *grand* 'large', and [œ̃] in *un* 'one'.

In describing vowel sounds, only the presence of secondary modifications must be noted, not their absence. Vowels are conventionally described in terms of the position of the tongue and lips; [ɑ], for example, is described as low, tense, back, and unrounded, but it is not necessary to mention that it is not nasalized.

2.9 DIPHTHONGS

The vowels that have been discussed thus far are technically called **monophthongs**, i.e. the symbols and descriptions imply an articulation at a single position in the vowel quadrilateral. However, a vowel articulation may begin at one position of the vowel quadrilateral and end in another. Such articulations, called **diphthongs**, are usually transcribed with two vowel symbols, indicating the beginning and end points of the articulation. To show that these vowel symbols represent a diphthong, they are connected by a subscribed arc. Thus, the vowels in the words *high* and *how* are commonly represented by [ai] and [au], respectively. Alternatively, a subscribed (and inverted) arc can be written under one of the symbols in order to denote that one of the vowels is pronounced with less prominence than the other. Thus, the vowel of *high* can be transcribed [ai̯] and that of *how* [au̯].

The diphthongs in which the movement is across the vowel quadrilateral are called **diagonal diphthongs**. The diphthong [ai̯] moves from the central region to the front (Figure 2.8); [au̯] moves from the central region to the back (Figure 2.9). The diphthong [ɔi̯], commonly heard in pronunciations of the English word *boy*, moves from back to front. Figure 2.10 shows the direction of motion of the diagonal diphthongs [ai̯], [au̯], and [ɔi̯]. Additional diagonal diphthongs found in some English dialects include [ʊi̯] in *push* and *bush* and [ɒi̯] in *wash* and the first syllable of *lawyer* and *caution*.

In contrast to the movement in diagonal diphthongs, the movement in **vertical diphthongs** is within the same region, front, central, or back. The direction of movement in vertical diphthongs is always upward. Most dialects of English have the vertical diphthongs [ei̯] and [ou̯] as in *say* and *go*, respectively. These vertical diphthongs are shown in Figure 2.11. The

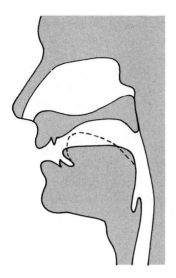

Figure 2.8
Position of the Speech Organs for [ai̯]

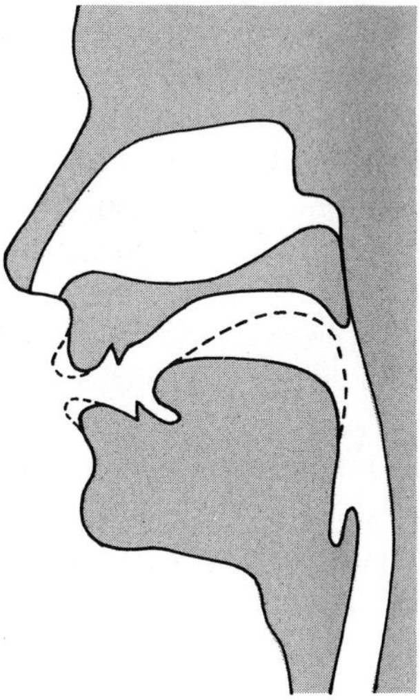

Figure 2.9
Position of the Speech Organs for [au̯]

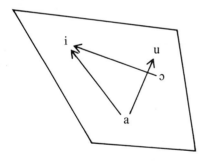

Figure 2.10
Diagonal Diphthongs

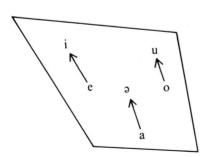

Figure 2.11
Vertical Diphthongs

diphthong of *go* may be rounded throughout: [oʊ̜]; or it may be the diagonal dipththong [əʊ̜]. The latter is common in British English and in some east central region dialects of the United States. The diphthong [ɑə̯] is sometimes heard as the vowel of *spa*, *la*, and *pa*. Many speakers also have the vertical diphthong [æi̯] in such words as *bang*, *bag*, and *bash*. Some speakers in the southern United States pronounce *grass*, *class*, *half*, *dance*, and the like with [æi̯]. Some speakers also have [ɛi̯] in such words as *leg* and *fresh*. Also heard is [ʊi̯] in *fish* and *wish*. The back vertical diphthong [ɒɒ̯] is heard in many Gulf States pronunciations of *law* and *dog* as well as in the final syllable of such words as *Utah* and *Arkansas*.

Besides diagonal and vertical diphthongs, there are **centering diphthongs**, which move from the periphery to the mid central region of the vowel quadrilateral. A number of centering diphthongs are shown in Figure 2.12.

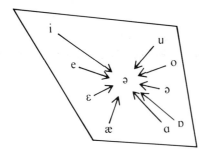

Figure 2.12
Centering Diphthongs

The diphthong [ɪə̯] often occurs in such words as *bid* and *sit*, [ɛə̯] in words like *bed* and *net*, [æə̯] in words such as *bass*, *bad*, and *have*. In the Pacific Northwest (and in some other areas) words like *law* and *la* are usually homonyms pronounced with the diphthong [ɑə̯]. Many Northwesterners also use [ɑə̯] in *cot* and *caught*, *don* and *dawn*, and the like. Speakers in various areas have [ɒə̯] in *dog*, *caught*, and *law*. Some New Yorkers have [ɔə̯] as the diphthong of *dog*. Speakers in many areas have [ʊə̯] in *hood* and *good*.

Diphthongs occur in many languages and dialects all over the world. The centering diphthongs [eə̯] and [oə̯] are found, for example, in the Norwegian of Bergen in *brev* 'letter' and *båt* 'boat'. Among American Indian languages of the Northwest, Coeur d'Alene has the diagonal diphthongs [ɔi̯] in [hɔi̯] 'stop', and [ui̯] in [xʷui̯] 'he went'. Quileute has [ai̯] in [həwai̯škə] 'deer', [iu̯] in [kiu̯tad] 'horse', and [au̯] in [xʷaʔau̯] 'find'. The vertical diphthong [ɛi̯] occurs in Coeur d'Alene [ʔɛcmɛi̯sən] 'I know it', and [oʊ̯] occurs in [tɔu̯šačtqən] 'six heads'. Finnish has several diphthongs involving secondary vowels, such as [öi̯] in *söi* 'he ate', [öü̯] in *löydän* 'I find', and [æü̯] in *näy* 'is not to be seen'.

2.10 VOWEL LENGTH

Most of the vowels described thus far can be produced in relatively longer or shorter forms. In some languages, such as English, the relative length of a vowel has little significance, but in others it is very relevant indeed. In German, for example, certain words are distinguished from others primarily on the basis of vowel length. Thus, the German words *Staat* 'state' and *Stadt* 'city' are distinguished by the length of their vowels, the former having a vowel which is considerably longer than that of the latter. The same is true of the word pairs *Rose* 'rose'/*Rosse* 'steed', *Beten* 'beets'/*Betten* 'beds', and *Ruhm* 'glory/*Rum* 'rum'.

In phonetic transcription, long segments are followed by a colon [:]. Thus, long *a* is written [a:]. Alternatively, long vowels may be transcribed with a sequence of two of the symbols for the corresponding short vowel: [aa] = [a:]. In addition to long and short vowels, there are vowels intermediate in length. Vowels that are neither fully long nor short are called **half-long vowels**. Half-long vowels are indicated by a single raised dot [·] after the vowel. Thus, half-long *e* is written [e·]. In English, vowels are frequently half-long before a voiced stop but short before a voiceless one. Consider, for example, the following pairs of words:

[ɑ·] ∼ [ɑ]	*mob — mop*	
[æ·] ∼ [æ]	*sad — sat*	
[e·i̯] ∼ [ei̯]	*maid — mate*	
[a·i̯] ∼ [ai̯]	*side — site*	
[a·u̯] ∼ [au̯]	*loud — lout*	
[ɛ·] ∼ [ɛ]	*bed — bet*	
[i·] ∼ [i]	*heed — heat*	
[ɩ·] ∼ [ɩ]	*hid — hit*	
[u·] ∼ [u]	*rude — root*	
[ʋ·] ∼ [ʋ]	*pudding — putting*	

The vowel in the first word of each pair sounds less clipped than that in the second. This length difference, while not as noticeable as that in the German examples given above, is nevertheless quite easy to detect.

2.11 VARIETIES OF VOWELS

The symbol [˃] (**chevron**), when properly oriented, is used together with a vowel symbol to show slight modifications of one sort or another. Where [V] represents any vowel, [V˂] is a fronted variety of [V], [V˃] is a retracted variety, [V˄] is a closer variety, and [V˅] is a more open variety. For example, a transcription of *bait* with [e˄] indicates a pronunciation of the vowel with a closer [e] than the symbol by itself represents; [e˃] represents a retracted [e]. Combinations of these diacritics can be used where necessary; thus, [e˃˄] represents a retracted and close variety of [e].

Since vowels are typically voiced, the unmodified vowel symbols imply voicing. Some languages, such as Japanese and Cheyenne, have in addition to their voiced vowels a set of voiceless vowels. To indicate that a vowel is voiceless, a small circle [̥] is placed under the vowel symbol. Thus, [ḁ] represents voiceless [a].

Other voice modifications are possible. In normal voicing only a small amount of air escapes through the vocal cords. In what is called **breathy voice**, the vocal cords vibrate normally along part of their length while the remaining portion of the vocal cords are held too far apart to vibrate. This permits a large amount of air to escape. Breathy vowels are indicated by a small plus [$^{+}$] placed above a vowel symbol. A breathy voice [a] is symbolized [$\overset{+}{a}$]. Breathy vowels occur in some of the languages of Southeast Asia, for example, Vietnamese.

Another voicing modification is **laryngealization** or **creaky voice**. In the production of creaky voice, the vocal cords vibrate normally along part of their length and the remaining part of the vocal cords vibrate at a much slower rate. A raised comma is used to indicate laryngealization. The symbol [a̓] represents a laryngealized [a]. In Puget Salish, for example, [lab] means 'whiskey' or 'rum' and [la̓b] means 'very'.

2.12 ALTERNATIVE VOWEL TRANSCRIPTIONS AND TERMINOLOGY

The International Phonetic Association has developed a transcription system, known as the International Phonetic Alphabet (IPA), which differs in certain significant ways from the system presented here. (The IPA is presented in the *Principles of the International Phonetic Association*, 1949.) Particularly significant is the Association's recognition of four vowel heights where we have recognized but three. In the IPA, the primary vowels are represented as in Figure 2.13.

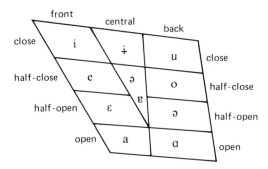

Figure 2.13
IPA Primary Vowels

Notice that the IPA divides our mid area into higher and lower sections. The vowels in the higher section are called **half-close**; those in the lower section, **half-open**. We consider the difference between the IPA half-open and half-close vowels to be primarily a difference in tenseness, rather than height, although the vowels in question differ both in height and tenseness.

To transcribe the vowel that we transcribe with [ʋ], the Association suggests the symbol [ɷ]. As alternatives to [ɿ] and [ɷ] they permit [ɪ] (**small capital i**) and [ᴜ] (**small capital u**) respectively, but express a preference for the former two.

The IPA also differs from the system presented here in the treatment of low vowels. The IPA does not have a low central vowel. In the IPA system [a] is front. And further, [æ] is regarded as a vowel intermediate between [ɛ] and [a]. We, on the other hand, regard [æ] as a low front vowel. Both the IPA classification and our own are reasonable; [æ] is both somewhat higher and somewhat more front than IPA [a]. We take the greater degree of fronting of [æ] to be more pertinent than its relative closeness. Our classification is compared with the IPA's in Figure 2.14. In our system, line *xz* of the IPA chart is replaced with the dotted line *xy*, and line *bd* with the dotted line *bc*. These minor changes put [æ] into the low front area and extend the central triangle into the low area.

The IPA recommendations for secondary vowels, which also differ somewhat from ours, are set forth in Figure 2.15. Notice that the Association's treatment of the mid vowels is the same as in the case of the primary vowels. We regard the primary distinction between [ʌ] and [ɤ] to be one of tenseness; they take it to be one of height.

Our choices of secondary front vowel symbols are also different from those of the IPA. We use [ü] and [ö] for IPA [y] and [ø]. We have rejected

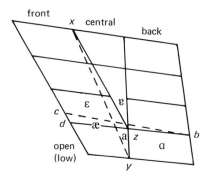

Figure 2.14
Variant Classifications

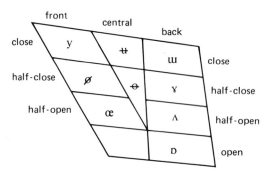

Figure 2.15
IPA Secondary Vowels

IPA [y] as a vowel symbol because English speakers so easily confuse it with the consonant *y* of the orthography. We have decided not to use [ø] for the mid front unrounded vowel because of its similarity to the mathematical null symbol ∅ which is used also in phonological descriptions. Our symbols [ü] and [ö] are used in the IPA as alternatives to [ʉ] and [ɵ]. The IPA has [ʏ] as the symbol for the lax high front rounded vowel. Neither we nor IPA provides a symbol for a lax counterpart of [ɯ]. Such a symbol is unnecessary because no language distinguishes tense high back unrounded vowels from their lax counterparts.

In the IPA system the symbol [˛] is used to indicate positional varieties of vowels instead of [']. Other diacritical symbols are also recommended. A dot placed below a vowel symbol can be used instead of [ˆ] or [˄] to indicate a close variety of that vowel. For example, [ẹ] indicates a closer

variety of [e̞]. The symbol [ˌ] as in [e̞], can be used instead of [ˇ] to show a
more open variety of a vowel. A plus sign placed either under ([e̟]) or after
([e⁺]) a vowel, indicates a fronted articulation, and a minus sign [-] placed
either under or after ([e̠] or [e-]) indicates a retracted variety. In some
systems, a macron [ˉ] is used instead of a colon to indicate a long vowel,
for example [ē].

2.13 VOWEL CLASSIFICATION AND PHONOLOGY

Classifying vowels according to the area of the mouth in which they
are produced and according to their secondary modifications has a valuable
and practical effect. It allows us to develop a characterization of vowels
that is independent of the orthography of any given language. Phonetic
alphabets make it possible to portray sounds for which we have no orthographic symbols, to read and comprehend pronunciations of words which
we have never heard, and to compare pronunciations across languages and
dialects in a consistent way.

The necessity for a phonetic alphabet becomes apparent when we
compare different uses of the same letter in various traditional orthographies
from language to language or even within the same language. For example,
the letter *u* as employed in the English orthography represents, among other
things, [ʌ] in *nut*, [ʊ] in *put*, [u] in *rule*, and the consonant-vowel
sequence [yu] in *use* (compare *Yukon*, where the phonetic [y] is overtly
represented). In French, however, the letter *u* represents [ü] as in *lune*
'moon', while in Norwegian *u* represents [ʉ] as in *hus* 'house'.

Vowel classifications also play a valuable role in phonology. Although
it sometimes happens that a single vowel takes part in a phonological process, most phonological processes involve groups of sounds which can be
classed together because they are articulated in the same part of the oral
cavity or share secondary modifications.

As an illustration of the role of vowel classifications in phonology,
consider the following example from Kikuyu, a Bantu language of Kenya
(based on Armstrong, 1967). The vowel system of Kikuyu includes the tense
vowels [a, i, u, e, o] and the lax vowels [ɛ] and [ɔ]. A verb suffix which
contains [e] when it follows a stem with a tense vowel will have [ɛ] instead
when it follows a stem containing a lax vowel. The perfect aspect suffix,
for example, has the form [eet] in the following words. (We have omitted
indication of the tones.)

(1) nyiteetɛ   'I have strangled'
(2) nyeteetɛ   'I have called'
(3) nyakeetɛ   'I have built'

(4)   nyokeetɛ   'I have come'
(5)   nyuukeetɛ   'I have slandered'

However, in forms with lax stem vowels the perfect suffix is [ɛɛt]:

(6)   nyɔɛɛtɛ   'I have lifted'
(7)   ndɛmɛɛtɛ   'I have cut'

The form of the suffix in examples (6) and (7) is the result of a very common phonological process called **assimilation**, in which a sound changes to become more like other sounds near it. Here the vowel of the suffix assimilates to the lax vowel of the stem.

Without a knowledge of phonetics we would be at a loss to understand why [ɛ] and [ɔ] have a similar effect on the suffix vowel. But since phonetics tells us that [ɛ] and [ɔ] are both lax mid vowels, it is not surprising that they function alike. The process which occurs in the Kikuyu examples above can be described as follows:

(1) The tense vowel [ee] becomes lax if preceded by a lax vowel.

Statements such as this, which describe phonological processes, are called **phonological rules**. In writing phonological rules, symbols are commonly used to represent notions such as 'becomes' or 'if preceded by'. Thus, a more formal statement of the Kikuyu rule would be:

(1') ee → lax/lax vowel _____

The arrow → in this rule is read as 'becomes' and the diagonal / as 'in the environment of'. The underscore _____ marks the position of the sound undergoing the change. In this case, the underscore is to the right, indicating that the [ee] follows a lax vowel. As it is written, rule (1') accounts for examples (1) through (6). To account for example (7), which has a consonant, *m*, between the stem vowel and the vowel of the suffix, we must expand our rule as follows:

(1") ee → lax / lax vowel (consonant) _____

The parentheses here indicate an optional element. Thus, rule (1") accounts for all Kikuyu examples given above. It is read "ee becomes lax (i.e. becomes ɛɛ) in the environment of a preceding lax vowel which may or may not be followed by a consonant."

2.14 SUMMARY

Vowels, speech sounds made by shaping the oral cavity in such a way that air may pass through it more or less freely, are classified according to the position of the tongue and lips and the degree of muscular tension (particularly of the tongue) necessary for their production. Vowels made with the tongue body extended are called **front vowels**; those made with the tongue body retracted, **back vowels**; and those made with the tongue neither extended nor retracted, **central vowels**. Vowels made with the tongue near the roof of the mouth and with a narrow jaw opening are **high vowels**; those with the most open articulation are **low vowels**; and those with moderate tongue height and jaw opening, **mid vowels**. **Tense vowels** are those whose production involves tension of the muscles of the vocal tract. Vowels articulated with little tension are **lax vowels**.

Some vowels are produced with the lips rounded. The most natural situation is for high back and mid back vowels to have accompanying lip rounding and for all others to be unrounded. **Primary vowels** are those made with the expected lip rounding; **secondary vowels** are those made with rounding opposite of that for the primary vowels.

In addition to these basic vowel types, vowels may be modified in various ways. Vowels articulated with the velum lowered, allowing air to exit through the nose, are **nasalized vowels**, and those made without accompanying vibrations of the vocal cords are **voiceless vowels**.

All of the basic vowels are **monophthongs** (vowels articulated with a tongue position that is essentially constant). **Diphthongs** are vowels that show a change in tongue position during their articulation. They can be classified in terms of the direction of change. The tongue rises for a **vertical diphthong**, moves laterally (e.g., from central to front) for a **diagonal diphthong**, and moves toward [ə] for a **centering diphthong**. Classifying vowels according to their phonetic properties allows us to characterize them independently of the orthography of any given language and to group them in phonologically relevant ways.

EXERCISES FOR CHAPTER 2

1 **a.** How is the nasalized mid front tense vowel symbolized?
 b. Given the terminology of Chapter 2, describe the articulation represented by [ɒ].
 c. How would a vertical diphthong with a mid back unrounded lax beginning and a high rounded lax end point be transcribed?

2. In this exercise, each word is spelled in regular English orthography except for the segment in brackets, which is given in phonetic symbols. These symbols may correspond to one or more letters of the English spelling. The transcriptions represent common American English pronunciations, but not all are necessarily from the same dialect. Identify each word.

1. h[æ]t	13. sh[ɑ]t	25. b[oṷ]l
2. h[ɑ]t	14. sh[ʌ]t	26. p[i]t
3. h[i]t	15. sh[u]t	27. p[ɪ]t
4. h[aɪ]t	16. ev[eɪ]de	28. p[ɛ]t
5. h[ʌ]t	17. av[ɔɪ]d	29. p[eɪ]te
6. p[ɪ]ll	18. b[oṷ]t	30. p[æ]t
7. p[ʊ]t	19. b[aṷ]t	31. p[ɑ]rt
8. r[ɛ]d	20. b[aɪ]t	32. p[ʌ̃]t
9. r[ɪ]d	21. b[ɒ]ll	33. p[aṷ]t
10. r[i]d	22. b[ɪ]ll	34. p[ɑ]t
11. sh[aṷ]t	23. b[ɛ]ll	35. [ɐ̯ɪ]ce
12. sh[ɔ]rt	24. b[ʊ]sh	36. n[aṷ]

3. Transcribe the italicized portion of each of the following words.

1. n*o*t	5. c*o*in	8. f*oo*d
2. b*u*s	6. b*e*d	9. n*o*te
3. c*a*t	7. l*ea*k	10. f*i*ght
4. r*i*ch		

4. Given the terminology of Chapter 2, classify each set of vowels as narrowly as possible. For example, [ö, œ, o, ɔ] is a set of mid rounded vowels.

1. [æ, a, ɑ, ɒ]	6. [i, ι, ü, ü]
2. [u, o, ɒ, ɯ]	7. [i, ʉ, ɵ, a]
3. [u, ü, ɑ, ʋ, o, ö, ʉ, ɔ, œ]	8. [ü, ö, ü, œ]
4. [i, u, ü, ɯ, ι, ʋ, i, ʉ]	9. [u, ɔ, o, ʋ, ɑ]
5. [ι, ü, ɛ, œ, æ]	10. [u, ɯ, i, ʋ, ʉ]

5. Using phonetic classes, describe as concisely as possible the processes indicated in 1 through 10 below. The arrow (→) is read 'become'. For example, the process by which [i, u, e, o] → [ι, ʋ, ɛ, ɔ], respectively, can be described as: nonlow tense vowels become lax.

1. [u, o, ɔ, ɑ] → [i, e, ɛ, æ]	6. [eɪ, oṷ] → [aɪ, aṷ]
2. [ɛ, ɔ] → [ι, ʋ]	7. [aɪ, aṷ] → [e, o]
3. [ʌ, ɒ] → [ɔ, a]	8. [u, o, ɔ] → [ü, ö, œ]
4. [ι, ɛ, ɔ] → [i, e, o]	9. [ü, ö, œ] → [i, e, ɛ]
5. [i, e, ɛ] → [ü, ö, œ]	10. [ɛ, æ] → [ɛɪ, æɪ]

6. In the Eskimo of Labrador (Labrador Inuttut), the vowels [i] and [u] become [ι] and [ʋ], respectively, before a sequence of two consonants. Use phonetic classes to describe this process. In this same language, [i] and [u] become [e] and [o], respectively, at the end of words. Use phonetic classes to describe this process. (Based on Smith, 1975.)

3 phonetics: consonants

3.1 INTRODUCTION

The system linguists use to describe the articulatory properties of consonants is somewhat different from that for vowels because consonants and vowels are produced in different ways. As we have seen, vowel sounds are made by altering the shape of the oral cavity through which air from the lungs is allowed to flow more or less freely. Consonants, on the other hand, are produced by constricting the vocal tract at some point thereby diverting, impeding, or completely shutting off the flow of air in the oral cavity.

Consonants are traditionally described and classified according to five major criteria: (1) the point in the vocal tract where the greatest constriction occurs, called the **point of articulation**; (2) the organ used to alter or block the vowel tract, called the **articulator**; (3) the way the various organs of speech are employed to produce sound, called the **manner of articulation**; (4) the state of the vocal cords, whether vibrating, closed, or open; and (5) the source of the airstream, whether from the lungs or not.

3.2 POINTS OF ARTICULATION

Figure 3.1 shows some of the most common points at which consonants are articulated. The point of articulation for the initial sounds of the words

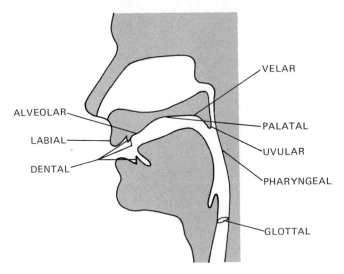

Figure 3.1
Points of Articulation

pea, be, and *me* is the upper lip. Sounds articulated at the upper lip are called **labial sounds,** or simply **labials.** The initial sounds of *thigh* and *thy,* which are articulated at the upper teeth, are called **dental sounds** or **dentals.** The sounds that begin *tip, dip, nip, sip, zip,* and *lip* are articulated at the alveolar ridge (the gum ridge being the upper teeth); hence, such sounds are called **alveolar sounds** or **alveolars.** The initial sound of *rip,* which is articulated at the hard palate, is called a **palatal sound.** The initial sounds of *ship, chip,* and *gyp* are either articulated at the palate, as for *r,* or at the extreme front of the palate near the alveolar ridge. When pronounced in the latter fashion, these sounds are called **alveopalatals.** The initial sounds of *call* and *gall* and the final sound of *song,* being articulated at the soft palate or velum, are called **velar sounds** or **velars.**

The uvula, the pharynx, and the glottis can also be points of articulation. Sounds made at the uvula are called **uvular sounds.** English has no uvulars, but the initial segment of the French word *repas* and the final segment of French *fenêtre* are uvular sounds. Sounds whose point of articulation is the pharynx are called **pharyngeal** sounds. Although there are no pharyngeals in English, they do occur in certain American Indian and Semitic languages. For example, the Coeur d'Alene words *Rust* 'lost' and *Rɛwp* 'drip' begin with a pharyngeal sound, as does the Arabic word *ʕazza* 'strong'.

The vocal cords can also be adjusted to form a constriction. Consonants whose point of articulation is the glottis are called **glottal** sounds. In English, the initial sound of *hen* and *hip* is glottal.

3.3 THE MAJOR ARTICULATORS

Consonants may also be classified according to the organ (or part of an organ) used to constrict the vocal tract. The major articulators used in the production of consonants, shown in Figure 3.2, are the lower lip, the tip or

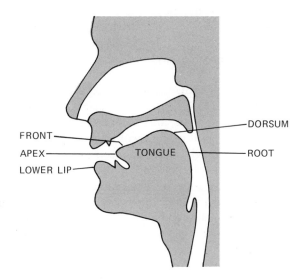

Figure 3.2
Major Articulators

apex of the tongue, the front of the tongue, and the dorsum. The root of the tongue is also used in the production of some sounds. Sounds articulated with the lower lip, as well as those articulated at the upper lip, are called **labial** sounds; those using the apex of the tongue are called **apical**; those employing the front of the tongue exclusive of the apex are **frontal**; and those using the dorsum, **dorsal**. When these terms are used to describe consonant articulations they are ordinarily compounded with one of the terms for point of articulation. Thus, a speech sound having the lower lip as its articulator and the upper teeth as its point of articulation, such as the initial sound of *fee*, is classified as **labiodental**. Similarly, a sound which has the dorsum as its articulator and the velum as the point of articulation is classified as **dorsovelar**. The first segments of *call* and *gall* are dorsovelar sounds. A special term is employed when the lower lip is the articulator and the upper lip the point of articulation. Sounds made in this manner, such as the first sounds in *pea*, *bee*, and *me*, are classified as **bilabials**. There is also a special term for sounds which are made by placing the tip of the tongue near or against the hard palate. A sound so produced is called **retroflex**. The initial sound of *red* is typically retroflex.

3.4 MANNER OF ARTICULATION: OBSTRUENTS

A third criterion important to the classification of consonants is the manner of their articulation. Manner of articulation includes such factors as the degree of closure (that is, whether the articulator actually shuts off the flow of air or only modifies it in some way) and other modifications such as nasal resonance.

According to their manner of articulation, language sounds may be divided into two general categories: obstruents and resonants. **Obstruents**, sounds made by obstructing the flow of air, are characterized by an extreme narrowing or constriction at some point in the vocal tract.

If the constriction is severe enough to interrupt completely the outflow of air from the lungs (or in the case of a few rather rare sounds, the inflow of air), the obstruent is classified as a **stop**. The initial sounds of *pea*, *tea*, and *key* are stops. If the constriction is sufficiently small that the air must be forced through it, creating turbulence and air friction noise, the obstruent is classified as a **fricative**. The first segment of *fee* is a fricative, as is the initial segment of *sea*. Notice that the fricative in *sea* and the stop in *tea* are made at the same point in the mouth—the alveolar ridge. Both are also made with the apex of the tongue. These sounds differ then only in the manner of their articulation, the initial of *sea* being an apicoalveolar fricative and that of *tea* an apicoalveolar stop. Sounds which are made at the same point of articulation and with the same articulator but with different manners of articulation are said to be **homorganic**.

In addition to simple stops and fricatives, there is a third type of obstruent, called an affricate. **Affricates** are complex segments composed of a stop closely followed by a fricative. Most commonly, the stop and the fricative that make up an affricate are homorganic. The words *church* and *judge* begin and end with affricates.

The phonetic symbols for a number of basic obstruents are given in

Table I. Notice that when compound terms such as labiodental and apico-palatal are employed, the first member of the term identifies the articulator and the second the point of articulation. There is no need to identify the articulator for velar and uvular sounds because velars are always articulated with the dorsum and uvulars with the root of the tongue. (The reason for this will become immediately obvious if you attempt an apicouvular stop.) The identification of an articulator for glottal sounds is also unnecessary, since the only possible articulations involve the vocal cords themselves. The articulator designations are often omitted when referring to bilabial, apicodental, apicoalveolar, and frontopalatal sounds. In many informal classifications, the labiodental and bilabial classes are referred to jointly as labials, since they have the same articulator.

As you can see in Table I, obstruents often occur in voiced and voice-less pairs. These pairs of sounds have the same articulator, point of articula-tion, and general manner of articulation; they differ primarily in whether or not their production involves vibration of the vocal cords. In general, the symbols for voiceless sounds also imply tenser articulations than do the ones for the corresponding voiced sounds. To represent lax (or **lenis**) voiceless stops, we use the symbol for the voiced stop plus the diacritic mark for voicelessness [ˌ]. Thus, the symbols [b̥, d̥, g̥] represent the lax counterparts of the tensely articulated (or **fortis**) sounds [p, t, k].

It should also be noted that the symbols for stops given in Table I imply quiet release; that is, the stop closure for these sounds is made and released in such a way that there is no audible burst of air. If an audible burst of air is produced, the stop is said to be **aspirated**. Aspiration is symbolized by writing a raised *h* after the consonant symbol, for example, [kʰ] and [tʰ]. The symbols in Table I represent only unaspirated sounds. This should be kept in mind since in English words stops are usually aspirated in initial position. In most normal pronunciations of *pin, tin, kin,* and the like, the aspiration can be heard quite plainly and can be felt if you hold the palm of your hand several inches from your mouth. The *p, t,* and *k* in such words are therefore transcribed [pʰ, tʰ, kʰ]. Compare the aspirated stops of *pin, tin,* and *kin* with the unaspirated stops of *spin, star,* and *skin.*

3.4.1 Stops

Stops are made by a complete blockage of the airstream at some point in the vocal tract. Of course, this blockage alone does not produce the sounds associated with stops. Rather it is the act of forming and releasing the blockage which produces sound.

In forming the bilabial stops [p] and [b], the lips are completely closed, trapping the flow of air in the oral cavity. The voiced member of the pair, [b] also has vibration of the vocal cords.

Table I SOME BASIC OBSTRUENTS

		(BI)LABIAL	LABIODENTAL	(APICO)DENTAL	(APICO)ALVEOLAR	APICOPALATAL (RETROFLEX)	(FRONTO)ALVEOPALATAL	(FRONTO)PALATAL (RETROFLEX)	DORSOPALATAL	VELAR	UVULAR	GLOTTAL
STOP	Voiceless	p		t̪	t	ṭ			k̟	k	q	ʔ
STOP	Voiced	b		d̪	d	ḍ			g̟	g	ɢ	
FRICATIVE	Voiceless	φ	f	θ / s̪	s / ɫ	ṣ	š / ṣ	ṣ̌	ç	x	ẋ	h
FRICATIVE	Voiced	β	v	ð / z̪	z	ẓ	ž / ẓ	ẓ̌	ʝ	ɣ	ʁ	ɦ
AFFRICATE	Voiceless		f̂		c / ƛ		č	č̣				
AFFRICATE	Voiced				ǰ / λ		ǰ	ǰ̣				

32

Apicodental sounds are produced by placing the tip of the tongue near or against the back of the upper teeth. These sounds are represented by placing the diacritic [ˌ] under the symbol for the corresponding alveolar sound. The voiceless and voiced apicodental stops [t̪] and [d̪] do not occur in most dialects of English, but they are common in many other languages, including Spanish, where the initial sound of the words *taco* 'light snack' and *tengo* 'I have' is apicodental.

The apicoalveolar stops [t] and [d] are extremely common in languages of the world. They are produced by placing the tongue tip against the alveolar ridge. The *t*'s and *d*'s of English are usually apicoalveolar.

Apicopalatal, or retroflex, sounds are produced by curling the tongue tip back from the alveolar position. The apicopalatal stops [ṭ] and [ḍ] are found in a number of languages, including Vietnamese, Sanskrit, and Tamil. A dot placed under a consonant symbol means that the sound being represented is articulated one position behind that implied by the symbol. Since [t] implies an alveolar position, [ṭ] indicates an apicopalatal, i.e., retroflex one.

Dorsopalatal sounds are made by placing the back of the tongue near or against the hard palate. They are symbolized by adding the diacritic [ˌ] to the symbol for the corresponding velar sound. The voiceless and voiced dorsopalatal stops are thus symbolized [k̰] and [g]. These sounds occur at the beginning of the English words *keep* and *gain*.

The velar stops [k] and [g] are articulated by placing the back of the tongue against the velum. Sounds produced in this manner occur at the beginning of the English words *cop* and *gone*. The difference between dorsopalatal and dorsovelar sounds is quite noticeable. Compare the pronunciation of the [k̰] in *keep* with that of the [k] in *cop*. You will find that the tongue begins in a position considerably closer to the front of the mouth for *keep* than it does for *cop*.

The uvular stops [q] and [ɢ] are made by retracting the root of the tongue well beyond the position assumed for articulating velars. In forming uvulars, the root is closed against the uvula, thus blocking the flow of air before it reaches the oral cavity. The voiceless uvular stop [q] is found in Arabic and in many American Indian languages (including Coeur d'Alene, Quileute, and Puget Salish). The rarer voiced uvular stop [ɢ] is found primarily in North American Indian languages such as Kwakiutl, Gitksan, and Eskimo.

The glottal stop [ʔ] is the only one of the voiceless stops that does not have a voiced counterpart. This is because glottal stops are made by interrupting the outflow of air by closing the vocal cords together. Such a manner of articulation does not allow the vibration of the vocal cords necessary to the production of voiced sounds. Glottal stops are common in many languages including English. In the expression *oh-oh*, for example, a glottal stop is usually heard both before the first vowel and as the catch between the two syllables. Similarly, each of the vowels in the negative expression *uh-uh* is normally preceded by a glottal stop. However, glottal stops are not restricted to essentially gestural expressions. Perhaps the most frequently occurring pronunciations of words such as *fountain* and *mountain*, for example, have [ʔ] rather than [tʰ] where the orthographic *t* occurs.

3.4.2 Fricatives

The voiceless and voiced bilabial fricatives are indicated by the symbols [ɸ] (**phi**) and [β] (**beta**), respectively. In the production of these sounds, air is forced through the lips, which are constricted enough to create friction. These sounds do not occur in all varieties of English, but some speakers have [β] rather than [v] in *obvious* and [ɸ] rather than [f] in *nymph*. Bilabial fricatives are very important sounds in languages such as Ewe (a West African language), Japanese, and Spanish.

The voiceless labiodental fricative [f], as in *fee* and *phone*, is made by placing the lower lip close enough to the upper teeth so that the airstream must be forcefully ejected between the lip and the teeth. Its voiced counterpart is [v], as in *vase*.

The voiceless apicodental fricative is represented by the Greek letter **theta** [θ]. This sound is made by forcing air through a constriction between the apex of the tongue and the tips or back of the upper teeth. The sound thus produced is rather rare in languages of the world, but occurs in Greek and English. The initial consonant of the word *thin* is a voiceless dental fricative. The voiced counterpart of [θ] is represented by the symbol [ð] (**eth**). Eth occurs as the initial consonant of the word *this*. Notice that although in modern English both [θ] and [ð] are represented orthographically by *th*, these sounds are just as distinct as [f] and [v]. They differ in precisely the same way (namely, in voicing). Further, the fact that [θ] and [ð] are written *th* in English does not mean that these sounds are related somehow to [t] and [h]. In written English, *th* never represents a *t* followed by an *h* except when the two sounds appear in separate syllables, as in *hothead* and *pothole*.

The apicoalveolar fricatives are represented by the symbols [s] and [z]. As the orthography suggests, [s] occurs at the beginning of *sue* and [z] at the beginning of *zoo*. These sounds are made by closing off the airstream at the sides of the tongue, allowing passage of air only through a narrow constriction over the center of the tongue. Any fricative made in this way is said to be **grooved**. By placing your hand in front of your mouth, you can compare the narrow stream of air that is emitted when the grooved fricative [s] is produced and the much wider stream accompanying the production of [θ]. Fricatives, such as [θ], which have a wide airstream, are said to be **flat** or **slit**.

The dental counterparts of [s] and [z] are [s̪] and [z̪]. These sounds have as their point of friction the back of the upper teeth. Both [s̪] and [z̪] are grooved apicodental fricatives. The difference in tongue shape seems to be the principal distinction between them and the flat fricatives [θ] and [ð]. The *s*'s in the spelling of the French words *sept* 'seven' and *oiseau* 'bird' represent the voiceless and voiced apicodentals [s̪] and [z̪], respectively.

An inverted circumflex [ˇ] (called a **wedge**) is often used to signify palatal sounds. The symbol [š] (**s-wedge** or **esh**) represents the voiceless (fronto)alveopalatal fricative. Its voiced counterpart is symbolized [ž] (**z-wedge**). The voiceless member of this pair is a common sound in English. It is often spelled *sh*, as in *ship* and *fish*. The [ž] occurs much less frequently but is found in the middle of such words as *vision, measure,* and *leisure.* In the production of the fricatives [š] and [ž], friction is created as air passes through a narrow opening between the tongue and the hard palate. In articulating these grooved fricatives, the apex of the tongue is tipped down and is near the lower teeth.

The retroflex counterparts of [š] and [ž] are the grooved frontopalatal fricatives [ṣ̌] and [ẓ̌]. These fricatives are made by placing both the tip and the front of the tongue near the forward part of the hard palate. A distinction between [š] and [ṣ̌] is apparently quite rare but is reported for the Mayan language Jacaltec (Day, 1973) in, for example, the words *ẍila* 'chair' (*ẍ* = [š]) and *xil* 'saw' (*x* = [ṣ̌]).

The grooved fricatives [ṣ] and [ẓ] are the retroflexed counterparts of [s] and [z]. They are made with the apex of the tongue in close proximity to the front of the hard palate. The [ṣ] occurs in some of the languages of India, both ancient and modern. In Europe, [ṣ] is found in Swedish as the sound written with *s* in *fars* 'farce', *kurs* 'course', and *först* 'first'.

Most **lateral** sounds are made by closing the tongue tip against the roof of the mouth in such a way that the airstream is diverted around the tongue. The symbol [ɬ] (**fricative-l**) represents the voiceless apicoalveolar lateral fricative, and the symbol [ɮ] its voiced counterpart. Voiceless lateral fricatives are found in a number of languages including Welsh, Navajo, Quileute, and Couer d'Alene. Voiced lateral fricatives, although quite rare, are reported to occur in Navajo and in Xhosa, a South African language.

The fricatives that are homorganic with the velar stops [k] and [g] are symbolized with [x] for the voiceless sound and [γ] (**gamma**) for the voiced one. In articulating velar fricatives, the dorsum is not allowed to close off the airflow completely as it does in producing [k] and [g]. Instead of complete closure, there is a severe constriction which causes air friction. Most dialects of English have no sounds produced in this manner, although [x] does occur in the Scots dialects in words such as *loch.* The [x] is also

common in such German words as *Bach* 'brook' and *machen* 'make' and in the
Spanish words *junta* 'group' and *ojo* 'eye'. The sound [ɣ] occurs in the Spanish
words *agua* 'water' and *cigarro* 'cigar' and in such Danish words as *kage* 'cake'
and *dager* 'days'. The sound [ɣ] is spelled *g* in both Spanish and Danish.

The dorsopalatal fricatives [ç] (**c-cedilla**) and [ɣ] (**front gamma**)
are the counterparts of the stops [ḵ] and [g̱], respectively. The voiceless [ç]
occurs in German *ich* 'I', *Becher* 'cup', and *Mädchen* 'girl'. It is also found in
some of the Scots dialects of English in words such as *sight* [sɪçt]. Both [ç]
and the voiced [ɣ] occur in Chiricahua Apache.

The uvular fricatives that are homorganic with [q] and [ɢ] are [x]
(**back-x**) and [ɣ] (**back gamma**). These sounds do not occur at all in
English. The voiceless uvular fricative [x] occurs in Quileute and Coeur
d'Alene, and [ɣ] as well as [x] occurs in Chipewyan, Kwakiutl, and Gitksan.

The symbol [h] represents a voiceless glottal fricative as in the English
words *head* and *hit*; [ɦ] represents its voiced counterpart, as in *ahead* and
ahoy. In the production of English [h] and [ɦ], the position of the tongue and
lips is identical with that of the vowel following. Compare the [h] of *heat*
with the [h] of *hot* and the [ɦ] of *ahead* with the [ɦ] of *ahoy*.

3.4.3 Affricates

Affricates, as we have said, are sounds made by completely stopping
the flow of air and then releasing it into a fricative. The dental affricate [f̂]
is produced by pressing the lower lip against the upper teeth, then releasing
the built-up pressure through an *f*-like fricative articulation. This affricate
occurs in German, where it is spelled with *pf*, as in *Pferd* 'horse' and *Kopf*
'head, top'.

The symbol [c] represents the voiceless alveolar affricate produced by
forming a [t] and releasing it through an [s]. This affricate is found in final
position in English words such as *cats*. It also occurs in German, where it is
written as *z* in such words as *zehn* 'ten', *Zahne* 'teeth', and *Herz* 'heart'. The
symbol [j] represents the corresponding voiced alveolar affricate. In English
this sound is written as *ds* in *cads* and *dz* in *adze*. The alveolar affricates have
as alternate representations the symbols [t͡s] and [d͡z], where the arc under
the symbols shows that the two elementary sounds are combined into an
affricate.

Lateral alveolar affricates are found in a number of North American
Indian languages. The voiceless one is symbolized by [ƛ] (**barred-lambda**)
and the voiced one by [λ] (**lambda**). As with [c] and [j], the production of
the lateral affricates involves forming an alveolar stop, but in this case the
airstream is released into a lateral fricative. Thus, [ƛ] is equivalent to the
combination [t͡ɬ] and [λ] to [d͡ɮ].

The (fronto)alveopalatal affricates are symbolized by [č] (**c-wedge**) and [ǰ] (**j-wedge**). For most speakers of English the final consonant of *beach* is [č] and the final consonant of *bridge* is [ǰ]. The affricate [č] is produced by forming a *t*-like stop followed closely by an alveopalatal fricative [š]. Therefore, this sound is sometimes represented as [t̬š] or [t̬š]. Similarly, [ǰ], which is produced by forming a *d*-like stop followed by a voiced alveopalatal fricative [ž], has the alternate representations [d̬ž] and [d̬ž]. These compound symbols can be used to emphasize the composition of the affricates when this is of importance.

The affricates discussed thus far are all homorganic. **Heterorganic affricates**, affricates for which the stop and fricative elements are not made at the same point of articulation, are much less common. In Homeric Greek there are two heterorganic affricates: ξ = [k̬s] and ψ = [p̬s], as in ξίφος 'sword' and ψῡχή 'soul, life'.

3.5 MANNER OF ARTICULATION: RESONANTS

In addition to the obstruents, there is a second major class of sounds, the resonants. **Resonants** are made by shaping the vocal tract rather than obstructing it. In the production of resonants, the outflow of air, either through the mouth or nose, is unobstructed. If there is accompanying friction, it is incidental and not a defining characteristic. Hence all vowels, as well as some consonants, are resonants.

3.5.1 Nasals

Among the most common resonant consonants are the nasals. The production of nasals involves the complete diversion of the airstream through the nasal cavity. This is achieved by lowering the velum while at the same time closing off the oral cavity at some point. Some of the more common nasal articulations are given in Table II.

In the production of the bilabial nasal [m], the oral cavity is large and internally unobstructed since it is closed off only at the lips. In Figure 3.3 the positions of the velum for [m] and [b] are shown. The lowered velum of [m] allows air to enter the nasal cavity; the bilabial closure causes the airstream to be diverted entirely through the nasal cavity.

In the articulation of the alveolar nasal [n], the oral cavity is partitioned into two subcavities, one in front of the closure made by the apex of the tongue at the alveolar ridge, the other above and behind the tongue (Figure 3.4).

TABLE II NASAL CONSONANTS

	BILABIAL	LABIODENTAL	ALVEOLAR	APICOPALATAL (RETROFLEX)	(FRONTO)ALVEOPALATAL	VELAR	UVULAR
RESONANT	m	ɱ	n	ṇ	ñ	ŋ	ɴ
PRENASALIZED STOP	ᵐb		ⁿd			ᵑg	

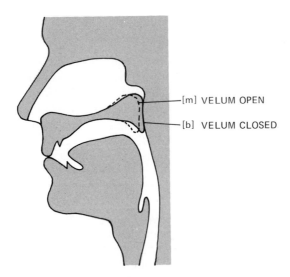

—[m] VELUM OPEN

—[b] VELUM CLOSED

Figure 3.3
Position of the Speech Organs for [b] and [m]
(Oral and Nasal Bilabials)

The (fronto)alveopalatal nasal [ñ] (**enya**) and the velar nasal [ŋ] (**eng**) are also made by partitioning the oral cavity. In producing [ñ], the partition is made by pressing the front of the tongue to the palate; for [ŋ] the partition is made by the dorsum of the tongue at the velum (Figures 3.5 and 3.6). In languages of the world, [n] is by far the most commonly occurring nasal, but [m] also occurs in many languages. The velar nasal [ŋ] is found

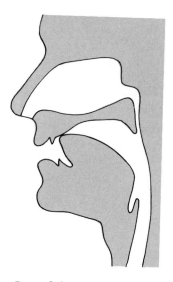

Figure 3.4
Position of the Speech Organs for [n]

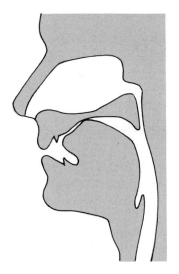

Figure 3.5
Position of the Speech Organs for [ñ]

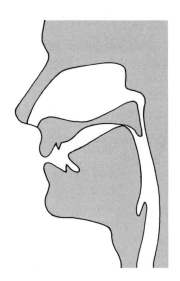

Figure 3.6
Position of the Speech Organs for [ŋ]

in many English words, such as *singer* and *hang*; in English orthography this sound is often represented by the two letters *ng*. In a number of words, such as *finger, angle, think,* and *tank,* however, the *n* alone represents [ŋ] and the *g* or *k* is pronounced with the normal [g] or [k] value. The alveopalatal sound [ñ] occurs in the Vietnamese (Saigon dialect) words [ñæ̀] 'house' and [ñiù] 'much', as well as the French words *ligne* 'line' and *montagne* 'mountain' (*gn* is the usual spelling for [ñ] in French). In English, [ñ] occurs only before another alveopalatal sound in the same syllable, as in *plunge* and *singe*.

Many English speakers have the labiodental nasal [ɱ] (written *m*) in the words *nymph* and *symphony*. The retroflex nasal [ɳ] occurs in many languages of India and Australia. The uvular nasal [ɴ] is rare, but occurs in Eskimo and a few other languages.

If, in the production of [m], the velum is raised for a significant length of time before the oral closure is released, the result is a complex segment called a **prenasalized stop**. What remains after the nasalization is terminated is essentially a [b]. Therefore, the symbol for a bilabial pre-nasalized stop is [ᵐb]. Prenasalized stops may also be made at the alveolar and velar positions. The symbol [ⁿd] represents the alveolar prenasalized stop, and [ᵑg] the velar one. Because they involve interruption of the air-stream, prenasalized stops are considered obstruents rather than resonants. These sounds occur in some of the languages of the Pacific (Fijian and Yapese, for example) and in a number of African languages.

3.5.2 Lateral Resonants

Not all lateral sounds are made with the severe constriction employed in the production of [ɬ] and [ɮ]. For the [l] in *leap* the lateral articulation serves merely to shape the oral cavity rather than to impede or block the flow of air. Laterals such as [l] are therefore resonants. Normally, the sound that appears at the beginning of *leap*, *late*, and *last* is produced by placing the apex of the tongue against the alveolar ridge but leaving one or both sides down to allow the air to flow out around the tongue. The tongue body is not elevated. A lateral articulated in this way is called a **clear-l**. The sound [ɫ] (**velarized-l** or **dark-l**), which begins words like *law* and *loose*, is articulated in much the same way as [l] except that the dorsum is elevated toward the velum. In English, [l] occurs before front vowels and [ɫ] occurs before back vowels.

Lateral resonants may also be articulated against the back of the upper teeth. Dental laterals are symbolized by placing the diacritic [ˌ] under the symbol [l]. The dental *l*, which appears in French words like *loup* 'wolf' and *foule* 'crowd', is, like [l], referred to as a clear l. A few languages have dorsovelar laterals. The resonant velar lateral can be symbolized [ʎ].

3.5.3 *r*-Sounds

Sounds made by constricting the pharynx while at the same time articulating with either the apex or the tongue root are called **r-sounds**.

For all *r*-sounds, the pharyngeal constriction is primary, the accompanying apical and uvular articulations being only of secondary importance. There are two distinct types of *r*. **Apical-r**, symbolized [r], is produced in somewhat the same manner as [l]. The apex and front of the tongue are elevated for both, but in the forming of [r] this elevation does not result in closure. Instead, air is permitted to pass freely over and around the apex of the tongue, which is simply raised or curled back to a point behind the alveolar ridge (Figure 3.7). In English, the initial sound of words such as *red, rock,* and *ride* is typically made in this way but with the lips rounded. Pure apical *r*'s occur in words like *fear* and *wear* (in dialects of English that do not drop final *r*).

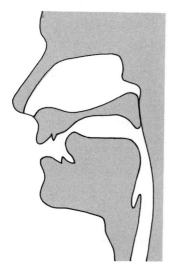

Figure 3.7
Position of the Speech Organs for the [r] in red

Continuant **uvular-r**, symbolized [ʀ], is made by constricting the oral cavity at the uvula as well as at the pharynx. The resulting sound, although predominantly resonant, tends also to be slightly fricative. The initial sound of the French word *rouge* 'red' is a uvular *r*.

R-sounds that are made with more friction than uvular-*r* are denoted by inverted symbols. Thus, [ɹ] represents a voiced apical fricative *r*, and [ʁ] a uvular one. The *r* of the English word *dream* is actually a voiced apical fricative. The quality of the *r* sounds in the words *dream* and *ream* are distinctly different. The word *trip* contains the voiceless fricative [ɹ̥]. The diacritic [̥], when used in conjunction with symbols for either vowels or consonants indicates voicelessness (see section 2.11). The *r* of the French word *autre* 'other' represents the voiceless uvular fricative [ʁ̥].

Several types of *r*-sounds are characterized by one or more momentary interruptions of the flow of air through the vocal tract. If this interruption in the airflow is accomplished by flicking the apex rapidly against the point of articulation, the sound is called a **flap**. A **flapped-r**, symbolized [ř], is made by flapping the apex once against the alveolar ridge, while articulating the necessary pharyngeal constriction. The sound in the middle of the Spanish word *pero* 'but' is a flapped *r*. The [ř] is classed as a resonant rather than an obstruent because, even though the airstream is completely closed off momentarily, the flap can be considered a secondary articulation.

A **trill** consists of several rapid interruptions of the airstream. If the tongue tip vibrates against the alveolar ridge, the result is an **apical trill**. This is the sound small children often make when imitating an airplane motor. The apical trill, which occurs in the Spanish *perro* 'dog' and in Swedish *röd* 'red', is symbolized [r̃].

Yet another kind of *r*-sound is produced by trilling the uvula. Understandably, a sound made in this manner is called a **uvular trill**. The uvular trill occurs in some dialects of German in *rot* 'red', *Regen* 'rain', *rund* 'round', and the like. It is symbolized [ʀ̃]. Trilled *r*'s, like flapped *r*'s, are classified as resonants since the trilling of either the apex of the tongue or of the uvula does not impede the airflow significantly.

The resonant *r*'s and the resonant laterals together form a class called the **liquids**.

3.5.4 Pharyngeals

Another group of sounds, the **pharyngeals**, are closely related to the *r*-sounds just discussed. Pharyngeals, as you might expect, are also produced by constricting the pharynx, but without an accompanying uvular or apical articulation. Although these sounds are resonants, the constriction of the pharynx is often severe enough to produce some audible friction. The voiced pharyngeal is represented by the symbol [ʕ] (**ayn**) and its voiceless counterpart by [ħ] (**barred-h**). Pharyngeal sounds are relatively rare; however, they occur in Arabic, some Northwest Indian languages, and certain languages of the Caucasus.

3.5.5 Glides

Glides are sounds produced by gliding the tongue toward or away from a more prominent adjacent vowel. These sounds are sometimes called **semivowels** because their articulation involves a constriction of the oral cavity which is greater than that for the highest vowels but not great enough to produce friction.

The palatal glide [y] occurs in such words as *yet* and *yarn*. It is made with the blade of the tongue at the palate. The glide beginning the French word *huit* 'eight' is articulated in the same way but with the lips rounded. The symbol [ɥ] (**inverted-h**) is used to indicate the rounded palatal glide. The velar glide [w] occurs in English *wet* and *woo* and in French *oui* 'yes'. It is made with the body of the tongue raised toward the velum and with the lips rounded. Because of the lip rounding, [w] is sometimes considered a labial sound.

The glide [y] is made in much the same way as the vowel [i]. In both, the tongue is raised and extended and the lips unrounded. The glide [w] and the vowel [u] correspond in a similar manner, as do [ɥ] and [ü].

In diphthongs in which the first element (i.e., the beginning point) is more prominent than the second element, the motion away from the beginning point can be considered a glide. Diphthongs such as [ai̯, au̯, oi̯] are often transcribed as [ay, aw, oy].

3.6 AIRSTREAM MECHANISMS

The vast majority of speech sounds, including all of those discussed so far, are made with outgoing, or **egressive** air from the lungs. Expelling air from the lungs is, however, only one of the airstream mechanisms used in the production of speech sounds. There are a number of sounds that are made with other mechanisms.

In some languages egressive oral cavity sounds are produced by closing the glottis, then rapidly raising the larynx. Such sounds are called **ejectives**. Raising the larynx compresses the air in the oral cavity. Upon release of the primary articulation, air is ejected, producing a sound quite different from that made with lung air. Ejective sounds have a sharp popping quality. They are symbolized by a raised comma or by an exclamation mark, so that an ejective *t* is represented as [t'] or [t!] and an ejective lambda affricate by [ƛ'] or [ƛ!]. The most common ejective sounds are the voiceless stops and affricates found in a number of American Indian languages (especially in the Pacific Northwest) and in some of the languages of the Caucasus.

Some sounds are not made with egressive air but with **ingressive** air, that is, with air flowing into the mouth. It should be emphasized that ingressive air flows only into the oral cavity—not into the lungs. It is possible to make sounds while inhaling, but this seems to be done only for special purposes and only in a few languages. In Swedish, for example, one sometimes hears the word *ja* uttered with ingressive lung air, meaning 'I understand. Go on'.

The sounds made with ingressive air result from the creation of a partial vacuum in the mouth; this vacuum can be produced by closing the glottis and lowering the larynx rapidly while making an oral stop articulation, thereby increasing the displacement of air in the vocal tract. When the primary articulation for the stop is released, air is drawn into the mouth, creating a characteristic dull popping sound. Sounds made by lowering the larynx are called **implosive stops**. Implosive sounds are typically voiced. The symbols for implosives are the same ones used for the corresponding egressive stops but with a hook added at the top. Thus, the symbols [ɓ], [ɗ], and [ɠ] represent the voiced implosives *b*, *d*, and *g*. These sounds occur most commonly in certain African languages, but are also found in such diverse languages as Thai, Sindhi (a language of Pakistan) and Gitksan.

Ejectives and implosives are mirror-image sound types. In the case of ejectives the glottis is closed and the larynx is rapidly raised; in the case of implosives the glottis is closed and the larynx is rapidly lowered.

Besides implosion, there is another ingressive airstream mechanism, called **velaric**. Sounds made with this airstream mechanism are called **clicks**. In the production of a click a velar closure is made, as for a *k* or *g*, and an additional primary closure is made in front of the velar closure. A partial vacuum is created by pulling back the tongue while the primary closure is maintained. When the primary closure is released, a sharp click is heard as air rushes into the mouth.

Although English speakers do not use clicks in forming words, they do use them as nonlinguistic gestures of various sorts. For instance, the sound used by English speakers to express mild disapproval, often written 'tsk-tsk', is a dental click. The symbol for this dental click is an **inverted t** [ʇ]. The lateral click, symbolized [ʖ], is the sound used by English speakers to urge a horse forward. Clicks may also be bilabial, in which case they resemble a smacking or kissing gesture. An example of a voiceless labial click is [p⁻]. The symbol for a retroflexed click is [ʗ]. In addition, clicks may be voiced, aspirated, or nasalized. When no special symbol is available, a raised arrow may be added as a diacritic to indicate a click, as for [p⁻] above. Thus, [n⁻] represents an alveolar nasal click. Clicks are quite rare in languages of the world, occurring only in certain languages of southern Africa. The best known languages with clicks are Zulu, Xhosa (where the *Xh* represents an aspirated lateral click), and Hottentot.

3.7 SECONDARY ARTICULATIONS

Many of the basic speech sounds described above may be modified in various ways. Modifications which are imposed on the primary articulation of a sound are called **secondary articulations**. Aspiration of voiceless stops (discussed in section 3.4) is one type of secondary articulation. Aspiration can accompany obstruents other than voiceless stops. The initial affricate of *chip*, *church*, and the like is aspirated [čʰ]. When voiced stops and affricates are aspirated, the aspiration sounds somewhat like a voiced *h*. The voiced aspirates [bʰ, dʰ, gʰ, ǰʰ], for example, are found in Sanskrit and in other languages of India.

Another secondary articulation is **labialization**, which involves lip rounding and a high back tongue position. Labializing a consonant causes it to take on a *w*-like quality. The words *quench*, *quick*, and (in most dialects) *quart* all begin with *k*'s which are labialized. Labialization is represented by a superscript [ʷ]. A [k] with labialization is therefore written [kʷ]. The initial sound of *quench* and *quick*, which has aspiration as well as labialization, is symbolized [kʷʰ].

The adjectives *labialized* and *labial* must be kept distinct. The stop [p] is labial but not labialized. A labialized *p*, i.e., a labialized labial, is symbolized [pʷ], and a clear *w*-like sound is heard when the stop is released. Some English speakers pronounce *Pueblo* with an aspirated, labialized *p*: [pʷʰ].

Consonants may also be modified by extending the body of the tongue into the high front position; this produces a *y*-like modification called **palatalization**. The initial sounds of *few*, *hue*, *cue*, and *mule* are all produced in this manner. Compare these sounds with the initial sounds of *fool*, *hoot*, *cool*, and *moon*, all of which are made without palatalization. A raised *y* directly after a symbol indicates palatalization: the palatalized consonants in *few*, *hue*, and *mule* are symbolized [fʸ, hʸ, mʸ]. When lip rounding and palatalization occur simultaneously, as in the French word *suis*, the symbol [ɥ] is used: [sɥi].

Another modification of consonant sounds, called **velarization**, is achieved by raising the back of the tongue toward the velum during articulation. As we noted in section 3.5.2, the *l*'s at the beginning of the words *law* and *loop* have this velar articulation whereas those beginning *leap* and *late* do not. Arabic has a series of velarized consonants which are distinct from its plain ones. Velarized sounds are represented by adding the diacritic [˜] or a slash mark to the symbol for the sound in question. Thus, [ṭ] indicates a velarized [t], and [ɫ] a velarized or dark [l].

Consonant sounds may also be modified by constricting the pharynx during articulation. This secondary articulation is called **pharyngealization**. Pharyngeal constriction was mentioned previously as the primary articulation of *r*-sounds and pharyngeals. When a secondary pharyngeal constriction is superimposed upon a consonant articulation, the diacritic symbol [˜] is used. This is the same diacritic used to denote velarization. It is possible to use the same diacritic for these two secondary articulations because velarized and pharyngealized sounds are very similar and do not seem to be differentiated in any language.

Many speech sounds can be produced with a simultaneous tight closure of all or part of the glottis. Obstruents with this secondary modification are said to be **glottalized**; resonants, including vowels, modified in this manner are said to be **laryngealized**. The diacritic for glottalization and for laryngealization is a raised comma [']. Thus, [m̰] represents a laryngealized [m], and [p'] and [k'] represent glottalized [p] and [k]. Laryngealized resonants are made with a type of glottal action which sounds quite different from ordinary voicing. As discussed in section 2.11, this action is often termed *creaky voice*.

In section 3.6, both the symbols [t'] and [t!] are used to represent ejective *t*. Ejective consonants are, of course, glottalized. When it is necessary to distinguish simple glottalization from ejective glottalization, the symbol [t'] can be used for a simple glottalized *t* and [t!] for an ejective. Ordinarily, however, [t'] will serve for both types of glottalization. We know of no language that distinguishes simple glottalization from ejective glottalization. Indeed, in the linguistic literature the terms *ejective* and *glottalized* are often used indiscriminately.

A secondary articulation, then, is any articulation superimposed upon a more basic or primary articulation. The most common secondary articulations are listed in Table III. The use of the term *secondary* in this context is not to be confused with its use in speaking of vowels (see section 2.7).

Table III

SECONDARY ARTICULATION	SYMBOL
Labialization	[ʷ]
Aspiration	[ʰ]
Palatalization	[ʸ]
Palatalization and Rounding	[ᵁ]
Velarization	[˜]
Pharyngealization	[˜]
Glottalization (obstruents)	[']
Laryngealization (resonants)	[']

3.8 CONSONANT LENGTH

Consonants, like vowels, may occur in relatively longer and shorter forms. A colon is used to denote length in consonants as well as in vowels.

Thus, the symbol [n:] indicates a longer version of [n]. Swedish has both long and short consonants and long and short vowels. For example, in the Swedish word [tʰɑ:kʰ] 'roof' the vowel is long and the final consonant short, whereas in [tʰakʰ:] 'thanks' the vowel is short and the final consonant long. Between vowels, long consonants are subject to a process which changes them into two of their short counterparts. This process is called **gemination**; and doubled consonants or vowels, from whatever source are called **geminates**. Italian, for example, contrasts geminates with short consonants intervocalically (that is, between vowels):

can*ó*ne	'big cane'	can*nó*ne	'cannon'
ca*p*èlla	'nanny goat'	ca*pp*èlla	'chapel'
rá*t*o	'ratified'	rá*tt*o	'rat'
pò*s*a	'rest'	pò*ss*a	'power'

A similar distinction is found in Estonian, as the following word pairs illustrate:

ki*n*o	'movie'	ki*nn*o	'to the movies'
ma*j*a	'house'	ma*jj*a	'to the house'
ka*v*a	'program'	ka*vv*a	'into the program'

However, in Estonian three consonant lengths are possible: short, long, and overlong. Intervocalically, an overlong consonant resolves itself into a sequence of consonants, the first long and the second short. All of the doubled consonants in the examples above result from the gemination of overlong consonants. Thus, in Estonian it is possible to have a triplet of words: one with a short consonant, as in *lina* 'flax'; one with a long consonant (geminated in this case to two short consonants), as in *linna* 'city's'; and one with an overlong consonant (geminated to a long and a short), as in *linna* 'of the city'. In transcription, overlong consonants, when they are not geminated, can be symbolized [C::]. Thus [n::] is the transcription for overlong final *n*, as in Estonian *linn* 'city'.

3.9 VARIANT ARTICULATIONS

To indicate that a consonant is articulated at a position near but not at the one implied by the basic symbol, a properly oriented chevron is used, as for vowels (see section 2.11). Thus, a [k] articulated at a point somewhat toward the back of the velum can be represented by [k']; and one made toward the front of the velum by [kʻ].

As was noted above, [̥] indicates the voiceless variety of a segment whose symbol implies voicing. Thus, a voiceless *m* is transcribed [m̥]; a voiceless *b* (as opposed to *p*, which is tenser), is transcribed [b̥]; and a voiceless, nonfricative *l* is transcribed [l̥]. Note that the symbol [l̥] represents an unvoiced [l], not the fricative [ɬ], which is naturally unvoiced. The symbol [l̥] implies a laxer articulation with much less friction than does the symbol [ɬ].

Sometimes a small subscript symbol [ˬ] is used to indicate the voiced counterpart of a voiceless sound. Thus, [s̬] can be used to represent [z] in a language in which [z] occurs only as a predictable variant of [s]. Similarly, [x̬] can be used for [ɣ], [ɬ̬] for [ɮ], and so forth.

The symbols and diacritics presented in this chapter and in Chapter 2 allow us to represent many nuances of articulation. A transcription that records as many features of an utterance as can be ascertained by the person doing the recording is called a **narrow transcription**. For many uses, however, a less subtle transcription is perfectly suitable. A transcription that omits many of the irrelevant and predictable details of pronunciation is called a **broad transcription**. Most of the transcriptions presented in this book are broad.

3.10 ALTERNATIVE CONSONANT TRANSCRIPTIONS AND TERMINOLOGY

The consonant symbols introduced in this chapter are for the most part those in common use in American linguistics. However, in your reading you will no doubt encounter transcription systems which differ somewhat from that outlined here. For instance, the IPA uses the symbol [j] for the glide [y] rather than for the voiced alveolar affricate it represents in our system, and the symbol [y] is reserved for the vowel we have represented as [ü].

A number of other symbols recommended by the IPA also differ from those we have suggested. For instance, the IPA recommends the symbols [ɲ] and [N] for the nasals [ñ] and [ŋ]; and [ʃ], [ʒ], and [χ] for the fricatives [š], [ž], and [x]. The IPA also uses [ɕ] and [ʑ] for the palatalized dental fricatives [s̬ʸ] and [z̬ʸ]. To indicate retroflexion the IPA uses a small hook instead of [.]. Thus, [s̩, z̩, t̩, d̩] are written [ʂ, ʐ, ʈ, ɖ] in IPA transcription. For *r*-sounds, IPA uses plain symbols to indicate trills, and [ɾ] for the flap [ř]. And finally, the IPA transcribes affricates with digraphs: [ts] for [c]; [tʃ] for [č]; [dz] for [j]; [dʒ] for [ǰ]; and so forth.

You may also encounter symbols that have been created from regular typewriter characters. For example, the more exotic phonetic symbols are sometimes replaced by typewriter symbols modified by a hyphen. Thus, the [ɬ] is represented by [ł], [ɣ] by [g̶], the [ɸ] by [p̶], the [β] by [b̶], and the [ð] by [d̶]. The symbols created in this way are often referred to as *barred-l, barred-g, barred-p*, etc.

In the older literature, you will also find transcription systems and terminology no longer in use. In the 1920's, for example, those working with American Indian languages customarily utilized the symbols [c] for [š], [tc] for [č], [x] for [x], [x] for [x̣], and [L!] for [x̌']. In this same period the glottal stop [ʔ] was shown as [ˀ]. In the older literature, different terminology is also common. For instance, the term 'spirant' is used for *fricative*, 'mute' is used for *stops* and *nasals*, 'surd' for *voiceless sound*, and 'sonant' for *voiced sound*. Because of disparities of the sort indicated above, it is necessary to note carefully the descriptions of the sounds being symbolized in any book or article containing phonetic transcriptions.

3.11 CONSONANT CLASSIFICATION AND PHONOLOGY

This and the preceding chapter have been devoted primarily to providing two things necessary to the study of phonology: the classificatory descriptions of language sounds and the phonetic symbols used to represent these sounds. Compared to phonology, phonetics is a relatively well-developed science. The reader interested in pursuing the study of phonetics might begin with such works as Abercrombie, 1967; Brosnahan and Malmberg, 1970; Malmberg, 1968; and Pike, 1943.

Phonetic symbols are obviously of great practical value in transcribing the utterances of various languages and in making clear certain similarities and differences among languages. However, the classification of speech sounds is of far greater theoretical significance. It was pointed out in section 1.2 that phonological processes do not involve random sets of sounds; rather, they are based on sets of sounds characterizable in terms of phonetic classes. In section 1.1, a rule of German phonology involving the classes of voiced and voiceless stops was discussed. In this example, the voiced stops [b, d, g] become their voiceless counterparts [p, t, k] in word final position.

English also has processes involving voiced and voiceless consonants: in English the sounds [l] and [r], which are usually voiced, are voiceless when they follow *p*, *t*, or *k*, as in *play, pray, tray, clay, crayfish*. It is significant that the sounds [l] and [r] form a set characterizable in terms of the classifications provided earlier in this chapter (as do [p], [t] and [k], of course). The consonants [l] and [r] are resonant but not nasal. Therefore the class of English nonnasal resonant consonants consists of [l] and [r], just as the class of English voiceless stops consists of [p], [t], and [k]. In English, there is an assimilatory process which causes voiced nonnasal resonants to become voiceless after voiceless stops. It is thus not an accident that these two classes of sounds interact in the way they do.

Sanskrit provides us with another example of a process involving classes of sounds. In Sanskrit there is a class of sounds made up of the dental stops and the dental nasal [ṭ, ṭʰ, ḍ, ḍʰ, ṇ]. This class is paralleled by a set of retroflex consonants [ṭ, ṭʰ, ḍ, ḍʰ, ṇ]. Whenever a dental stop or nasal immediately follows a retroflex sound, it is replaced by its retroflex counterpart. For example, the past participle ending -*ta* becomes -*ṭa* when suffixed to the roots *dviṣ* 'hate', which ends in a retroflex *ṣ*, thus giving *dviṣṭa* 'hated'.

This rule of Sanskrit phonology, like those of English and German, involves sets of phonetically similar sounds. The similarities revealed by phonetic descriptions of speech sounds such as those presented in this chapter allow us to frame the rules of phonology in a general and plausible way. A rule that devoices resonant consonants after [p], [t], and [k], for example, is plausible phonetically, since [p], [t], and [k] are all voiceless. However, one that devoiced resonant consonants after, say, [p], [z], and [i] would be quite implausible. In fact, a rule that specified any process in the environment of a class made up of [p, z, i] would be implausible, since these sounds cannot be shown to be phonetically similar in any meaningful way. In the absence of the classifications provided by phonetic theory, however, [p, z, i] would be just as meaningful a collection of sounds as [p, t, k] and no more ad hoc. Phonology, then, if it is not to be a mysterious art, must rely on phonetics to provide the sound classes essential to the formulation of phonological rules.

3.12 SUMMARY

Speech sounds are divided into two major categories: **vowels**, which are sounds made by altering the shape of the oral cavity without significant constriction; and **consonants**, sounds produced by constricting the vocal tract in such a way as to divert, impede, or stop the flow of air. In describing and classifying consonants, five criteria are usually employed. These are: (1) the **point of articulation**, that point in the vocal tract where the greatest constriction occurs; (2) the **articulator**, the organ used to impede the airflow; (3) the **manner of articulation,** how the sound is produced; (4) the state of the vocal cords; and (5) the source of the airstream.

The points of articulation are the upper lip, the upper teeth, the alveolar ridge, the hard palate, the velum, the uvula, the pharynx, and the glottis. Sounds produced at these points are called, respectively, **labial, dental, alveolar, palatal, velar, uvular, pharyngeal,** and **glottal** sounds.

The major articulators are the lower lip, the apex of the tongue, the front of the tongue, and the dorsum. Consonants produced with these articulators are called, respectively, **labial, apical, frontal,** and **dorsal.**

The manner of articulation is very important in classifying consonants. Consonantal sounds characterized by a constriction which either interrupts the airflow or causes friction are called **obstruents.** Those with constrictions which are part of a shaping articulation are called **resonant consonants**.

Obstruents are of three types: **stops**, those sounds made by completely blocking off the flow of air and then releasing it; **fricatives**, sounds made by forcing air through a narrow passageway, thus causing friction; and **affricates**, sounds made by stopping the airflow and then releasing it into a fricative.

Resonant consonants include the **nasals**, sounds produced by lowering the velum and blocking the oral cavity, thus diverting the airstream through the nasal cavity; the **laterals**, sounds made by positioning the tongue in such a way that air can flow out along one or both sides; **r-sounds**, those sounds made by tightening the pharynx while articulating with either the tip of the tongue or the uvula; **pharyngeals**, those sounds made by constricting the pharynx without any accompanying oral articulation; and **glides**, sounds made by moving the tongue toward or away from a more prominent adjacent vowel.

Most speech sounds are made with an outgoing or **egressive** airstream. Those made with an ingoing flow of air are called **implosives** and **clicks**.

In addition to these primary forms of articulation, consonants may also be classified in terms of **secondary articulations**. These include **labialization, palatalization, velarization, pharyngealization, glottalization**, and **laryngealization**.

EXERCISES FOR CHAPTER 3

1. Given the terminology of Chapters 2 and 3, classify as narrowly as possible the following sets of sounds.

1. [i, n, l, r, y]		6. [t, l, d, n]
2. [y, w]		7. [g, ɣ, ŋ]
3. [h, ʔ]		8. [i, e, ɛ, æ]
4. [t, s, r]		9. [i, ü, u, ɯ]
5. [b, d, g, v, ð, z, ž]		10. [p, t, k, q]

2 a. Without consulting the text, try to write out the names of the following symbols.

1. [ʔ]	7. [ʎ]	13. [ḷ]
2. [β]	8. [ŋ]	14. [ð]
3. [š]	9. [θ]	15. [ɥ]
4. [ç]	10. [č]	16. [ř]
5. [ʕ]	11. [ɣ]	17. [ɓ]
6. [ř]	12. [ʀ]	18. [fʸ]

    b. Check any answers you are unsure of. Memorize those you did not know.

    c. Describe how each of the sounds symbolized above is produced.

3. Give the symbols for two sounds which fall into each of the following categories.

1. voiced stops	7. voiced affricates
2. r-sounds	8. grooved fricatives
3. dental fricatives	9. nasals
4. voiceless bilabials	10. semivowels
5. velars	11. prenasalized stops
6. liquids	12. laterals

4. Identify the following words. The transcriptions represent common American English pronunciations. Stress and length are not represented.

a.

1. [θr̃i]	11. [wɔrt]	21. [stɹeit']
2. [fɔr]	12. [hɑt']	22. [smuð]
3. [tʷʰaịs]	13. [k̟lin]	23. [rau̯di]
4. [ʔɒɫ]	14. [tɹaị]	24. [θu̯k̟']
5. [mɛni]	15. [dʌɫ]	25. [kʰʌ̃m]
6. [blæk̟']	16. [šɑrp']	26. [fɒɫ]
7. [rɛ̯ʒd]	17. [pʸʰur]	27. [gou̯]
8. [hʷaịt']	18. [łaịt']	28. [pʰɛlt']
9. [gʊ̯ʒd]	19. [łɒŋ]	29. [dæ̃c']
10. [sɪt']	20. [šɔrt']	30. [dɹæịg̰]

b.

1. [kʰau̯]	11. [kʰʊk']	21. [wɪ̃k']
2. [gɪ̯ʒv]	12. [dip']	22. [sɪ̃ŋ]
3. [hʸuǰ]	13. [lɛft]	23. [læf]
4. [slæp']	14. [hʷɛ̃n]	24. [kʰɒf]
5. [tʰeịk̟']	15. [fɒ̯ʒg]	25. [łʌ̃ŋz]
6. [rʌb]	16. [ʔaịs]	26. [rut']
7. [skɹæč']	17. [snou̯]	27. [pʰãị̃n]
8. [šut']	18. [pʰæθ]	28. [fłaị]
9. [splɪt']	19. [sʌ̃n]	29. [ʔɛłk']
10. [hʌ̃t']	20. [yɪr]	30. [dɒ̯ʒg]

5. What are some of the consistent features of the dialect represented in Exercise 4? Where do glottalized stops appear? What is the nature of the voiceless stops that precede vowels? What kind of *r* occurs initially before vowels? After *t*? After *d*? What kind of *t* and *d* occur before *r*? How is orthographic *ng* rendered? Answer these questions and make any other observations that you can about the systematic characteristics of the sample.

6. Keeping in mind the observations you made concerning the pronunciations above, transcribe the following words as you say them. Your pronunciation may vary in a few or even many respects from that presented in Exercise 4.

a.

1. work	11. pay	21. full
2. arm	12. bind	22. dull
3. box	13. bleak	23. stand
4. hill	14. blow	24. four
5. bath	15. alive	25. for
6. child	16. book	26. try
7. ask	17. buy	27. floor
8. keep	18. bread	28. take
9. need	19. both	29. hair
10. leg	20. this	30. stitch

b.

1. poor	11. down	21. real
2. pour	12. well	22. our
3. yeah	13. next	23. eye
4. call	14. boy	24. which
5. skirt	15. talk	25. mist
6. clock	16. pump	26. deaf
7. strong	17. shoe	27. one
8. free	18. cute	28. jump
9. smell	19. tree	29. comb
10. lunch	20. this	30. calm

7. Describe the following processes. The arrow is read 'become(s)'.

1. [b, d, g] → [p, t, k], respectively
2. [z, ž] → [s, š], respectively
3. [x, γ] → [k, g], respectively
4. [t, d] → [č, ǰ], respectively
5. [i, u, ü] → [y, w, ɥ], respectively
6. [n] → [ñ] immediately before a palatal stop
7. [n] → [m] immediately before [p, b]
8. [d] → [l] immediately before [l]
9. [t, θ, k, x] → [d, ð, g, γ], respectively, before a voiced sound
10. [k, g, x] → [kʷ, gʷ, xʷ], respectively, after [u, o, ɔ]

8. The regular past tense ending in Swedish is basically -*de* as in examples 1–10 below. In examples 11–18, however, -*de* has become -*te*. Examine

the final sound of each verb stem and determine the conditions under which *d → t*. In the examples, e=[ə], å=[o], ä=[ε], y=[ü], and öj=[öy].

1. baka-de	'baked'	10. glad-de	'pleased'
2. fråga-de	'asked'	11. köp-te	'bought'
3. ställ-de	'put'	12. ryck-te	'pulled'
4. bygg-de	'built'	13. läs-te	'read'
5. gräv-de	'dug'	14. möt-te	'met'
6. glöm-de	'forgot'	15. tänk-te	'thought'
7. kän-de	'knew'	16. kyss-te	'kissed'
8. höj-de	'raised'	17. krymp-te	'shrunk'
9. hör-de	'heard'	18. försök-te	'tried'

9. The consonants of Nyangumarda (a Pama-Nyungan language of Western Australia) are arranged below into nine classes. Using such articulatory parameters as voiceless, nasal, alveolar, stop, glide, etc., specify each of these nine classes. (Based on Hoard and O'Grady, 1976.)

	(5)	(6)	(7)	(8)	(9)
(1)	p	t		t^y	k
(2)	m	n		n^y	ŋ
(3)		l	r	l^y	
(4)				y	w

10. The Nyangumarda consonants *t*, *n*, and *l* become retroflexed in some environments; *l* and *r* are devoiced in yet another environment. Based on the following examples, determine the environments in which these processes occur. On the voicing of *t* see Exercise 11 below. (Based on Hoard and O'Grady, 1976.)

1. karta	[kɑrdɐ]	'sleep (n.)'
2. pirntil	[pirṇdɨ̩]	'back, spine'
3. partarl	[parḍarḷ]	'in vain'
4. larlka	[larḷgɐ]°	'dry'
5. parir	[parɨ̥r̃]	'hand'
6. karlu	[karḷṷ]	'soft mud'
7. pala	[palɐ]	'that (nearby)'
8. kata	[kadɐ]	'more, again'
9. yanamarna	[yanɑmɑrṇɐ̥]	'I was about to go'

11. In Nyangumarda, *p*, *t*, *tʸ*, and *k* become [b], [d], [dʸ], [g], respectively, in one environment but are unchanged in another environment. Examine the following examples to determine what these environments are. (Based on Hoard and O'Grady, 1976.)

1. mampu   [mambu]   'hair'
2. kata   [kɑdɐ]   'more, again'
3. katʸa   [kadʸɐ]   'far'
4. puka   [pugɐ]   'rotten'
5. kaku   [kɑgu]   'deep'
       ([kɑk' y̦], if said in isolation)
6. yurpa   [yurbɐ]   'to rub'
7. ŋalpa   [ŋalbɐ]   'to enter'
8. kalku   [kɑlgu]   'to care for'
9. yukurru   [yuguř y̦]   'dog'
10. milpinʸ   [mɪlbinʸ]   'fingernail'
11. ralʸup   [ralʸʊp']   'whoosh'
12. kartku   [kɑrt'k'y̦]   'river gum tree'
13. partanʸ   [pɑrɖanʸ]   'child'
14. nurta   [nurɖɐ]   'blunt, dull'

4 syllables

4.1 INTRODUCTION

In the preceding two chapters we discussed the phonetic properties of sound segments, which are the building blocks of speech. However, spoken language is not simply a linear sequence of sound segments. Rather, vowels and consonants group together to form larger units of sound such as syllables, words, phrases, and sentences. In this chapter we will be concerned with the nature and properties of a more complex phonetic structure: the syllable.

4.2 THE PSYCHOLOGICAL REALITY OF THE SYLLABLE

There are many indications that the syllable is a psychologically real unit. For instance, speakers of unwritten languages, if asked to divide a word into its constituent parts, will usually divide it into syllables rather than individual sound segments. Indeed, it may prove difficult to convince them that further divisions are possible. The same is true of English-speaking children before they are introduced to the alphabetic writing system.

56

Furthermore, in any language a given word will be divided into the same number of syllables by nearly all speakers (although they may not always agree as to where the syllables begin and end). Any speaker of English could tell you that the words *articulation, astronomical,* and *serendipity* have five syllables each, whereas *communal, advertise,* and *occupy* have only three.

The ease with which speakers with no linguistic training can identify the number of syllables in a word is even more striking when one considers the difficulty these same speakers have in determining the number of individual sounds in a word. If you ask a linguistically naïve speaker how many syllables the word *singer* has, for example, you will almost invariably be told that there are two. But if you ask how many sounds this word has, you may receive a variety of answers ranging from two to six. (Actually, there are four in most dialects.)

Speakers of all English dialects agree on the number of syllables in most words. But even in those words with a variable number of syllables, there is generally agreement within a given dialect concerning the number of syllables a word contains. Although British and American speakers would disagree on the number of syllables in *secretary,* British speakers consistently divide it into three and Americans just as consistently divide it into four. Of course, even speakers of the same dialect may vary somewhat in the number of syllables they ascribe to certain words, but this too falls within predictable limits. Thus, some speakers pronounce *reckoning* and *wobbly* with two syllables and some with three; but no speaker would pronounce these words with four syllables or one.

Further evidence of the psychological reality of the syllable may be found in the writing systems of a number of languages. Unlike English, French, or Russian—all of which have symbols for individual sounds—some languages have writing systems that are syllable based. For example, the writing system devised by the Cherokee scholar Sequoya for his native language has a symbol for each syllable. Sequoya was familiar with the Latin alphabet, but apparently could not read and write English. In any event, he took the Latin alphabet, added a number of additional symbols (most are variations of Latin letters), and assigned syllable values to the symbols. The Cherokee syllabary is given in Figure 4.1. In this syllabary system *Sequoya* is spelled with three symbols and can be transliterated as *si-kwo-ya.* A syllabary is well suited to Cherokee, since its syllabic structure is predominantly of the consonant plus vowel (CV) type.

The Cherokee example is not an isolated case. The writing systems of the ancient Assyrians and Persians consisted of a combination of syllable and word symbols, as does that of modern Japanese. Since writing systems are attempts to characterize the nature of speech, the inventors of these syllabic systems must have perceived the syllable as a real and basic speech unit.

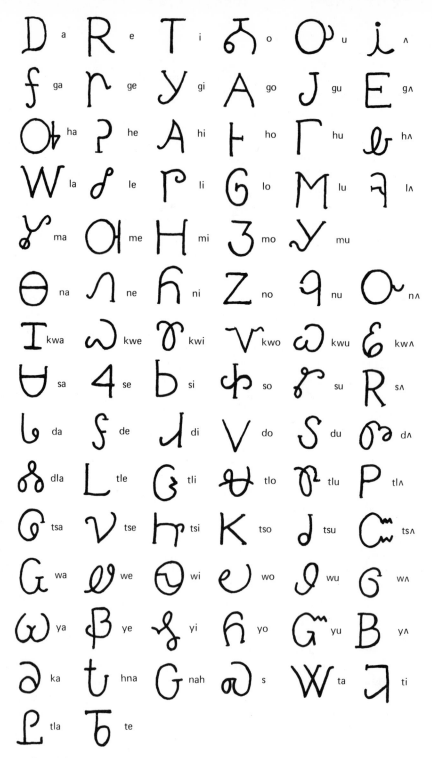

Figure 4.1
The Cherokee Syllabary

4.3 SYLLABLE PRODUCTION AND RECOGNITION

It seems clear that the syllable is a genuine and easily recognized unit of speech. What is less clear is how speakers produce and recognize these units. It has been said of the syllable that it is easy to identify but impossible to define. What precisely is a syllable? How do speakers determine the number of syllables in any given utterance? How do speakers segment a given utterance into discrete syllables? Various answers to these questions have been offered, none of which is completely satisfactory. It has been hypothesized (Stetson, 1951) that a syllable is a group of sounds which is made with a single puff of air. According to this approach each syllable is produced by a chest pulse, a single small contraction of the muscles between the ribs, which forces a puff of air from the lungs through the vocal tract.

However, it is not clear that every syllable invariably involves a chest pulse. For example, the word *city* may be produced with only one chest pulse if the division into two syllables is effected by introducing a flap in the middle of a single pulse. On the other hand, a word like *pots* might have only one syllable so far as English speakers are concerned but consist of two chest pulses, one for *pot*, terminated by the stop *t*, and an additional, weaker pulse for the final *s*. Even if there were a one-to-one correspondence of chest pulses and syllables, the difficulty speakers often have in determining which of two adjacent syllables contains a particular consonant segment belies the claim that syllables are neatly separated by the termination of one chest pulse and the start of another. Despite these difficulties Stetson's proposal is not unreasonable. Certainly, any theory concerning syllable production must take into account the fact that the production of speech sounds requires the controlled expulsion of air from the lungs.

In all probability, we recognize syllables through a combination of factors, including sonority (relative prominence), stress, length, pitch, and certain phonetic features characteristic of the beginnings and endings of syllables (such as the aspiration of syllable initial voiceless stops in English).

4.4 SYLLABIC SEGMENTS

Each syllable centers around one prominent segment, typically a vowel or resonant, which may be preceded and/or followed by other, less prominent segments. This central most prominent part of the syllable is called the **syllabic** segment. The most commonly occurring syllabics are vowels. Consider the following single-syllable words and you will discover the most prominent sound in each to be the vowel:

cot	sill
bat	corn
neck	push

Because vowels are almost always syllabic, the usual vowel symbols imply syllabicity. In cases where vowels are nonsyllabic, they are marked with a diacritic [͜]. The glides [y] and [w] are sometimes written as nonsyllabic vowels [i̯] and [u̯], so that *wet* is transcribed [u̯ɛt] and *yet* [i̯ɛt].

In contrast to vowels, consonants are usually nonsyllabic. Since consonant symbols do not imply syllabicity, syllabic consonants must be marked by a diacritic [ˌ]. Thus, a syllabic *r* is written [r̩]. The majority of syllabic consonants are either liquids or nasals. English has a number of words, such as *fur* [fr̩], *pert* [pr̩t], and *bird* [br̩d], in which the only syllabic segment is the liquid [r̩]. The spelling of these words might suggest that they are pronounced with a [ʊ], [ɛ], or [ɪ], but this is not so.

Trilled *r*'s, as well as plain *r*'s, can be syllabic segments. In Serbo-Croatian, for instance, a trilled *r* is the only syllabic in words such as *hrt* 'dog' and *vrh* 'hill'. Similarly, in Czech, [ř̩] appears in words like *krk* 'neck' and *prve* 'first'.

As a rule, a resonant consonant will become syllabic if it is neither preceded nor followed by a syllabic segment. But there are exceptions to this generalization. French, for example, has resonant nonsyllabic consonants in final position after a consonant, as in [tabl̥] 'table'.

Although most syllabic consonants are resonants, fricatives may also be syllabic. Syllabic fricatives do not occur in English except in a few isolated instances, such as the attention-getting interjection *pst!* [ps̩t]; but in a few languages, such as Bella Coola, they occur quite frequently. The Bella Coola word [ɬ̩k'ʷ] 'big', for example, has as its only syllabic a lateral fricative.

While outside of a few interjections English does not have words whose only syllabic segment is a consonant, there are a large number of English words of two or more syllables which contain both vowels and syllabic consonants. In each of the following disyllabic words the second syllable contains a syllabic consonant.

butter	[bʌdr̩]	smitten	[smɪt'n̩]
caller	[kɒlr̩]	sudden	[sʌdn̩]
pickle	[pɪkl̩]	beckon	[bɛkn̩]
battle	[bædl̩]	cotton	[kɑt'n̩]

A resonant consonant is also present in the first syllable of words like *contain* [kn̩tein] and *comply* [km̩plai̯]; and, in rapid speech, in words like *parade* [pr̩eid]. Compare the syllabic *r* of *parade* to the nonsyllabic and voiceless *r* of *prayed* [pr̥ɹeid].

There are more syllabic consonants in rapid speech than in slow, careful speech. This is so because speakers have a tendency to drop segments in rapid speech, and if the segment dropped is a vowel, an adjacent consonant may become syllabic. For example, in rapid speech the English conjunction *and* usually takes the form of a syllabic nasal, either [n̩], [m̩], or [ŋ̩], depending on the adjacent consonants.

[n̩]	room and board
[n̩]	pots and pans
[m̩]	up and back
[ŋ̩]	back and forth

The division point between syllables, called the syllable juncture, is marked with a hyphen [-]. For the word *parade*, then, the syllabication is [pr̩-eid]. We know that the word *mistake* is divided after the first vowel, [mɪ-steik], because the lack of aspiration in the *t* indicates that it is in the same syllable as the *s*. *Mistime*, on the other hand, must be syllabicated [mɪs-tʰaim] because the aspiration of the *t* of *time* indicates that it is the initial sound in the syllable. The segments within a single syllable are said to be **tautosyllabic**. In *mistake*, then, the *s* and *t* are tautosyllabic, but in *mistime* they are not.

Syllabic segments as a class are often represented by the symbol V, although V is also sometimes used to denote vowels only. Nonsyllabics are represented by the symbol C.

4.5 SYLLABLE STRUCTURE

Structurally, the syllable may be divided into three parts: the peak, the onset, and the coda. The most prominent part of the syllable—that which contains the syllabic segment—is called the **syllable peak**. The word *parade* [pr̩-eid] has two peaks, [r̩] and [ei]. Sometimes a syllable may be composed of only a peak, as in the last syllables of *bottle*, *butter*, and *city*. More frequently, however, a syllable will also have segments preceding and/or following its peak.

The **onset** of a syllable consists of all the segments that precede the peak and are tautosyllabic with it. The **coda** consists of all the tautosyllabic segments that follow the peak. The first syllable of *parade*, [pr̩], has an onset [p] but no coda, whereas the second syllable, [eid], has a coda [d] but no onset. A syllable that has no coda is called an **unchecked** or **open syllable**; one with a coda is called a **checked** or **closed syllable**. Thus, the first syllable of *parade* is open and the second, closed.

The word *stop* consists of a single syllable with [st] as its onset, [ɑ] as its peak, and [p] as its coda. The peak and coda of a syllable form a unit called the **syllable core** (Pike and Pike, 1947). The word *stop* thus has the following syllabic structure:

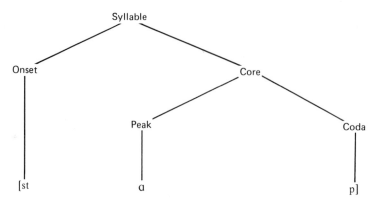

Figure 4.2
Syllable Structure of stop

4.6 CODA RESTRICTIONS

Individual languages differ a great deal in the kinds of syllables they have. Some of these differences stem from language-specific restrictions placed upon the structure of onsets and codas.

Apparently, no language has only syllables without onsets. Every language has at least some open syllables with a single consonant as onset, such as those in the following list:

English	do	
French	tu	'you (familiar)'
Mandarin	ma	'horse'
Swahili	la	'no'
Spanish	si	'yes'
Turkish	su	'water, juice'
Twi	ka	'to remain'
Eastern Ojibwa	na	'go on, do'
Hausa	ke	'you (fem. sing.)'
German	da	'there'

Some languages, such as Hawaiian, have only open syllables. Every syllable in Hawaiian ends in a vowel. Japanese is somewhat like Hawaiian in this respect. Some closed syllables do occur in Japanese but they are of a very limited sort. There are many Japanese words, such as *shika* 'deer', *suidoo* 'channel', and *ni* 'cargo, baggage', which end in a vowel, and a smaller number of words like *kisen* 'steamship' and *kyooben* 'teaching position' which end in a syllablic nasal, but no words that end in an [r] or a [k], for instance.

In Finnish, the situation is more complex. The final syllable of a Finnish word can end in a vowel (by far the most common situation) or a single alveolar consonant (*t, s, n, l,* or *r*), as in the words *sanot* 'you (sing.) say', *taas* 'again', *tulin* 'I come, am coming', *sammal* 'moss', and *kinner* 'Achilles tendon (nom. sing.)'. Finnish tolerates a somewhat wider range of consonants as the last sound of a syllable within a word including, in addition to those noted for final syllables, *p, m, k,* and *h*. In the examples below, syllables are again separated by a hyphen.

lap-si	'child'	pois-sa	'away'
läm-pö	'heat'	lin-na	'fortress, jail'
mak-sa	'to pay, cost'	pul-lo	'bottle'
lëh-ma	'cow'	par-ta	'beard'
nät-ti	'pretty'		

Within words, coda clusters consisting of a resonant (*n, l, r,* or *m*) followed by a voiceless obstruent (*s, p, t,* or *k*) also occur. Thus, the clusters *ns, nt, nk, lk, lp, lt, rt, rp, rs, rk,* and *mp* are found at the end of medial syllables (as the following examples show) but never at the end of words.

tans-ka	'Danish'	kort-teli	'a city block'
kynt-tilä	'candle'	torp-pa	'cottage'
kink-ku	'ham'	myrs-ky	'storm'
silk-ki	'silk'	mark-ka	'mark'
help-po	'easy'	komp-pania	'an army company'
kilt-ti	'nice'		

English is even more complex than Finnish in the types of codas it allows. In final position an English syllable may have no coda, as in *spa*, or may be checked by from one to four consonants, as in *top*, [tɑp], *apt* [æpt], *arched* [arčt] and *sixths* [siksθs].

4.7 ONSET RESTRICTIONS

Languages also differ in the kinds of syllable onsets they allow. In some languages, all of the syllables have onsets. This is true of Quileute, Coeur d'Alene, and Puget Salish, for example. Most languages, however, have at least some syllables that lack onsets. Hawaiian, Japanese, Finnish, and English all have syllables that begin with vowels. Thus, in Hawaiian we find such words as [ahi] 'fire' and [ola] 'life'; in Japanese, [aoku] 'to be blue' and [aimasu] 'to meet'; in Finnish, [on] 'is' and [iso] 'large'; and in English, *of* and *angry*.

All of the four languages just mentioned allow syllables beginning with either one or no consonants, but only English allows more than one consonant in the onset. English syllables may have onsets of from one to three consonants, as the words *ray*, *pray*, and *spray* illustrate. In English, three-consonant onsets are highly restricted in their composition. The first consonant in such onsets must be an *s*, the second a voiceless stop, and the third a liquid (as in *split*, *spry*, *scream*, and *sclerosis*). Moreover, if the second consonant is *t*, the third must be *r* (as in *stream*, *stroke*, and *stray*).

Some other languages allow more varied onsets. Serbo-Croatian has onsets of up to three consonants, but these are less restricted in their composition than are their English counterparts. In Serbo-Croatian, the first consonant of a three-part onset is not limited to *s*, but may be any of the fricatives [s, z, š, ž, h] or [g]; the second may be a voiced or voiceless stop, or [m] or [v]; and the third may be a glide, a liquid, or [v] or [n]. The following words illustrate the variety of onsets possible in Serbo-Croatian. In these words *j* represents [y].

smràad	'filth'	ždrijébac	'stallion'
svjèdok	'witness'	žglòb	'joint'
štrìk	'rope'	htjèti	'to want'
škrìn'a	'box'	gdjè	'where'
zgn'eéčiti	'to crush'	zdvòjiti	'to get together'

Serbo-Croatian, then, reaches the upper limits of diversity and length for syllable onsets. Although some languages allow onsets of more than three consonants, very long onsets are rare even in the languages that allow them.

4.8 WEAK AND STRONG SYLLABLES

Depending upon the composition of its core, a syllable may be said to be weak or strong. The syllable onset has no bearing on this matter at all. The core of a **weak syllable** contains a short vowel followed by no more than one short consonant. Thus, the second syllables of *sofa*, *bullet*, and *method* are all weak. The space of time occupied by a single weak syllable is termed a **mora** (plural **morae**). In certain languages—Southern Paiute, for instance—the mora is an important unit in the determination of stress placement (Sapir, 1930).

A **strong syllable** occupies more than one mora. Its core is composed of one of the following:

(a) a long vowel, with or without a coda of any length;
(b) a short vowel followed by two or more consonants;
(c) a short vowel followed by at least one long consonant.

In some languages, such as Latin, the distinction between strong and weak syllables is important in stress placement. A number of recent works (Chomsky and Halle, 1968; Ross, 1973; Hoard and Sloat, 1973; and Sloat, 1974) assume that syllable structure is also relevant to stress placement in English words. In languages such as English, which distinguish vowels on the basis of whether they are tense or lax rather than long or short, weak and strong syllables are defined according to whether they contain tense or lax vowels. This is not an unexplainable fact; as we noted in section 2.10, tense vowels are intrinsically longer than lax ones. The definitions of weak and strong syllables given above can be made to apply to languages such as English by simply substituting *lax* for each occurrence of *short*, and *tense* for each occurrence of *long*.

The English words *mean* and *almost* have strong final syllables of type (a). The words *indent* and *arrest* have final strong syllables of type (b). When situated before a syllable with an onset, a syllable containing a VC core is termed **strong by position**. Whereas the final syllables of *indent* and *arrest* are strong by nature; the first syllables of *al-most*, *ad-vise*, and *tor-ment* are strong by position. In the word *Adirondack* the next to last syllable, *ron*, would be weak if it did not precede a syllable beginning with a consonant. The first syllable of *mi-stake* is weak since *st* forms the onset of the final syllable. English has no examples of type (c) strong syllables. Swedish does, however, in *vitt* 'white (neut.)', *hack* 'notch', *skinn* 'skin', and *tagg* 'spine, barb', each of which ends in a long consonant.

4.9 SUMMARY

In this chapter we have considered the structure and function of a very basic unit of sound—the syllable. Evidence from a number of sources strongly suggests that the syllable is a psychologically real unit of language. Most speakers, including speakers of unwritten languages, can divide words into syllables quite effortlessly. It is difficult to determine exactly how speakers do this, however. A combination of factors is probably involved, including sonority, stress, length, pitch, and certain phonetic features characteristic of the beginnings and endings of syllables. There has been a good deal of discussion in the linguistic literature about rules for syllable division and the place of the syllable in phonological descriptions. (See, for example, Pulgram, 1970; Hoard, 1971; Hooper, 1972; Newman, 1972; Vennemann, 1972.)

Syllables are divided into two main parts—an onset and a core. The core is further divided into a peak and a coda. The **peak** is the most prominent segment in the syllable. It may consist of a vowel (by far the most common situation), a resonant, or, infrequently, a fricative. Consonants that form the peak of a syllable are called **syllabic** consonants. The **onset** of a syllable consists of all the segments in that syllable up to the peak; the **coda** consists of all the segments in that syllable which follow the peak. A syllable that has no coda is called an **unchecked** or **open syllable**; one with a coda is called a **checked** or **closed syllable**.

Languages place different restrictions on the structure of their syllable onsets and codas. Some languages, such as Hawaiian, strictly limit the syllable types they will allow; others, such as English, admit a wide variety.

A syllable may be either weak or strong, depending on the type and number of segments in its core. Syllable strength is important in some languages for determining stress placement.

EXERCISES FOR CHAPTER 4

1. Below is a list of rather uncommon English words. How many syllables do you think each of these words contains? Check your answers against the syllabification provided in a large, unabridged dictionary. How often did you determine the correct number of syllables, even in words you had never encountered before?

Mishnical	rachitomous
lituiform	incomity
humic	gyve
fimbria	dothienenteritis
nowy	boltel
Palatinate	crinitory
dush	hoppet

2 **a.** Using the Cherokee syllabary given in Figure 4.1, transliterate the following English words into Cherokee script.

1. go	6. seamy
2. you	7. iota
3. yo-yo	8. yucca
4. emu	9. sully
5. saga	10. gay

b. See how close you can come to transcribing your name in Cherokee script.

c. Would the Cherokee syllabary be a satisfactory writing system for English? Why or why not?

3. Which of the following words in each pair contains a syllabic consonant?

1. rotten   rattan
2. card   curd
3. cattle   cattail
4. firm   farm
5. wobbly   wobble
6. burr   bear

4. Divide each of the following one-syllable words into its component onset and core. Then divide each core into its peak and coda. Note the syllables that lack one or more of these parts.

fact	[fækt]	pay	[peɪ]
spleen	[splin]	plot	[plɑt]
fraud	[frɒd]	hand	[hænd]
old	[old]	milk	[mɪlk]
bring	[brɪŋ]	strict	[strɪkt]
stump	[stʌmp]	cats	[kæts]
art	[ɑrt]	to	[tu]
fern	[fr̩n]	and	[ænd]

5. Determine every possible syllable onset in the following list of Swedish words. Do the same for the word final codas. Can you make any general statements about the configurations of Swedish onsets and codas such as those made for English and Finnish in sections 4.6 and 4.7? Which Swedish clusters would never occur in English onsets and codas?

splittra	[splɪt-třa]	'splinter'
springa	[spřɪŋ-ŋa]	'run'
spjut	[spyʉ:t]	'spear'
ström	[střö:m]	'stream'
skri	[skři:]	'scream'
skvätta	[skvɛt-ta]	'squirt'
plikt	[plɪkt]	'duty'
björk	[byœřk]	'birch'
gnaga	[gnɑ:-ga]	'grow'
röd	[řö:d]	'red'
kniv	[kni:v]	'knife'
tämj	[tɛmʸ]	'tame (imperative)'
tänj	[tɛnʸ]	'stretch (imperative)'
långt	[lɔŋ:t]	'long (neut.)'

glovs	[glo:vs]	'globes'
glops	[glo:ps]	'stripling's'
vrede	[vře-:də]	'wrath'
fnissa	[fnɪs-sa]	'giggle'
kramp	[křamp]	'cramp'
tjäna	[çʸɛ:-na]	'to serve'

6. For the following words try to determine which *t*'s, *p*'s, and *k*'s are aspirated and which are not. Does the point of syllable division or the presence of a tautosyllabic consonant seem to determine (entirely or in part) the appearance of aspiration?

stop	pill	happy	police
top	still	misspell	ketone
spot	till	mis-total	satire
pot	skill	mistake	satirist
spar	kill	master	Hittite
par	ski	nifty	echo
spill	key	disturb	echoic

7. Determine the syllable strength of each of the syllables in the words given below. Which syllables are strong by position?

mun-dane	pen-cil
ve-to	for-mal-de-hyde
ob-long	At-lan-tic
hos-tile	wal-nut
po-lice	per-ma-nent

8. The Nyangumarda consonants were given in Exercise 3.9. Every Nyangumarda word and syllable begins with a single consonant. Most Nyangumarda words end in a vowel. Nyangumarda codas and medial sequences of consonants are given below. The sequences given in parentheses are not attested in the available data but their absence seems to be accidental rather than systematic. (Based on Hoard and O'Grady, 1976)

   a. single word-final consonants: n, nʸ, l, lʸ, r, p, t, tʸ, k.
   b. word final consonant clusters: rt, rn, rl.
   c. medial sequences of two consonants:

rp	np	lp	nʸp	lʸp	rr	mp
rt	nt	lt	nʸk	lʸk	rn	ŋk
rtʸ	ntʸ	ltʸ	nʸm	(lʸm)	rl	nʸtʸ
rk	nk	lk	(nʸŋ)	lʸŋ		lʸtʸ
rm	nm	(lm)	(nʸw)	(lʸw)		
rŋ	nŋ	lŋ				
rw	(nw)	lw				

d. medial sequences of three consonants:

rtp	rnp	rlp
rtt^y	rnt	rlt
rtk	rnt^y	rlt^y
rtm	rnk	rlk
rtŋ	rnm	rlm
rtw	rnŋ	rlŋ
	rnw	rlw

The point of syllable division of the two-consonant medial sequences is C–C; that of the three-consonant medial sequences is CC–C. With this syllable division in mind, state in general terms, such as liquid + stop, stop + stop, and so forth, the permissible Nyangumarda syllable codas, both medial and final.

5 prosodic elements

5.1 INTRODUCTION

The term *prosody* has traditionally been used in the analysis of poetry to mean 'metrical structure' or 'versification'. In linguistics, too, *prosody* involves the study of the rhythmic structure of speech sounds. However, whereas the student of metrics confines his notion of prosody to the form and style of poetry, the linguist uses the term more broadly to refer to the rhythmic nature of language in general. To a linguist, then, **prosody** is the study of (1) quantity, stress, and tone in relation to the syllable and (2) intonation in relation to phonetic phrases and sentences. Instead of prosody, some linguists use the term **suprasegmentals** in essentially the same sense (e.g., Lehiste, 1970).

5.2 QUANTITY

It was noted in section 1.3 that some sound segments intrinsically take longer to produce than others. Typically, tense vowels take longer than their lax counterparts, low vowels take longer than higher ones, and diphthongs take longer than simple vowels. However, such measures of intrinsic length are of limited interest in phonology. Of much more interest is the fact that most sounds, regardless of their intrinsic length, may be produced in relatively longer and shorter forms. The relative length or **quantity** of speech sounds is often utilized in languages to distinguish words. In section 2.10 we gave examples of German word pairs which are differentiated primarily by the relative length of their vowels. Also, in section 3.8 we gave Estonian word pairs which are distinguished by the length of their consonants. And, as noted in section 4.8, quantity also serves to separate syllables into the two types—weak and strong—which in some languages play an important role in the placement of stress.

5.3 STRESS

In many languages, including English, some syllables within a word are relatively more prominent than others. In the word *message,* for example, the first syllable is more prominent than the second. In the word *massage,* however, the reverse is true. In yet other words, such as *guitar* and *police,* either the first syllable or the second may be more prominent, depending on the dialect being spoken. A syllable that is more prominent than the other syllables in a word or phrase is said to be **accented** or **stressed**. Languages which have syllables that differ in stress are called **stress languages**.

English syllables seem to be stressed by a combination of raised pitch and increased loudness and length (Fry, 1955, 1958). Compare the pronunciation of the word *insert* in the sentence *Please insert tab A in slot B* with its pronunciation in the sentence *Today's newspaper had an insert advertising school clothes.* When used as a noun, as in the second sentence, *insert* has its first syllable strongly accented. The most strongly accented syllable of a word is said to carry **primary stress**, indicated by an acute accent mark [´]. The noun *insert,* which has primary stress on its first syllable, is transcribed [ínsɹt]. The word *insert* when used as a verb, as in the first sentence, has primary stress on the final syllable and is transcribed [ɪnsɹ́t].

Although the second syllable of the noun *insert* is less prominent than the first, it is not entirely unaccented. Rather, it has an intermediate or **secondary stress**. The grave accent mark [`] is used to indicate that a syllable carries secondary stress. Thus, a more precise phonetic transcription of the nominal form *insert* would be: [ínsɹ̀t].

The first syllable of the verb form *insert,* on the other hand, has neither primary nor secondary stress. Usually, unaccented syllables such as this are transcribed without an accent mark. Thus, the transcription of the verb *insert* given above, [ɪnsɹ́t], reflects precisely the correct stress pattern.

Distinguishing between syllables with secondary stress and those with no stress at all is sometimes a difficult task. But it is one which becomes easier with practice. In the following pairs of English words, the first member has a secondary stress on the last syllable; the second does not. Compare these words and attempt to establish for yourself the difference between syllables lacking stress and those carrying secondary stress.

cómmènt	móment
hálò	céllo
Bógàrt	Stéwart

Some authors use a breve [˘] to mark unaccented syllables, but this practice is somewhat confusing since the same symbol is used to indicate short vowels. As a rule, we will not mark unaccented syllables unless there is a need to call special attention to them, in which case we will follow a practice that is becoming increasingly common and mark them with a raised circle [°].

In marking a stressed syllable, American linguists usually place the accent mark over the syllabic segment, as we have done in the examples above. This practice is not ideal, however, since in an accented syllable the higher pitch and volume levels extend throughout all the segments, regardless of syllabicity. To mark only the syllabic segments suggests that they alone are accented when in actuality the scope of accent is the entire syllable. In some dictionaries, stress is marked at the end of the syllable; in others (and in the transcription system of the International Phonetic Association) stress symbols are placed before the syllable. These transcription practices are less likely to confuse the uninitiated than the one we have adopted. However, ours is the one most frequently found in the phonological literature; and once the fact is established that accent marks denote stress over the whole syllable and not just on the syllabic segment, such a system seems entirely adequate.

In some transcriptions of stress (e.g., that used by Chomsky and Halle, 1968), numbers are used instead of accent marks. A raised one [1] is used to indicate primary stress, [2] to indicate secondary stress, [3] to indicate so-called tertiary stress, [4] to indicate the next lower degree of stress, and so on.

A word, if long enough, may have several nonprimary stresses. But regardless of length, no word has more than one primary stress. With the exception of clitics (words that have been incorporated into the stress pattern of an adjacent word) every word in a language which uses stress accent has a primary stress. This being the case, counting the number of primary stresses in a sentence reveals the number of independent words the sentence contains. When stress is used to ascertain the number of words in a sentence, it is being used in a **culminative function**.

Words like *insert* and *present*, which are stressed differently when used as different parts of speech, and words like *guitar* and *police*, which are stressed differently by speakers of different dialects (or even by the same speaker on different occasions), show that in English, accent is **variable**; that is, its position cannot be predicted given only the phonetic structure of a word. English is not unique in this respect. Other languages with variable accent include Sanskrit, Greek, and Coeur d'Alene. There are languages, however, in which the accent pattern is fixed rather than variable. The position of a **fixed accent** is completely predictable from the phonetic structure of the word. In Finnish, for example, primary stress always falls on the first syllable of a word, as in *léhmä* 'to ride' and *énsin* 'at first'. Other languages with fixed stress include Hawaiian, Czech, and Southern Paiute. In such languages, the accent not only serves the culminative function of indicating the number of independent words in an utterance, but also marks the beginning and ending points of words. This is referred to as the **demarcative function** of accent.

do limitative

5.4 TONE

In the previous section we noted that in English and other stress languages, pitch acts together with volume and length to place accent on certain syllables. There are languages in which pitch plays a different role, however. In these languages, the same sequence of segments may have different meanings if uttered at different relative pitches. For example, in Twi, a language of Ghana, the consonant-vowel sequence [pe] means 'to like or be fond of' if spoken with a low pitch. But if spoken with a high pitch, it means 'exactly' (Redden *et al.*, 1963). Pitch variations used in this way are called **tones**, and languages that use pitch in this way are called **tone languages**.

The function of tone is quite different from that of stress. All stress systems are culminative and some are also demarcative; by definition tone systems are neither. Tones do not mark the beginning and ending of words, nor do they even indicate to the speaker how many words there are in an utterance. The highest pitch may occur on more than one syllable of a word. In the Twi forms [kúrú] 'a sore' and [sísí] 'a bear', for example, both syllables have high tones. What is more, not every word in a tone language has a syllable with the highest-pitched tone. The Twi forms [kuru] 'to thatch' and [sisi] 'to cheat' have a low tone on both syllables. Therefore, it is clear that the number of high tones in an utterance cannot be equated with the number of words.

Twi has the simplest possible tone system. It consists of two contrastive tones, high and low. One of these tones marks each syllable in a Twi word, and a difference in tone on a single syllable is enough to distinguish two words. Thus, in Twi the sound sequence [papa], spoken with a high tone on each syllable, means 'good'. But if the tone on the first syllable is low, this sequence means 'father', and if the tones on both syllables are low, it means 'a fan made of woven palm leaves'.

There are several different ways of transcribing tones. For two-tone languages like Twi, the simplest system is to mark the syllables with high tones and leave those with low tones unmarked. We do this by placing an acute accent ['] over the syllabic segment of the syllable with high tone:

high-high	pápá	'good'
low-high	papá	'father'
low-low	papa	'palm-leaf fan'

For the more complex three-tone systems, such as that of Yoruba (Stevick and Aremu, 1963), two diacritics are necessary: an acute accent to mark high pitch and a grave ['] to mark low. Syllables with mid tones are left unmarked.

high	kán	'to break'
low	kàn	'to reach'
mid	kan	'sour, acid'

In both Twi and Yoruba, the pitch of a tone usually remains level throughout the syllable. Languages in which the majority of syllables maintain the same level or register are called **register tone languages**. In many languages, however, the pitch may rise or fall, so that a syllable that begins on a low tone may end on a high one, or the reverse. Register tones and falling and rising tones are called **simple tones**.

In addition to simple tones, some languages have **complex tones**, which both rise and fall in a single syllable. Complex tones may begin with low or mid pitch, rise to a higher pitch and then fall; or they may begin with a mid or high pitch, fall to a lower pitch and then rise. For obvious reasons, tones with a rise-fall contour are often transcribed with the diacritic [^], and those with a fall-rise contour with the diacritic [ˇ].

Tones that rise, fall, or change direction within a syllable—that is, all tones other than register tones—are called **contour tones**. Languages with a predominance of such tones are called **contour tone languages**.

Mandarin, probably the most widely studied tone language, has four contrastive tones, high (written without a diacritic), rising ['], falling ['], and fall-rise [ˇ]. These tones distinguish four different meanings for some sound sequences:

high	[mɑ]	'mama'
rising	[má]	'numb'
falling	[mà]	'scold'
fall-rise	[mǎ]	'horse'

In addition to the diacritics we have been using, there are at least two other devices often used to transcribe tones. In some transcriptions, level tones are indicated by numbers. In such a system, the number 1 corresponds to the tone with the lowest pitch, 2 to the next higher tone, and so forth. The numbers are usually placed directly before the syllable whose tone is being indicated. Numbers are particularly useful in transcribing languages with more than two or three tones. The Chinese language Tái Gǒng is reported to have five level tones, a falling tone, and two rising tones (Wang, 1967). Clearly, diacritics could represent such a system only very awkwardly. However, using numbers, we can easily show the following five-way contrast:

^{1}la 'candle'
^{2}la 'move away'
^{3}la 'cave'
^{4}la (classifier)
^{5}la 'short'

Taking the numbers 5, 3, and 1 to represent high, mid, and low tones, respectively, we can also use numbers to transcribe contour tones. Simple rising and falling contours are represented by two numbers, one denoting the beginning tone, the other the ending tone of the contour. Thus, a tone falling from the high to the mid region is transcribed 53, and a tone rising from a low region to the mid is 13. Complex tones are represented by a set of three numbers, indicating the tones at the beginning, middle and end of the contour. Therefore, a complex tone which begins in the mid region, rises to the high, then falls again to mid is a 353 tone. A 313 tone would also start in the mid region, but would then fall to low and rise to mid.

Another way of representing tones is to use the tone letters proposed in 1920 by the Chinese linguist Y. R. Chao. **Tone letters** are symbols depicting the shapes of the various tones. In transcription, they are placed at the end of a syllable or word. The tone letters are given below, together with their corresponding numerical designations:

Level	˥ =	5,	˦ =	4,	˧ =3,	˨ =2,	˩ =1		
Rising	˩˥ =	35,	˩˧ =	13					
Falling	˥˩ =	53,	˧˩ =	31					
Falling-Rising	˥˧˥ =	535,	˧˩˧ =	313					
Rising-Falling	˧˥˧ =	353,	˩˧˩ =	131					

5.5 STRESS-PITCH LANGUAGES

A third class of languages, which shares features of both stress and tone languages, is referred to as **stress-pitch languages** (Pike, 1948). In these languages, tones can occur coincidently with the primary stress. In Swedish, for example, most stressed syllables are spoken with a rising tone, symbolized [´]. This contour is evident in such words as *ánd* 'duck', *idé* 'idea', *analýs* 'analysis', *igén* 'again', and *égen* 'own'. In some words of two or more syllables, however, the syllable with primary stress is spoken with a falling tone instead. This falling contour, symbolized [ˋ], occurs, for example, in *ànde* 'spirit', *pòjke* 'boy', *flìcka* 'girl', and *bàka* 'to bake'. Sometimes the only difference between two Swedish words is tone. Compare, for instance, *ánden* 'the duck' and *ànden* 'the spirit'. It should be noted, however, that tone is not a major means of distinguishing words in Swedish, as it is in Mandarin or Twi. Rather, it is a secondary phenomenon and only occasionally distinguishes words. Other stress-pitch languages include Norwegian, Serbo-Croatian, Ancient Greek, and Takelma (a Northwest Indian Language).

Stress-pitch languages are basically stress languages which use tone distinctions in a limited way. It appears that these types of languages never have more than two distinct tones. Furthermore, the point at which tone distinctions can occur is always coincident with the position of primary stress. Thus in stress-pitch languages, pitch serves a culminative function quite unlike its function in tone languages.

5.6 INTONATION

In addition to its role in stress and tone systems, pitch also functions in all languages to demarcate and distinguish phrases and sentences. Pitch differences that extend over phonetic units larger than the syllable are called **intonations**. One of the primary functions of intonation is demarcative. By means of intonation, syllables are grouped into phrases, and phrases into sentences. Intonation is what welds strings of syllables or groups of phrases together.

In English a phrase usually has one of two different terminations. The most common phrasal intonation ends on a falling pitch; the other ends on a more or less level pitch. In the expression *This is the cat that ate the rat*, the first phrase ends with a falling pitch.

This is the cat

(In the example and in those to follow, the level of the line drawn above each syllable represents its relative pitch.) But in the expression *This is the cat, however, that refused to eat the rat,* the same phrase terminates on a sustained mid-level pitch.

This is the cat

The falling termination of the first example indicates that the phrase is complete at that point. The sustained mid-level termination of the second indicates that it is to be interrupted and recommenced after the introduction of parenthetical material.

Intonation contours may also indicate the possible groupings of words in phrases. Consider the following phrases which may have their words grouped in more than one way.

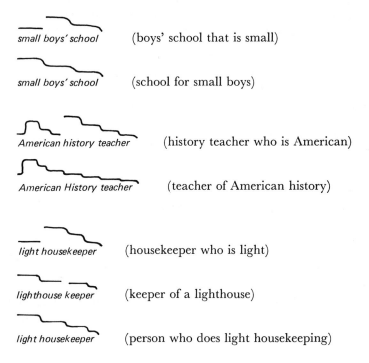

small boys' school (boys' school that is small)

small boys' school (school for small boys)

American history teacher (history teacher who is American)

American History teacher (teacher of American history)

light housekeeper (housekeeper who is light)

lighthouse keeper (keeper of a lighthouse)

light housekeeper (person who does light housekeeping)

Intonation may also serve to emphasize a certain word within a phrase or sentence. The first of the following sentences has a neutral intonation contour. Each of the others has a higher pitch on one word than would normally be expected. That word therefore takes on special importance in the sentence.

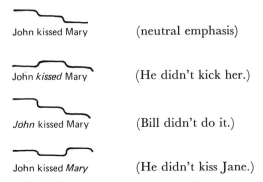

John kissed Mary   (neutral emphasis)

John *kissed* Mary   (He didn't kick her.)

John kissed Mary   (Bill didn't do it.)

John kissed *Mary*   (He didn't kiss Jane.)

Further, in English, the same sentence may mean quite different things when spoken with different intonations. For the most part declarative sentences terminate with a falling pitch and questions requiring a *yes* or *no* answer terminate on a rising pitch. Contour terminations are not the only significant factor, however. Exclamations are often characterized by a high pitch throughout. The following sentences illustrate these different intonations.

1. John is our new president.   (I'm informing you.)
2. John is our new president?   (I didn't know.)
3. John is our new president!   (That nincompoop?)

In many cases, single-word utterances may also be distinguished by intonation. Consider, for example, the following exchange:

1. Mumble-mumble   What?
2. Dad?   What.
3. I ran into the garage door again.   What!

The three instances of *what* uttered above mean quite different things. The first (with rising intonation) is a request for the previous utterance to be repeated; the second (with falling intonation) is a response meaning 'I'm listening'; and the third (with high pitch) is an exclamation denoting exasperation and disbelief. The fact that pitch is used here to distinguish three meanings of a single word does not mean that English is a tone language, but merely that some English phrases consist of only a single word.

5.7 SUMMARY

In this chapter we have discussed the major prosodic elements of language: quantity, stress, tone, and intonation. **Quantity** refers to the relative length of sound segments. Many languages have both long and short vowels and some have both long and short consonants.

Stress or **accent** refers to the relative prominence of syllables within a word. Languages that employ stress, either in its **culminative function** (to indicate the number of words in a sentence) or in its **demarcative function** (to mark the beginning and ending points of words) are called **stress languages**. Every independent word in a stress language has at least one stressed syllable. If two or more syllables in the same word are stressed, one will carry **primary stress** and the others **secondary stress**. A language is said to have **variable accent** if the location of primary stress cannot be predicted from the phonetic structure of the word. If stress is phonetically predictable, the language is said to have **fixed accent**.

Languages that use pitch differences to distinguish words are called **tone languages**. **Simple tones** have a pitch which is either level, rising, or falling. **Complex tones** have pitch which both rises and falls in a single syllable. Languages that distinguish words on the basis of level tones are called **register tone languages**. Those that have a predominance of tones that rise, fall, or change direction are called **contour tone languages**. **Stress-pitch languages** are stress languages that may have tonal distinctions on syllables with primary stress. Pitch contours that extend over phrases and sentences are called **intonation contours**.

EXERCISES FOR CHAPTER 5

1. Transcribe the stress patterns of the English two-syllable words given below. For example, the word *echo* has the pattern écho̊ and the word *nylon* has the pattern ný̀lòn.

1. bucket	11. accent
2. argon	12. admire
3. cadet	13. valley
4. bamboo	14. rupee
5. machine	15. second
6. pencil	16. balloon
7. kidnap	17. sofa
8. aside	18. alpine
9. baron	19. baboon
10. trapeze	20. sulphate

2. Transcribe the stress patterns of the following three-syllable English words. How many different stress patterns do you find?

1. separate	13. molluscoid
2. diphthongize	14. Virginia
3. bipartite	15. maniac
4. iconic	16. venison
5. salivate	17. Montana
6. Katmandu	18. Japanese
7. Florida	19. banana
8. bookkeeper	20. Timbuktu
9. bagatelle	21. hydroxide
10. morphemic	22. shoelaces
11. Arabic	23. abstraction
12. misconstrue	24. generic

3. The stress pattern of many English words varies from dialect to dialect. Transcribe your own pronunciation of the words given below and determine from an unabridged dictionary the full range of possible stress patterns. For example, for some speakers *perfume* is accented *pĕrfúme*, while for others it is *pérfùme*.

1. address (noun and verb)	9. permit (noun and verb)
2. expletive	10. Caribbean
3. substantive	11. epicurean
4. applicable	12. transplant (noun and verb)
5. adult	13. perfume (noun and verb)
6. locate	14. torment (noun and verb)
7. inquiry	15. recondite
8. advertisement	16. transfer (noun and verb)

4. Transcribe the intonation patterns of the following English questions. Contrastive stress is indicated with an acute accent.

1. Do you have any bananas?
2. How much does it cost?
3. Do you want coffee or tea? (i.e., which do you want?)
4. Do you want coffee or tea? (i.e., do you want either one?)
5. They shoot horses, don't they?
6. When did John gó?
7. When did Jóhn go?
8. Does he have pláns to leave?
9. Does he have plans to léave?
10. Who are you calling, Matilda? (direct address)
11. Who are you calling—Matilda?
12. Why are you calling Matilda?
13. Why are you calling, Matilda? (direct address)

5. Transcribe the prosodic elements of the following English sentences. Transcribe both the stresses and the intonation patterns.

   1. John went from Tonawanda to Toronto in a birchbark canoe, hurtling over Niagara Falls in a furious frenzy.
   2. The cautious referee gingerly threw the ball up at midcourt as ten seven-footers converged with alacrity.
   3. My father slew a kangaroo and he gave me the grisly part to chew.
   4. Jack and Jill went up the hill to look at the view and to fetch a pail of water.
   5. On the road to Mandalay, the travelers found a hitherto unknown tribe which spoke a perfectly delightful language.
   6. Even though Robert spoke no English, many of his teachers, we are sad to say, did not seem to notice why he did poorly on his exams.
   7. One of Shakespeare's sonnets deals with old age and contains in each quatrain an image that expresses the theme in a similar and contrasting manner.

6. In each of the following pairs of sentences how do the stress and intonation patterns of the italicized words differ?

   1a. John lives in *Tennessee.*
    b. John has a *Tennessee* walking horse.
   2a. *New York* is the largest city in the United States.
    b. *New York* City has five boroughs.
   3a. *Chinese* is difficult to write.
    b. The *Chinese* language most widely taught is Mandarin.

6 distinctive features and natural classes

6.1 INTRODUCTION

The traditional system of articulatory phonetics outlined in the preceding chapters is basic and necessary to an understanding of the phonological literature. But in formulating phonological rules, it is sometimes helpful to have another way of talking about speech sounds. Instead of treating sound segments as indivisible or atomic entities (as the symbols of the phonetic alphabet would suggest they are), linguists often describe sounds as complexes of properties or features. Each of these **distinctive features**, as they are called, represents one of the simultaneous (or nearly simultaneous) activities occurring in the vocal tract during production of a speech sound. When a speaker pronounces a [b], for example, he goes through a set of motions which include completely closing the lips, raising the velum against the back of the throat, and vibrating the vocal cords. Any one of these activities may be relevant to some phonological process. For instance, there may be a process involving only sounds made at the lips (that is, [p, b, β, ɸ, m]); or only sounds made with complete closure (i.e., stops); or sounds made with the velum raised (oral sounds); or sounds made with accompanying vocal cord vibration (voiced sounds); or sounds involving some combination of these activities (such as voiced stops). It is therefore

82

useful to be able to discuss the properties of sounds separately. The main advantage of distinctive features is that they provide a convenient way to discuss what phonologists have known for a long time: that sounds may be grouped together in a number of different ways, depending on which of their properties are being considered. Arguments that distinctive features are a necessary part of phonological descriptions have been advanced in a number of publications, e.g., Halle, 1959, 1962; Chomsky, 1964; Chomsky and Halle, 1968.

The primary goal of linguists working on the distinctive features theory has been to find a relatively small number of features that can be used to characterize just those sound classes which take part in phonological processes and no others. At this point, however, the perfect set of distinctive features has yet to be found. A set suggested some years ago by Jakobson, Fant, and Halle (1952) has subsequently been shown to be inadequate in certain ways; and a number of linguists have since proposed revised sets. In 1968 Chomsky and Halle put forth a significant reformulation of the distinctive features theory, which, while not ideal, represents a considerable improvement over earlier work. The discussion of features which follows is based primarily on their work.

Chomsky and Halle list thirty-six individual features which they feel "together represent the phonetic capabilities of man." Of these thirty-six features, we will discuss only those most commonly found in the phonological literature. Our list, then, does not purport to be exhaustive. Most distinctive features are **binary**, that is, they can have only one of two values—plus or minus. Thus, a sound is classed as either voiced or voiceless, tense or lax, but not 'partially voiced' or 'somewhat tense.' Thus, if a segment is nasal, it is said to carry the value plus (+) for the feature [nasal] or to be [+ nasal]. If a segment is not nasal, on the other hand, it still has the feature name [nasal] as part of its description, but this time accompanied by the minus specification: [− nasal]. Notice that distinctive features and their values, like phonetic symbols, are enclosed in square brackets.

6.2 THE MAJOR CLASS FEATURES

Three features, [consonantal], [sonorant], and [syllabic], interact to yield the major sound classes. The [+ consonantal] sounds are produced either with contact between articulator and point of articulation, or with a degree of closure severe enough to produce friction. This feature distinguishes the true consonants (stops, fricatives, affricates, nasals, laterals, and trills) from the glides and vowels. The [+ sonorant] sounds are made by shaping the vocal tract so that the airstream passes essentially unimpeded through either the oral or the nasal cavity. Vowels, glides, nasal consonants, laterals, and *r*-sounds are [+sonorant]. Stops, fricatives, and affricates are [−sonorant].

That nasals and laterals are both [+consonantal] and [+sonorant] may appear contradictory, but actually it is not. Although nasals have a consonantal obstruction in the oral cavity, the airstream is free to pass through the nasal cavity. Similarly, lateral resonants have an obstruction at the midline of the oral cavity, but the airstream can pass relatively freely around it.

Both vowels and glides are [+sonsorant] and [−consonantal]. A third feature is therefore necessary to distinguish between these two classes. The feature [syllabic] characterizes the segments with the greatest prominence in a syllable. As we noted in Chapter 4, vowels are normally syllabic and all other sounds are normally nonsyllabic. Liquids, nasals, and fricatives, however, may be [+syllabic]. Stops are always [−syllabic].

Diphthongs are composed of two [−consonantal, +sonorant] segments, the first of which is [+syllabic] and the second [−syllabic]. The matrix in Table I shows the relationship between the features [consonantal] [syllabic], and [sonorant] and the speech sound classes they define.

Table I   MAJOR SPEECH SOUND CLASSES

	CONSONANTAL	SONORANT	SYLLABIC
Liquids and nasals	+	+	−
Vowels	−	+	+
Glides	−	+	−
Obstruents	+	−	−

6.3 TONGUE BODY FEATURES

Three features relate to the position of the body of the tongue. These are [high], [low], and [back]. Chomsky and Halle define a position of the tongue body that they call neutral. The **neutral position** is approximately the position at which the vowel of the English word *bed* is articulated. We have transcribed this vowel as [ɛ]. Vowels made in positions higher than the neutral position are characterized as [+high]. Those made in positions lower than the neutral position are [+low]. This means that mid vowels are [−high, −low]. Sounds made in positions which require the retraction of the tongue from the neutral position are [+back]. Thus both central and back vowels are [+back].

6.4 THE FEATURE ROUNDED

The feature [rounded] distinguishes sounds with lip rounding from those without. Sounds with lip rounding are [+rounded]. Table II shows how the tongue body features and the feature [rounded] interact to characterize certain vowels.

Table II FEATURE SPECIFICATIONS FOR SOME COMMON VOWELS

	i	u	ü	æ	ɑ	ɒ	e	ö	ə	o
High	+	+	+	−	−	−	−	−	−	−
Low	−	−	−	+	+	+	−	−	−	−
Back	−	+	−	−	+	+	−	−	+	+
Rounded	−	+	+	−	−	+	−	+	−	+

6.5 CONSONANTS AND THE FEATURES HIGH AND BACK

The features [high] and [back] serve to characterize consonants as well as vowels. Velar consonants, such as [k], [g], and [x], like the glide [w] and the vowel [u], are [+high, +back]. Uvulars such as [q], [ɢ], and [x], like the velars, are [+back]; but unlike velars, they are [−high]. Labial, dental, and alveolar consonants such as [p], [θ], and [t] are [−high, −back]. Dentals and alveolars are [−high] because in their production it is the apex or front of the tongue, not the body, that is raised. The neutral position is defined in relation to the body of the tongue not to the apex or front. Palatals such as [č] and [k̡] are [+high, −back]. In the production of [č], as opposed to [t], both the front and the body of the tongue are elevated. Table III shows the values that certain consonants have for the features [high] and [back].

Table III CONSONANTS AND THE FEATURES HIGH AND BACK

	p	b	f	θ	t	d	s	l	n
High	−	−	−	−	−	−	−	−	−
Back	−	−	−	−	−	−	−	−	−

	č	ǰ	š	k	g	x	q	ɢ	x
High	+	+	+	+	+	+	−	−	−
Back	−	−	−	+	+	+	+	+	+

6.6 FEATURES AND SECONDARY ARTICULATIONS

The features [high], [low], [back], and [rounded] also characterize certain secondary articulations of consonants. Labialization, velarization, palatalization, and pharyngealization involve the superimposition of various combinations of these features onto a consonant articulation. Labialization is characterized by the set of feature values [+back, +high, +rounded]. Velarization involves a [+back, +high, −rounded] articulation. Palatalized sounds are [−back, +high], while pharyngealized sounds are [+back, +low]. Table IV compares several plain consonants with their labialized, velarized, palatalized, and pharyngealized counterparts.

Table IV   SECONDARY ARTICULATIONS

	t	tʸ	tʷ	ɫ¹	ɫ²	k	kʸ	kʷ	m	mʸ	l	ɫ
Low	−	−	−	−	+	−	−	−	−	−	−	−
Back	−	−	+	+	+	+	−	+	−	−	−	+
High	−	+	+	+	−	+	+	+	−	+	−	+
Rounded	−	−	+	−	−	−	−	+	−	−	−	−

¹ Velarized t.
² Pharyngealized t. (The same symbol is used for both types of t.)

6.7 MANNER FEATURES

There are a number of features which distinguish sounds on the basis of the manner of their articulation. The features [interrupted] and [strident] allow us to distinguish the classes of stops, fricatives, and affricates. The feature [interrupted] characterizes sounds in which the airstream is completely blocked during part of their articulation. Thus, stops and affricates are [+interrupted] whereas fricatives, nasals, liquids, glides, and vowels are [−interrupted]. The feature [continuant] is often used (with opposite values) in place of [interrupted]. Thus, [+continuant] is equivalent to [−interrupted], and vice versa.

The feature [strident] marks sounds which are produced in such a way as to permit the airstream to pass through only a narrow opening in the center of the vocal tract. This manner of articulation creates a large amount of friction, resulting in the hissing sound characteristic of strident segments. Certain pairs of sounds, such as [s] and [θ], and [š] and [ç], can be distinguished on the basis of stridency. In the production of [s] the contact that the tongue makes with the alveolar ridge is nearly complete; only a small groove in the middle of the tongue allows for the passage of the air-stream. In the production of [θ], on the other hand, the opening is much wider from side to side and contact between the tongue and the roof of the mouth is less complete. The [s] is therefore specified as [+strident], and [θ] as [−strident]. The main difference between the palatal fricatives [š] and [ç] is also their relative degrees of stridency; [š] is considerably more strident than [ç].

The features [interrupted] and [strident] can also be used to distinguish some affricates from their corresponding stops and fricatives. Among the alveolars, [t] is [+interrupted, −strident] and [s] is [−interrupted, +strident]. The affricate [ts], also symbolized [c] can be distinguished from both [t] and [s] because it is [+interrupted, +strident].

The feature [distributed] identifies consonants articulated with a constriction which is relatively long from front to back. Sounds that are [+distributed] include the dental fricatives [θ] and [ð], the palatal fricative [ç], and the bilabials [p, b, ϕ, β, m].

In distinctive feature theory, as in traditional phonetics, any speech sound produced with the velum lowered so that some or all of the airstream passes out through the nose is nasal. Thus, nasal consonants and both vowels and consonants with secondary nasalization have the feature [+nasal].

The feature [lateral] also has the same definition in both distinctive feature theory and traditional phonetics: sounds made by diverting the airstream laterally around the tongue are [+lateral].

6.8 THE FEATURES VOICED AND TENSE

The feature [voiced] characterizes sounds whose articulations include periodic vibrations of the vocal cords. Vowels, glides, nasals, and liquids are normally [+voiced], as are the obstruents [b, d, g, v, ð, z, ǰ, ž, γ, ɣ, ɦ].

The feature [tense] is a property of speech sounds made with relatively high tension in the muscles of the oral cavity. Sounds that are [−tense], or lax, involve much less muscle tension. Because the greater muscular effort expended in producing tense sounds is time-consuming, tense sounds are generally longer in duration than their lax counterparts. Lax sounds are typically articulated rapidly and with somewhat indistinct articulatory gestures. They therefore do not have the maximal displacement from the center of the oral cavity which characterizes tense sounds. The tense vowels [i] and [u], for example, are produced nearer to the extreme of the vowel production area than are their [−tense] counterparts [ɪ] and [ʊ]. Typically, voiced obstruents are [−tense] and voiceless ones are [+tense]. However, the feature [tense] is relevant mainly to the production of vowels and is rarely used in rules to identify classes of consonants. Table V shows how the feature [tense], along with the tongue body features and the feature, [rounded], characterizes a number of common vowels.

Table V FEATURE SPECIFICATIONS, COMMON VOWELS

	i	ɪ	e	ɛ	æ	u	ʊ	o	ɔ
High	+	+	−	−	−	+	+	−	−
Low	−	−	−	−	+	−	−	−	−
Back	−	−	−	−	−	+	+	+	+
Rounded	−	−	−	−	−	+	+	+	+
Tense	+	−	+	−	−	+	−	+	−

	a	ə	ü	ü	ö	œ	ɯ	ɤ	ʌ	ɒ
High	−	−	+	+	−	−	+	−	−	−
Low	+	−	−	−	−	−	−	−	−	+
Back	+	+	−	−	−	−	+	+	+	+
Rounded	−	−	+	+	+	+	−	−	−	+
Tense	+	−	+	−	+	−	+	+	−	−

6.9 PLACE OF ARTICULATION FEATURES

Two features serve to distinguish the major positions of articulation. The feature [coronal] characterizes sounds made by raising the apex or front of the tongue to form a partial or total obstruction. Since these parts of the tongue can be used only in articulations involving the teeth, alveolar ridge, or palate, the [+coronal] sounds include interdentals, alveolars, and palatals, but exclude labials, velars, uvulars, and pharyngeals.

Sounds that are anterior are made at or in front of the alveolar ridge; all sounds articulated farther back than the alveolar ridge are [−anterior]. Labials, dentals, and alveolars are [+anterior]; vowels, palatals, velars, uvulars, and pharyngeals are [−anterior). In Figure 6.1 the tongue is shown in the neutral position. The part of the tongue between the lines that enclose the term *coronal* is what is elevated in the production of [+coronal] sounds. The line dividing [+anterior] from [−anterior] sounds is drawn just forward of the place of articulation of [š].

+ANTERIOR | −ANTERIOR

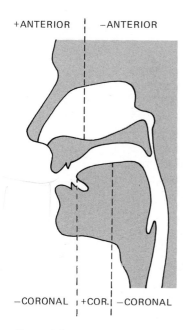

−CORONAL | +COR.| −CORONAL

Figure 6.1
The Features Anterior and Coronal

Table VI lists the distinctive features presented above and their abbreviations.

Table VI   THE DISTINCTIVE FEATURES AND THEIR ABBREVIATIONS

Consonantal	[cons]
Sonorant	[son]
Syllabic	[syl]
High	[hi]
Low	[lo]
Back	[bk]
Rounded	[rnd]
Interrupted	[int]
Strident	[str]
Distributed	[dist]
Nasal	[nas]
Lateral	[lat]
Voiced	[vd]
Tense	[tns]
Coronal	[cor]
Anterior	[ant]

Table VII SOME VOICELESS OBSTRUENTS

	p	ṭ	t	ṭ	ḳ	k	q	ʔ	f̂	χ	č	φ	f	θ	s	ṣ	š	ç	x	ẋ	h
int	+	+	+	+	+	+	+	+	+	+	+	−	−	−	−	−	−	−	−	−	−
str	−	−	−	−	−	−	−	−	+	+	+	−	+	−	+	+	+	−	−	−	−
dist	+	+	−	−	−	−	−	−	−	−	−	+	−	+	−	−	+	+	+	+	−
cor	−	+	+	+	−	−	−	−	−	+	+	−	−	+	+	+	+	+	−	−	−
ant	+	+	+	−	−	−	−	−	+	+	−	+	+	+	+	−	−	−	−	−	−
hi	−	−	−	+	+	+	−	−	−	−	+	−	−	−	−	−	+	+	+	+	−
bk	−	−	−	−	−	+	+	−	−	−	−	−	−	−	−	−	−	−	+	+	−
lat	−	−	−	−	−	−	−	−	−	+	−	−	−	−	−	−	−	−	−	−	−

All are [+cons, −son, −rnd, −nas, +tns, −lo, −vd]

The matrix in Table VII uses these features to describe a number of common obstruents. The matrix in Table VIII uses them to describe a number of common resonants.

Table VIII SOME RESONANT NONSYLLABICS

	m	ṇ	n	ñ	ŋ	ḷ	l	ř	r̃	R̃	y	ɥ	w
cons	+	+	+	+	+	+	+	+	+	+	−	−	−
dist	+	+	−	+	−	+	−	−	−	−	−	−	−
cor	−	+	+	+	−	+	+	+	+	−	−	−	−
ant	+	+	+	−	−	+	+	+	+	−	−	−	−
rnd	−	−	−	−	−	−	−	−	−	−	−	+	+
lo	−	−	−	−	−	−	−	+	+	+	−	−	−
hi	−	−	−	+	+	−	−	−	−	−	+	+	+
bk	−	−	−	−	+	−	−	+	+	+	−	−	+
nas	+	+	+	+	+	−	−	−	−	−	−	−	−
tns	−	−	−	−	−	−	−	−	+	+	−	−	−
lat	−	−	−	−	−	+	+	−	−	−	−	−	−

All are [+son, −str, −int, +vd]

6.10 PROSODIC FEATURES

The prosodic features, unlike the features discussed thus far, are relative in nature; that is, their presence or absence can be determined only by comparing one segment with another. The prosodic features include, in addition to the feature denoting syllabicity, the features required to describe quantity, tone, and stress.

The difference between the English words *wooed* [wud] and *wood* [wʊd] is primarily one of tenseness versus laxness. The contrasting vowels in these words differ also in quantity, but this difference is a concomitant of the tense/lax distinction. However, the high back vowels of the Finnish words *uuni* [u:ni] 'oven' and *uni* [uni] 'sleep' are both tense. The primary distinction between these two vowels is their length. We use the feature [+long] to designate a segment which has relatively greater duration than another segment otherwise phonetically identical.

The feature [stress] distinguishes stressed syllables (and segments) from unstressed ones. Syllables with stress are marked [+stress]. Various tone features have been suggested in recent years (Fromkin, 1972; Hyman and Schuh, 1974; Leben, 1971; Wang, 1967; Woo, 1969; Hyman, 1975), but at this time it appears that the Chao numbering system given in section 5.4 is the most satisfactory method yet devised for discussing tone.

6.11 OTHER SUGGESTED FEATURES

Other features which have been suggested in the literature include: labial, front, glottalized, heightened subglottal pressure, and delayed release. The feature [labial], abbreviated [lab], distinguishes sounds articulated with the lower lip from all other sounds. The feature [front], abbreviated [fr], is shared by the front vowels, the glides [y] and [ɥ] and the frontopalatals; it distinguishes front vowels from all other vowels. Glottalized and laryngealized sounds have the feature [glottalized], abbreviated [gl]. Aspirated sounds have been described as having the feature [heightened subglottal pressure], or [HSP]. The feature [delayed release], abbreviated [del rel], distinguishes affricates from stops. (For some proposals concerning possible alternative and additional features see Harms, 1968; Wang, 1968; Ladefoged, 1970; Hoard, 1977; Campbell, 1974; and Anderson, 1976.)

6.12 NATURAL CLASSES

Distinctive features are useful because they allow us to characterize not only individual sound segments but the natural classes of segments which undergo phonological processes. A **natural class** is a group of segments which have properties in common and therefore share distinctive feature values. For instance, all the consonants form a natural class, since they all share the distinctive feature specification [+cons]. A subclass of the consonants, the obstruents, also forms a natural class which has the feature specifications [+cons] and [−son]. The stops, which share the specifications [+cons], [−son], [+int] and [−del rel], form still another natural class. Among the obstruents, only stops and affricates have a plus value for the feature [interrupted]. Of these, the stops are [−del rel] and the affricates [+del rel].

If we wish to specify an even smaller natural class—the dental and alveolar stops, for instance—we need only add to the list of feature specifications for stops [+cor] and [+ant]. The following specifications are those necessary to distinguish dental and alveolar stops from all other sounds:

$$
\begin{bmatrix}
+\text{cons} \\
-\text{son} \\
+\text{int} \\
-\text{del rel} \\
+\text{cor} \\
+\text{ant}
\end{bmatrix}
$$

Secondary modifications such as labialization and palatalization aside, this set of features specifies the four plain stops [t], [d], [ṭ], and [ḍ]. To specify just the alveolar stops, we add the specification [−dist]:

$$
\begin{bmatrix}
+\text{cons} \\
-\text{son} \\
+\text{int} \\
-\text{del rel} \\
+\text{cor} \\
+\text{ant} \\
-\text{dist}
\end{bmatrix}
$$

To specify the particular alveolar stop [t], we simply add to this matrix the specification that distinguishes [t] from [d], namely [−vd]:

$$
\begin{bmatrix}
+\text{cons} \\
-\text{son} \\
+\text{int} \\
-\text{del rel} \\
+\text{cor} \\
+\text{ant} \\
-\text{dist} \\
-\text{vd}
\end{bmatrix}
$$

Since [t] is the only voiceless alveolar stop, these feature specifications distinguish [t] not only from [d] but from all other sounds as well.

Notice that the smaller the natural class, the larger the number of feature specifications necessary to describe it. It takes only one feature, [+cons], to represent the natural class of all consonants, whereas it takes at least eight features to represent the single sound [t]. This inverse correlation between the size of the class and the number of features necessary to its definition would seem to explain at least partially why phonological processes generally involve natural classes rather than single segments or random groups of segments. Since a large number of features are required to describe a process which applies to either a single sound or a group of unrelated sounds, the rules needed to describe such processes are quite complex, and, therefore, presumably difficult to store in the mind. Hence, they are less likely to occur than those involving natural classes.

6.13 REDUNDANT FEATURE VALUES

It is not always necessary to specify every feature value for a given natural class or sound segment. If the value for some feature always implies a certain value for another feature, it would be redundant to specify both. In writing feature matrices, as in other areas of phonology, we wish to avoid redundancy. Therefore, only those features necessary to distinguish a sound or sound class from all others are specified. **Redundant feature values**—those whose presence or absence can be inferred by the presence or absence of another feature—are simply not stated. For example, if a segment is [+str], it must be [−nas] because there are no strident nasals. The specification [+str], then, implies that the segment is [−nas]. Further, if a segment is [+nas], it must also be [+son], since all nasals are resonants. Therefore, we need only specify [+nas]. It would be possible to distinguish far more different segments with the same number of features if all the feature values were independent of each other. But as we mentioned above, distinctive feature theory attempts to provide a description of only those segments which distinguish words in some language, without allowing for sound types that are never distinctive or that can never occur because of limitations of the vocal tract.

Facts about which feature values co-occur can be represented by implicational formulas. The examples of redundant features given above can be restated in the form of two implicational formulas:

1.   [+str] ⇒ [−nas]
2.   [+nas] ⇒ [+son]

(The double shafted arrow is used to symbolize the notion 'implies.') The first of these formulas says, essentially, that if a segment is [+strident], you can assume that it will not be a nasal. The second says that if a segment is nasal, it will also have [+sonorant] as one of its features.

Some implicational formulas, such as the following, recognize physiological impossibilities:

3.   [+hi] ⇒ [−lo]
4.   [+lo] ⇒ [−hi]

Obviously, the implications in 3 and 4 are due simply to the fact that the tongue body cannot simultaneously be both raised from the neutral position and lowered from the neutral position.

Other implicational formulas reflect the fact that some features, by their very nature, subclassify others. Formula 2 is of this type, as are 5, 6, and 7:

5.   [+str] ⇒ [+cons]
6.   [+int] ⇒ [+cons]
7.   [+lat] ⇒ [+cons]

These last three formulas mean that only consonants can be strident, interrupted, or lateral: there are no vowels or glides with these features.

Implication 1 holds not only because there are no strident nasals, but also because no language seems to distinguish a nasalized from an unnasalized strident fricative, for example, [ž] from [z]. Similarly, rule 8 holds because there are no distinctively nasalized lateral sounds.

8. $[+\text{lat}] \Rightarrow [-\text{nas}]$

Implications, 1 and 8 express the hypothesis that, although certain combinations of features are physically possible, these combinations will never be used to distinguish words in any language.

The implications that hold between features have an effect on the specification of natural classes. As we have noted, rules describing phonological processes should have no redundant feature specifications. Obviously, in distinguishing sounds we need not express values for features whose values are known by implication.

A theory of distinctive features is intended to provide ultimately a complete set of properties sufficient to characterize all distinctive speech sounds and just the natural classes of sounds that take part in phonological rules. The features introduced in sections 6.2 to 6.11 are to be considered as illustrative rather than definitive. In any event, they are obviously insufficient to distinguish all speech sounds. No features are given, for example, to describe implosive or click consonants or to describe central vowels. Additional features have been suggested in the phonological literature. The problem is that proposed features are not justified merely by the fact that they can distinguish one sound from another. That could be done simply by assigning arbitrary labels. To justify features, it must be shown that they are required to specify the natural classes that are needed in phonological rules. A large amount of research on a wide range of languages is necessary before we can have complete confidence in any list of distinctive features.

6.14 SUMMARY

In this chapter we have introduced features of the following types: (1) features such as **consonantal, sonorant,** and **syllabic,** which classify segments into major classes; (2) tongue body features such as **low, high,** and **back;** (3) manner of articulation features such as **interrupted, strident, distributed, nasal,** and **lateral;** (4) place of articulation features such as **coronal and anterior;** (5) prosodic features such as **long, stressed,** and **syllabic** (also considered a major class feature); and (6) a number of diverse features such as **rounded, tense,** and **voiced.**

A **natural class** is a group of segments which share distinctive feature values. The more feature values specified, the smaller the natural class. Redundant, or predictable, feature values are not listed but are understood to be present because of implicational rules. For instance, vowels are never [+strident] or [+anterior]. Therefore, the specifications [−cons, +son, +syl], which identify the natural class of vowels, serve for [−cons, +son, +syl, −str, −ant]. The feature values [−str, −ant] are redundant because of the implicational rules [−cons] ⇒ [−str] and [−cons] ⇒ [−ant].

EXERCISES FOR CHAPTER 6

1. Determine the feature matrix which specifies the natural class for each group of sounds in 1 to 10 below. Use the distinctive features listed in Table VI.

    1. [æ, e, ε, ι, i]   6. [i, e, u, o]
    2. [p, t, k, b, d, g]   7. [ε, ɔ, œ, ʌ]
    3. [m, n, ŋ, b, d, g]   8. [t, d, r, l, b, s, θ]
    4. [s, š]   9. [k, q, x, χ]
    5. [y, w, i, u]   10. [p, b, k, g]

2. Describe the processes given in 1–10 below by means of feature value changes involving natural classes. It is only necessary to indicate to the right of the arrow the features that change value. Example: [u, o] → [ü, ö], respectively, can be expressed as

$$
\begin{bmatrix} -\text{cons} \\ +\text{son} \\ +\text{syl} \\ +\text{back} \end{bmatrix} \rightarrow [-\text{back}]
$$

    1. [p, t, k] → [ɸ, θ, x], respectively
    2. [i, e, u, o] → [ι, ε, ʊ, ɔ], respectively
    3. [s] → [š]
    4. [n] → [ŋ]
    5. [ɑ] → [æ]
    6. [e, o] → [i, u], respectively
    7. [i, u, ü] → [y, w, ɥ], respectively
    8. [t, d, k, g] → [tʷ, dʷ, kʷ, gʷ], respectively
    9. [t, d, k, g] → [tʸ, dʸ, kʸ, gʸ], respectively
   10. [l] → [y]

3. Assume that there is a feature [front] defined so that front vowels are [+front] and all other vowels are [−front]. Now describe a process whereby unstressed [ι, ʊ, ε, ɔ] → [ə].

4. Assuming that aspirated stops are [+HSP], describe a process whereby plain [p, t, č, k] become aspirated if they are initial in a syllable.

5. Construct feature value charts (similar to Tables V and VII) for the inventories given below in a–d. Assume that there is a feature [glottalized] for the languages that have a plain/glottalized distinction. Use only as many features as are necessary to distinguish the sounds in each of the inventories. Make use of the features [glottalized], [front], and [heightened subglottal pressure] if needed. Indicate redundant feature specifications in parenthesis.

Example: Nyangumarda has the segment inventory [p, t, tʸ, k, m, n, nʸ, ŋ, l, r, lʸ, w, y, i, a, u]. The segments can be characterized as follows:

	p	t	tʸ	k	m	n	nʸ	ŋ	l	r	lʸ	w	y	i	a	u
cons	+	+	+	+	+	+	+	+	+	+	+	−	−	−	−	−
son	−	−	−	−	+	+	+	+	+	+	+	(+)	(+)	(+)	(+)	(+)
syl	(−)	(−)	(−)	(−)	(−)	(−)	(−)	(−)	(−)	(−)	(−)	−	−	+	+	+
cor	−	+	+	−	−	+	+	−	+	+	+	(−)	(−)	(−)	(−	(−)
ant	+	(+)	(+)	−	+	+	+	−	+	−	+	(−)	(−)	(−)	(−)	(−)
nas	(−)	(−)	(−)	(−)	(+)	+	+	(+)	−	(−)	−	(−)	(−)	(−)	(−)	(−)
front	(−)	−	+	(−)	(−)	−	+	(−)	−	(−)	+	−	+	+	−	−
high	(−)	(−)	(+)	(+)	(−)	(−)	(+)	(+)	(−)	(−)	(+)	(+)	(+)	(+)	−	+

(Based on Hoard and O'Grady, 1976)

To determine the redundant features, a tree diagram can be constructed. A redundancy is found at any node where the tree does not branch (see Figure 6.2). Some of the redundancies are due to implicational rules. For example, vowels and glides are [−cor] and [−ant]. Other redundancies are specific to Nyangumarda (and to other languages with similar inventories). For example, all vowels are [−nas], and the obstruents, [p, t, tʸ, k], which are described by the natural class [+cons, −son, −syl], are [+int, −str].

a. German: [p, b, t, d, k, g, f, v, s, z, š, ž, c, m, n, ŋ, l, ʀ, y, h, i:, ɩ, e:, ɛ, u:, ʊ, o:, ɔ, ü:, ü, ö:, œ, a:, ɑ]. (Based on Moulton, 1962)

b. Swedish: [p, b, t, d, k, g, f, v, s, š, çʸ, m, n, ŋ, l, ř, y, h, i:, ɩ, e:, e, ɛ:, ɛ, ɑ:, a, ü:, ü, ö:, œ, ʉ:, ɵ, u:, ʊ, o:, ɔ]. (Based on Elert, 1964)

c. Quechua (Bolivia): [p, pʰ, p', t, tʰ, t', k, kʰ, k', q, qʰ, q', č, čʰ, č', s, š, h, m, n, nʸ, r, l, lʸ, y, w, i, u, a]. (Based on Orr and Longacre, 1968)

d. Telugu (a Dravidian language of India): [p, pʰ, b, bʰ, t, tʰ, d, dʰ, č, ǰ, ṭ, ḍ, ṭʰ, ḍʰ, k, kʰ, g, gʰ, m, n, ṇ, l, ḷ, r, s, ṣ, w, y, i:, i, u:, u, e:, e, o:, o, a:, a]. (Based on Wilkinson, 1974; Subbarao, 1971)

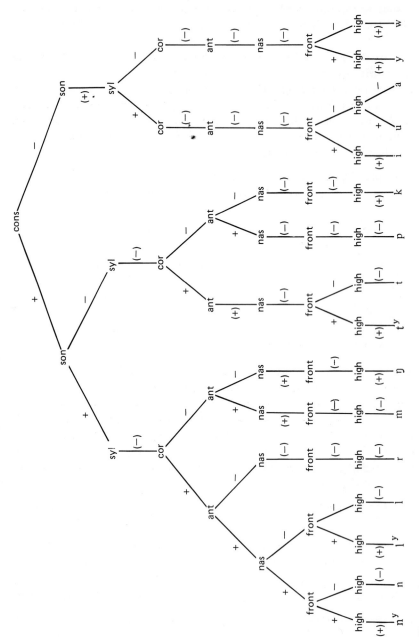

Figure 6.2

7 naturalness

7.1 INTRODUCTION

In Chapter 1 we saw that not all of the perceivable properties of speech sounds play equally important roles in phonology. Apparently, some properties, such as the absolute values of length, loudness, and pitch, never function distinctively in language at all. Furthermore, when the phonological features that do function distinctively are combined, the resulting sounds also vary in their phonological importance. As we noted in section 6.13, certain combinations of feature specifications are not found in the phonological inventory of any language. Obviously, some features do not occur together because the human speech apparatus is incapable of producing them simultaneously. There are no sounds that are both retroflexed and palatalized, since the tongue cannot be tipped back and extended to the front at the same time. Similarly, no sounds are labiopalatal, since only someone with a very unusual anatomy could close his lower lip against his hard palate.

There are other feature combinations, however, which seem perfectly feasible from an articulatory standpoint, yet are never found in the phonological systems of human languages. For instance, the derisive sound known as a Bronx cheer or "raspberry," although familiar to most English speakers, is not a part of English phonology. That is, it does not combine with other sounds to make English words. This sound, made by placing the tongue between the lips and ejecting air around it, does not seem to be incorporated into the phonology of any language, although it is a part of the gestural system of several. The same is true of the rounded, grooved labial fricative sounds made in whistling. No language has words composed partly of whistles.

Of course, this is not to imply that all sounds used gesturally lack phonological status. There are sounds which are phonologically relevant in one language but merely gestural in another. For instance, the voiceless lateral click used by some Americans to urge a horse forward, and the voiceless dental click used by English speakers to express mild reproach, function as speech sounds in some South African languages. Furthermore, even within the same language, a sound may be employed both phonologically and gesturally, as for instance, the sound [š] in English, which functions both as a phoneme in words like *share* and *ash* and as the hushing sound sometimes heard in libraries and theaters.

At any rate, the fact that sounds such as whistles and Bronx cheers are used gesturally but never phonologically suggests that sounds may be rejected as possible speech segments for some reason other than difficulty of articulation. That some potential distinctive features such as absolute pitch values never serve to distinguish words in any language and certain combinations of distinctive features never function together in speech sounds leads to the conclusion that the human mind is predisposed to utilize sounds in definite ways. In phonological systems, certain perfectly feasible feature combinations never occur; and even among the permissible combinations some are clearly preferred over others. The fricative [θ], for example, is relatively rare in the phonological inventories of languages. The fricative [s], on the other hand, is extremely common. We might assume, then, that the sound [θ] is in some way less natural to language than [s]. In this chapter we will be concerned with determining the relative naturalness of speech sounds. The literature on this topic is rapidly expanding. Some of the earlier and influential studies are: Cairns, 1969; Chomsky and Halle, 1968; Greenberg, 1966a, 1966b, 1970; Hockett, 1955; Jakobson, 1968; Postal, 1968; and Trubetzkoy, 1969.

7.2 IMPLICATIONAL LAWS

When related pairs of sounds such as the voiceless and voiced alveolar stops [t] and [d] are discussed, the more natural sound is referred to as the **unmarked** member of the pair. One important way of establishing which one of a pair of sounds is the more natural is to determine which can occur without the other in a given sound system. Where the presence of a given sound in a sound system nearly always implies the presence of another sound, we say an **implicational law** holds between those sounds. As a rule, a language does not have [d] in its sound inventory unless it also has [t]. But the converse is not true; there are languages that have a [t] without having a [d]. The Pohjanmaa dialect of Finnish, for example, has a [t] but lacks [d] entirely. In the case of [t] and [d], then, [t] is less marked than [d].

The status of [t] and [d] with respect to markedness is not an isolated phenomenon. Voiceless obstruents generally are more natural than their voiced counterparts. Among the stops, not only does the presence of a [d] in a language imply that language has a [t], the presence of [b] implies the presence of [p]; [g] implies [k]; and [ɢ] implies [q]. It can be said, then, that, in general, a language cannot have a voiced series of stops unless it also has a corresponding voiceless series.

Among fricatives as well, it is generally true that the presence of a voiced series such as [v, z, ž] implies the presence of a voiceless series [f, s, š]. Even the exceptions to this rule seem to have a consistent historical explanation. For instance, [v] often comes into a language as a change from [w]; and since [w] does not imply [f], neither does [v] in these cases. Classical Sanskrit has [v], from an earlier [w], but no [f]; the same is true of modern Finnish.

Just as voiceless obstruents are more natural than voiced obstruents, so are unaspirated stops more natural than aspirated ones. That is, unaspirated stops may occur in languages that do not have aspirated ones—such is the case in Finnish, French, and Spanish—but apparently no language has only aspirated stops. English has aspirated stops in syllable-initial position; but it also has unaspirated ones in other positions. The implicational law in this case is: the presence of aspirated stops in a language implies the presence of unaspirated ones.

As we have seen, voicelessness in obstruents is generally the unmarked condition. For resonants this situation is reversed: vowels, glides, liquids, and nasals are most commonly voiced. In fact, every language has voiced vowels. But only a small number of languages, such as Japanese, Cheyenne, and Nyangumarda, have voiceless vowels as well. Voiceless nasals, liquids, and glides also occur in fewer languages than do their voiced counterparts.

7.3 EVIDENCE FROM RANGE OF DISTRIBUTION

Sounds which are relatively unmarked not only occur in more of the languages of the world than do marked sounds, but they also typically have a wider distribution within a given language. That is, unmarked sounds occur in more types of environments than marked sounds. We can thus use evidence from within a single language to help establish the relative naturalness of sounds. But in doing so we must be careful to distinguish assimilatory environments from nonassimilatory ones.

Range of distribution in nonassimilatory environments is what counts in establishing relative naturalness. If the nature of the environment accounts for the presence of a sound, we cannot be certain about the capacity of that sound to function independently in a sound system. For example, if the labial nasal *m* occurs between a vowel and a *p* (as in *damp*) the labiality of the *m* may be due to assimilation to the labial *p*. However, if *m* occurs between a vowel and *d* (as in *slammed*) the *m* is in a nonassimilatory context, since the labiality of the nasal clearly cannot be due to any property of the vowel or of the alveolar *d*. That *m* occurs in *slammed*, then, is clear evidence concerning its range of distribution; but that it occurs in *damp* tells us nothing certain.

Historical change sometimes has an unusual effect on a language's distributional pattern. In Arabic, for instance, [b] has a wider distribution than [p], since [p] occurs only in voiceless environments. This unusual situation was brought about by the historical change of [p] to [f] in other positions. Apparently, the failure of evidence from range of distribution in a given language to converge with the evidence from distribution across languages is traceable to sound changes of this sort. In general, however, evidence from range of distribution within a language seems to lead to essentially the same implicational laws as does comparison of the sound inventories of various languages.

7.4 SYLLABLE STRUCTURE

Just as individual sounds and inventories of sounds differ in markedness so also do the patterns that sounds form within words. It is clear that some syllables are more natural than others; that is, they are composed of more natural combinations of sounds. And as with individual sounds, the presence in a language of certain syllables implies the presence of other less marked marked ones.

The least marked syllables are those beginning with a single consonant and ending in a vowel; somewhat more marked are syllables ending in a single consonant; and still more marked are syllables beginning or ending in various types of consonant clusters. Clusters of four or more consonants, either as onsets or codas, are extremely rare. Vowel initial syllables seem to be more marked than syllables beginning with a single consonant. There are languages—Nyangumarda and Quileute, for example—in which all syllables begin with a consonant, but there are no languages reported to have only vowel initial syllables.

Languages show a preference for syllables with short onsets and codas. But even onsets and codas of the same or nearly the same length, certain consonants and clusters of consonants are preferred over others. For instance, if a language has consonant cluster codas, it is expected to have some clusters composed of a resonant followed by an obstruent. Some languages have codas consisting of an obstruent followed by a resonant, but if they do, they also have resonant plus obstruent codas. French illustrates this implicational law. It has *table* [ṭabḷ] 'table' and *votre* [votṛ] 'your' with obstruent plus resonant codas. But French also has resonant plus obstruent clusters, as in *gorge* [goʁž] 'throat', *garde* [gaʁḍ] 'guard', *farce* [faʁṣ] 'farce', and *bulbe* [büḷb] 'bulb'.

The unmarked order for obstruents and resonants in onset clusters is the opposite of the order in codas. In onsets and codas, obstruents occur more naturally outside resonants than inside. One consonant of a consonant cluster is **outside** another if it is farther from the peak. The situation in English is typical: we find such initial clusters as: *pr, tr, kr, br, pl, bl, kl, gl, sl, fr, fl, θr, sn,* and *sm.* Swedish has these and also [kn] as in *kniv* 'knife', [gn] as in *gnaga* 'gnaw', and [fn] as in *fnissa* 'giggle'. At an earlier period in its history English also had [kn], [gn], and [fn] clusters. *Kn* and *gn* remain in the spelling of *knife* and *gnaw,* but not in the pronunciation. The cluster [fn] was changed to [sn]; Old English *fneosan* is the precursor of Modern English *sneeze.* The loss of *k* and *g* before *n* and the change of *y* to *s* before *n* illustrate a general preference for alveolar and dental consonants (see 7.5).

Many languages, including English, Swedish, Spanish, French, Sanskrit, and Mandarin, have clusters consisting of a consonantal segment outside a glide. This tendency is extremely strong. Puget Salish has typical codas consisting of glide followed by an obstruent, as the following words exemplify:

šawʔ	'bone'
X'layʔ	'canoe'
huyq	'fishnet'
síqews	'pants'
sqawc	'potato'
pʰədíwxʷ	'dirt' (Skagit dialect)

Puget Salish also has typical onsets consisting of an obstruent followed by a glide:

swátixʷtid	'earth, ground'
p'wayʔ	'flounder'

swidá^ʔx   'mountain huckleberries'
syæyæ^ʔ   'friend'
twaq'^w   'Mount Rainier' (Nisqually dialect)

In English and many other languages there is a preference for voiceless obstruents in clusters. English has initial *fr, šr, θr, sn, sm* but not **vr, *zr, *ðr, *žr, *zn, *zm*. (Note the use of an asterisk to mark an impermissible form, i.e. a form which violates rules in the language in question.) This is consistent with the preference languages generally show for voiceless obstruents over voiced obstruents. Serbo-Croatian, with its initial clusters *zr, zl, žl, vr, vl, zm, zn, dm, gm, dn*, and *gn*, also has the less marked *fr, sl, sm, šm, sn, šr, tm, km, pn*, and *kn*.

Even though they are somewhat less natural than clusters of resonants and obstruents, clusters composed entirely of obstruents are quite common. In onset clusters of obstruents, fricatives tend to occur before stops; clusters of obstruents with voicing (either the second member or both) are less common than voiceless clusters. English has the onsets *sp, st, sk*, and *sf*, but does not have **sb, *sd, *dg* or **zb, *zd, *zg*. All ten of these onsets occur in Serbo-Croatian. Notice also that English does not have any onset clusters of two stops like *pt, tk, bd, gd*. All of these also occur in Serbo-Croatian. Stop plus stop onsets also occur in a number of other languages, for instance, Ancient Greek (e.g., in [ptéron] 'feather, wing'). Languages that have onset clusters consisting entirely of stops seem also to have onsets consisting of a fricative followed by a stop.

In some languages, onsets consist of stop plus fricative as well as the reverse. Besides *sp, st*, and *sk*, Puget Salish also has *ts*, as in [tsolč] 'drum'.

In syllable final clusters, the sequence of fricative plus stop seems to be favored over stop plus fricative unless the fricative is *s*, in which case both orders seem equally likely. Both orders occur in English (*rasp, lapse*). Stop plus stop codas are also quite common. English has such codas as *pt* in *apt*, *bd* in *robbed*, *kt* in *act*, and *gd* in *sagged*.

In many languages, the segments of an obstruent coda must agree in voicing. Languages apparently do not have voiced obstruent codas unless they also have voiceless codas.

Clusters of resonants occur in some languages. English has the codas *lm, rm, ln* (for some speakers), *rn*, and *rl*, and the onset *mr* in noninitial syllables, as when *admirable* is pronounced [æd-mrə-bḷ]. Serbo-Croatian has the onsets *mr, ml*, and *mm*. Among resonant clusters there is a general preference for nasal plus liquid onsets and liquid plus nasal codas. Thus in both onsets and codas, nasals tend to be outside liquids.

In English at least, the restrictions given in this section seem to apply to clusters of three segments as well as to clusters of two. For instance, the three-consonant onset *spr* of *spring* has the obstruents outside the resonant and, of the two obstruents, the fricative is outside the stop. The coda *rps* of *harps* has just the reverse order of consonants, as expected.

7.5 NATURAL CONSONANT SYSTEMS

Within the classes of consonants, some subclasses are more natural than others. Obstruents are less marked than sonorants. All languages have several obstruents; but many have only a single liquid (*l* or *r*), and a few languages of the Pacific Northwest (Quileute, Makah, Twana, and Puget Salish) have no nasals at all. Within the set of obstruents, stops are the most natural subclass and fricatives are more natural than affricates. In all the subclasses, dentals and alveolars are more natural than the corresponding retroflex consonants, and velars are more natural than uvulars.

As we have mentioned, voiced obstruents are more marked than voiceless ones. For all classes of obstruents, those with secondary articulations are less natural than those without. For example, the presence of glottalized stops or pharyngealized stops in a language implies the presence of the corresponding plain stops. The most natural fricatives are [s] and [h]. The labial affricates (such as [f̂]) are less natural than the coronal ones (such as [č]). Among coronal affricates, the strident ones are the most natural, and of the strident affricates, the lateral ones (such as [ƛ]) are less natural than the sibilant types.

Among the sonorants, voiced segments are more natural than unvoiced ones and liquids seem to be more natural than nasals. Of the liquids, it is difficult to assess whether laterals or *r*-sounds are less marked; apparently languages can have either type without having the other. Hawaiian, for instance, has *l* and no *r*, while Japanese has *r* and no *l*. However, if a language has a dark (velarized) *l*, it apparently must also have a clear (plain alveolar or dental) *l*. Clear *l* is thus the more natural sound. English has both clear and dark *l*'s, but Spanish has only clear *l*'s.

Among the nasals, however, *n* is the preferred segment. This is consistent with the tendency that languages show for having more alveolar and dental consonants than other kinds.

Chomsky and Halle (1968: 413–14) have suggested that the least marked set of consonants is [p, t, k, s, n]. However, Hawaiian, which has a very minimal consonant system, lacks [t] and [s]. Instead of [s], Hawaiian has [h]. In the history of many languages [s] has changed to [h], which seems to suggest that [h] is at least as natural as [s]. Further, as we have pointed out, several Northwest American Indian languages, do not have [n], or any other nasal, as a part of their consonant systems. Some other American Indian languages, among them Cherokee, lack [p]. Thus, the Chomsky and Halle proposal seems unlikely to be correct. In fact, at present any attempt to pinpoint the set of least marked consonants seems premature.

7.6 NATURAL VOWEL SYSTEMS

Aside from the few rather general statements above, it is difficult as of now to make many defensible claims about the markedness of consonants. We are no more confident about the detailed markedness of vowels. However, it is possible to make some general observations.

Oral vowels are more natural than nasal ones. The presence of nasal vowels in a system implies the presence of oral vowels (and, almost certainly, of nasal consonants). Similarly, a lax vowel implies its tense counterpart. Languages which have lax vowels such as [ɪ], [ɛ], [ʊ] or [ɔ] also have the corresponding tense vowels. According to Greenberg (1966b) long vowels imply short ones.

The nonfront low vowels seem to be the most natural vowels. Apparently no language lacks a vowel of the quality of [a] or [ɑ]. The high front vowel [i] also seems to occur in every language. There is some evidence that [i] is less natural, however, than the low vowels. In Kabardian, for instance, the low central vowel occurs in nonassimilatory environments, but except in borrowings, the vowel [i] occurs only in assimilatory environments, after [y], laterals, and palatalized consonants (Kuipers, 1960).

Some phonologists would include [u] in the set of least marked vowels. However, it apparently does not occur at all in certain Straits Salish dialects, such as Saanich and Songish, spoken on the southern tip of Vancouver Island. Along with [ɑ] and [i], these languages have a mid front vowel [e] rather than [u] (Thompson, Thompson, and Efrat, 1974). Both [u] and [e], then, imply [i], and neither implies the other. However, the number of languages lacking [u] is much smaller than the number lacking a mid front vowel.

Low vowels appear to be most natural if unrounded, judging from the ubiquity of [a, ɑ]. Among nonlow vowels, back vowels are more natural if rounded: [u], [o], and [ɔ] are more natural than [ɯ], [ɤ], and [ʌ]. On the other hand, front rounded vowels imply front unrounded ones in the same system.

7.7 SUMMARY

Some sounds, although perfectly feasible from an articulatory standpoint, are never found in the phonological systems of human languages; others are found only rarely; and still others are found in almost every language. These facts suggest that the human mind is predisposed to use sounds in certain well-defined ways and that some sounds are more natural to human language than others.

One way of determining which of a pair of sounds is the more natural is to find which can occur independently of the other in sound systems. Some sounds almost never occur in a language unless certain related sounds are also present. If the presence of a given sound implies the presence of some other sound in a particular language inventory, an **implicational law** holds between them. A number of implicational laws have been found, including the following: (1) voiced obstruents imply voiceless obstruents; (2) obstruents with secondary articulations imply plain ones; (3) voiceless resonants imply voiced ones; (4) nasal vowels imply oral vowels; (5) front rounded vowels imply front unrounded vowels; (6) mid vowels imply high vowels; and (7) high back vowels imply high front vowels. Evidence for naturalness based on the range of distribution within a language seems to be generally consistent with the implicational evidence based on sound inventories.

Just as sound segments may be more or less natural, so may types of syllables. The most natural syllables are of the shape consonant plus vowel. Somewhat less natural are syllables ending in a single consonant. Other things being equal, the longer the syllable coda becomes, the less natural the syllable. The same is true of the syllable onset: onsets consisting of several consonants are less natural than those consisting of a single consonant. Further, some sound combinations within onsets and codas are more natural than others.

Entire sound inventories also seem to differ in degree of naturalness, but as yet it is difficult to pinpoint the optimum set of sounds.

EXERCISES FOR CHAPTER 7

1. Mark each of the following sound inventories either N (natural) or I (impossible). Underline the most natural consonant system and the most natural vowel system.

   a. Consonant inventories
   1. / p, t, q, f, s, š, č, l, r, n /
   2. / p, t, ʔ, f, s, r, m, n, w, y /
   3. / b, d, g, ɢ, v, z, l, r, n, y /
   4. / pʰ, b, tʰ, d, kʰ, g, f, v, s, z, l, r, m, n, ŋ, w, y /
   5. / pʰ, p, b, tʰ, t, d, f, v, s, z, š, č, l, r, m, n /
   6. / p, b, t, d, k, g, f, v, s, z, l, r /
   7. / ʔ, t, s, r, n /

8. / p, pʰ, t, tʰ, k, kʰ, kʷ, kʰʷ, m, n, l, ɫ, s, x, w, y /
9. / p, pʰ, b, t, tʰ, d, ṭ, ṭʰ, ḍ, k, kʰ, g, m, n, ṇ, ŋ, s, ṣ /
10. / p, k, d, g, f, z, l, r /

b. Vowel inventories

1. / ã, ĩ, ũ, ɛ̃, ɔ̃, æ̃ /
2. / a, i, u /
3. / ɯ, ö, ü, ɒ /
4. / a, i, u, e, æ /
5. / a, i, u, e, o /
6. / a, i, u, ü, ɯ, ɒ /
7. / a, ɐ, i, ɩ, u, ʊ /
8. / a, i, u, ü, ö /
9. / i, e, o /
10. / a, i, u, ɩ, ʊ /

2. Discuss each of the sound systems given below in terms of the naturalness of their consonant and vowel systems. The symbols given are not suffi-cient for a narrow transcription. Each symbol represents a class of similar articulations.

a. The Kuskokwim dialect of Eskimo (Based on Mattina, 1970)

p	t	k	q		
f	s	x	x̣	i	u
m	n	ŋ	ṇ̇		
	l ɫ			a	

b. Maori (Based on Hohepa, 1967; Maori is the aboriginal language of New Zealand and belongs to the Malayo–Polynesian family)

p	t	k		
m	n	ŋ		
f			i	u
		h	e	o
w			a	
	r			

c. Tagalog (Based on Lapid, 1969; Tagalog is the principal language of the Philippines and belongs to Malayo–Polynesian family)

p	t		k	ʔ		
b	d		g		i	u
	s		h		e	o
m	n		ŋ		a	
	l r					
w		y				

d. Nupe (Based on Hyman, 1970; Nupe is a Kwa language of Nigeria)

```
p    t          k
b    d          g
f    s    š          h
v    z    ž                i   ĩ              u   ũ
ᵏp   c    č                e                  o
ᵍb   j    ǰ                        a   a:     ã
m    n
     l
     r
w         y
```

e. Yuchi (Based on Crawford, 1973; Yuchi is an American Indian language thought to be distantly related to the Siouxan languages)

```
p    t    c    č    k    ʔ
pʰ   tʰ   cʰ   čʰ   kʰ
b    d    j    ǰ    g
p'   t'   c'   č'   k'        i   ĩ              u   ũ
f         s    ɫ    š    h    e   ẽ              o   õ
f'        s'   ɫ'   š'        æ   æ̃   ɑ   ɑ̃    ɒ
          n    l
          n'   l'
w              y
w'             y'
```

f. Arabic (Classical). (Based on Schramm, 1962.) A period placed below a consonant indicates pharyngealization. The symbol *b* represent a class of articulations including [p].

```
          t          k    q        ʔ
          ṭ
b         d    ǰ
          ḍ
f    θ    s    š    x         h    i   i:         u   u:
     ð    z    ɣ                       a   a:
     ḏ̣    ṣ              ḥ
m         n
w              y
          l    r          ʕ
```

g. Tibetan (Based on Shefts and Chang, 1967; Chang and Shefts, 1964)

p	t	c	ṭ	č	k	q				
pʰ	tʰ	cʰ	ṭʰ	čʰ	kʰ	qʰ				
m	n			nʸ	ŋ		i:		ü:	u:
m̥				n̥ʸ	ŋ̂			ι:	ʊ:	
	s			š			e:		ö:	o:
	l	r					ε:		ɔ:	
	l̥	ɽ̥								ɑ:
w				y			i	u	ì:	ũ: ũ:
							e	ʌ	o	ẽ: õ: õ:
							a			ɛ̃
										ã

3. In Yuchi, all syllables begin with at least one consonant and all words end with a vowel. From the following examples, determine the syllable structure of Yuchi and the possible sequences of consonants within a word. (Based on Crawford, 1973)

1.	byõštõ	'thunder'	18.	y'asek'wẽ	'she sings'
2.	getyoʔo	'belch'	19.	gok'yõwõ	'think'
3.	setʰwa	'she kills'	20.	ʔispi	'black'
4.	jætʰyõ	'raccoon'	21.	histaʔĕ	'flat'
5.	godyok'o	'back of knee'	22.	syašpa	'she is cold'
6.	tot'wẽ	'sand'	23.	s'yoʔi	'his tobacco'
7.	cʰwa	'I kill'	24.	špa	'blackberry'
8.	cʰyaso	'money'	25.	šta	'snow'
9.	jyoł'a	'my lungs'	26.	ʔišt'ĕ	'road'
10.	gočʰwẽ	'rub (once)'	27.	jiškili	'horned owl'
11.	č'wẽnẽ	'willow'	28.	y'õt'ašk'a	'post oak'
			29.	šwa dok'wẽ	'I break a
12.	nĕč'ya	'you cry'			piece off'
13.	kyop'a	'(go) look!'	30.	š'wæ	'pokeberry'
14.	gokʰwẽ	'tie'	31.	wešya	'manure'
15.	kʰafa	'behind'	32.	č'wahe	'five'
16.	sejogwa	'she told me'	33.	geš'wa	'wart'
			34.	ʔondi	'we (inclu-
17.	ʔagahe ʔagyanõ	'come			sive)'
		tomorrow!'	35.	hondi	'he'

4. Examples of Finnish word-final and syllable-final codas were given in section 4.6. On the basis of that data, discuss the naturalness of the codas permitted in Finnish.

5. The inventory of Moru (a Nilo–Saharan language of the Sudan) is given
   below. Discuss the naturalness of the Moru sound inventory. Some
   examples of initial consonant clusters are also given. On the basis of this
   limited data, make a general statement about the onset structure. Given
   this general statement, what further consonant onsets would you expect
   to find in the language? (Based on Cowan, 1965.)

   a. Inventory

p		t		č	k		i		ɯ	u
b	ɓ	d	ɗ	ǰ	g		e			
^{k}p								ɛ	ɔ	
^{g}b									a	
f	s					h				
v	z									
m	n			n^y	ŋ					
	ř	ř̆	l							
w				y						

   b. Initial clusters

hw	mb	ŋb	n^{y}ǰw
čw	mv	n^{y}ǰ	nzw
ǰw	nd	nr	
sw	nz	tr	
zw	ŋg	dr	

8 natural processes

8.1 INTRODUCTION

As we saw in Chapter 2, the individual sounds within a word or phrase often have an effect on one another. However, not all of the changes sounds undergo when in conjunction with one another are equally likely to occur. In fact, certain processes of sound change are extremely widespread in the languages of the world, whereas others are relatively rare. Thus, sound processes may be said to differ in naturalness just as do sounds and sound sequences.

8.2 ASSIMILATORY PROCESSES

No doubt the most common way a sound may change is to assimilate to another sound. The most natural sound processes, then, are various types of assimilation.

8.2.1 Nasalization

One of the most common types of assimilation is the nasalization of vowels (and sometimes of other resonants) which are adjacent to a nasal consonant. Nasalization is especially common in vowels that precede nasal consonants. In English, for instance, the nasalization of vowels and resonants is frequently conditioned by a following nasal consonant. The sound to which another assimilates is said to **condition** the change. The nasalization of English vowels can be heard in such words as *pen* [pẽn], *hand* [hæ̃nd], and *fine* [fãɪ̃n].

8.2.2 Nasal Assimilation

A second process which is extremely common is the assimilation of nasal consonants to the position of an adjacent consonant. In English, an *n*, as in the prefix *con-* of *control* and *consume*, often becomes labial ([m]) before the labials [p, b, f], as in *comfort, compel,* and *combine*, but velar ([ŋ]) before the velars [k, g], as in *congress* and *concubine*. Similarly, in Yoruba the *n*-suffix which marks the progressive aspect becomes [m] before labial sounds, as in [mbo] 'be hiding'; [ŋ] before velars, as in [ŋkan] 'be breaking'; [mⁿ] before double stops, as in [m gᵇa] 'be getting'; but remains [n] elsewhere, as in [nta] 'be selling'.

8.2.3 Palatalization

A third very common assimilatory change is **palatalization**. This process superimposes a palatal articulation on nonpalatal consonants which are followed by a front vowel or glide. Palatalization produces sounds such as the [pʸ], [mʸ], [kʸ], and [fʸ] in the words *pure, mule, cute,* and *few* from the plain consonants [p], [m], [k], and [f]. In terms of distinctive features, it involves the addition of the feature values [+hi, −bk] to a consonant.

The various front vowels and *y* do not condition palatalization with equal frequency, however. There are implicational laws which constrain palatalization. In a given language if palatalization occurs before low front vowels, we expect it to also occur before mid vowels (if the language has mid vowels); if it occurs before mid front vowels, we expect it to occur before high ones. In Japanese the palatalization of *t* takes place only before the high front vowel [i]. (The palatalizing of *t* is followed by the substitution of [č] for [tʸ]. This natural change of [tʸ] to [č] is discussed in the next section.) In Modern Russian, the palatalization of velars takes place before high and mid vowels; and in Old English the palatalization of velars is conditioned by front vowels at all three heights.

If a sound becomes more like a preceding sound, the assimilation is said to be **progressive**. If it assimilates to a following sound, the assimilation is **regressive**. The assimilatory processes involved in nasalization and palatalization may be of either the progressive or regressive type, but regressive assimilation seems more common in both cases. It appears that the occurrence of progressive nasalization or palatalization in a language implies that these processes will also occur regressively. In Old English, palatalization takes place both before and after a front vowel. In Japanese and Russian it takes place only before a front vowel. None of the languages has palatalization only after a front vowel. In Old English the palatalization process is extended to its limits, occurring both before and after all front vowels.

8.2.4 Assibilation

Palatalization is very often followed by another natural process called assibilation. In **assibilation**, the [ʸ] release of palatalized stops changes to a strident fricative. The stops [tʸ] and [kʸ] seem to be the segments which most often assibilate. The change of [tʸ] to [č] mentioned in section 8.2.3 for Japanese is a typical example of assibilation. Following assibilation, [č] may change to [š], which may in turn change to [s].

The chain of sound changes [t, k] → [tʸ, kʸ] → [č] → [š] → [s] is probably the source of the English alternations of [t] and [s] in word pairs like *democrat* and *democracy* and of [k] and [s] in pairs like *critic* and *criticism*.

8.2.5 Intervocalic Voicing

Another very natural process voices obstruents when they occur between vocalic segments. This process, which assimilates voiceless segments to the voicing of the neighboring sounds, changes [t] to [d] in some English dialects. The [t] of *meat*, for example, voices between vowels: *meaty* [midi]. Intervocalic voicing is not always limited to the environment V___V, however. It may also occur between a liquid and a vowel, as in *furtive* [fɹ̩dɪv] or between liquids, as in *myrtle* [mɹ̩dl̩].

8.2.6 Intervocalic Weakening

A related process, **intervocalic weakening**, assimilates stops to the continuancy of surrounding sonorants. Note the alternation of the stops *b*, *d*, and *g* with their corresponding fricatives in the following Spanish forms:

[b]: *b*rioso	'lively'	[β]: e*b*rioso	'intoxicated'
[d]: *d*icción	'diction'	[ð]: la *d*icción	'the diction'
[g]: *g*uerra	'war'	[γ]: la *g*uerra	'the war'

It has been suggested that intervocalic voicing and the change by which stops become continuants intervocalically are actually two aspects of the same process. In this view, if a voiceless stop is weakened by one degree, it assimilates to the voicing of the surrounding vowels; if it is weakened by another degree, it assimilates to their continuancy; and if it is weakened still more, it disappears altogether (becomes null, i.e. $\emptyset$). Between vowels, the following sets of changes are quite likely to occur:

$$p \rightarrow b \qquad b \rightarrow \beta \qquad \beta \rightarrow \emptyset$$
$$t \rightarrow d \qquad d \rightarrow \eth \qquad \eth \rightarrow \emptyset$$
$$k \rightarrow g \qquad g \rightarrow \gamma \qquad \gamma \rightarrow \emptyset$$

In Finnish, the weakening process has been carried out to different degrees for different voiceless stops, so that [p] alternates with [v] (which has replaced the less natural bilabial fricative [β]); [t] with [d] (or in some dialects with $\emptyset$); and [k] with $\emptyset$. Thus, *t* weakens one degree by becoming voiced to [d]; *p* weakens two degrees by becoming both voiced and continuant [β] (ultimately [v]); and *k* weakens all three degrees through the chain k → g → γ → $\emptyset$. In Finnish there is no direct evidence of the intermediate steps of this chain (k→g, g→γ, γ→$\emptyset$). However, because the weakening of [g] to [γ] is a well-known historical change in English, Greek, Spanish, and a number of other languages, and because the deletion of voiced fricatives is also a common process, it is reasonable to assume these intermediate steps, whether or not direct evidence for them exists. (See Zwicky, 1974, for a discussion of what he terms "false steps.")

8.2.7 Obstruent Voicing and Devoicing

The assimilatory voicing of obstruents in environments other than between sonorants is rather rare. Occasionally, for example in Sanskrit and Polish, voiceless obstruents become voiced in assimilating to a voiced obstruent. It is much more common, however, for voiced obstruents to lose their voicing in the context of a voiceless obstruent. In fact, if a language has a rule which assimilates voiceless obstruents to voiced ones, it will have an assimilatory devoicing rule as well. This implicational law allows us to predict that Sanskrit and Polish will have obstruent devoicing as well as voicing, which is indeed the case.

Whereas a language does not have obstruent voicing without also having devoicing, the opposite is not true. Many languages have only assimilatory devoicing of obstruents. In Swedish, for example, progressive devoicing of the past tense ending *-de* is seen in *köpte* 'bought', where the preceding [p] causes the [d] to become [t]. Compare *bakade* 'baked' from *baka + de*. However, Swedish has no parallel cases of obstruent voicing. The devoicing of obstruents in voiceless environments is consistent with the tendency of languages to have more voiceless than voiced clusters.

Word-final devoicing, such as occurs in Sanskrit and German, may be regarded as the assimilation of a stop to the voiceless pause which follows it. Not all instances of devoicing in word-final position are due to assimilation, however. Some apparently result from the devoicing constraint described by Harms (1973a). According to this constraint, a voiceless consonant can never be followed by a voiced one in a coda cluster. This generalization holds true not only for contiguous consonants, but for consonants at any distance from each other. In other words, once voicelessness is introduced into a syllable coda, voicing may not be reintroduced under any circumstances. There are, then, no syllables that end in [tm, tz, tʁ], etc., although syllables can end in [tm̥]: Swedish *rytm* [rüt:m̥] 'rhythm'; [ts]: Swedish *katts* [kʰat:s] 'cat's'; and [tʁ̥]: French *autre* [otʁ̥] 'other'.

8.2.8 Vowel Assimilation

The assimilation of vowels to each other is another very natural process. Kikuyu vowel assimilation (section 2.13) is an example of this. An assimilation or set of assimilations which restrict the vowel sequences that occur in a word by permitting only certain sets of vowels in successive syllables is called **vowel harmony**. Perhaps the best-known language with vowel harmony is Turkish. The plural suffix in Turkish is either *-lar* or *-ler*; the choice depends on the nature of the vowel in the immediately preceding syllable. Consider the examples in 1 and 2:

1		2	
güller	'roses'	*adamlar*	'men'
ziller	'bells'	*pullar*	'postage stamps'
eller	'hands'	*kollar*	'arms'
gözler	'eyes'	*kïzlar*	'girls'

The plural suffix is *-ler* when the preceding vowel is *ü, i, e,* or *ö,* and *-lar* when the preceding vowel is *a, u, o,* or *ï* ([ɯ]). Clearly, the set of vowels which occurs when the shape of the plural suffix is *-ler* is not random; *ü, i, e,* and *ö* are all front vowels. If we assume that the shape of the plural suffix is basically *-lar,* we can state the rule which governs the choice of *a* or *e* in the plural suffix as follows: *a* becomes *e* when preceded by a front vowel. We can also note that the change of *a* to *e* is an assimilation of a nonfront vowel to the front position of the vowel that precedes it. That is, given our understanding of the phonetics of vowel production, the change of *a* to *e* after a front vowel is a very natural assimilatory process.

Vowel assimilations can also be regressive. Coeur d'Alene has a rule that changes [i] or [ɛ] to [a] when the next vowel in the word is [a]. For example, the usual form of one of the prefixed articles is [xʷɛ] as in [xʷɛsut'ɛ:sút'ɛ] 'the rubber' and [xʷɛsdíluʔ] 'the switch'. However it becomes [xʷa] when it precedes a form whose first vowel is [a], as in [xʷamác'p] 'the bee'. A stem vowel also changes if a suffix is added which contains [a]. Without suffixes the forms for 'one' and 'gallop' are [nɛk'ʷɛʔ]

and [dəlím]. If the suffix [ɑlqʷ] 'log(s)' is added, we derive [nák'ʷaʔɑlqʷ] 'one log' and [čdəlámɑlqʷ] 'train' (literally, 'it gallops on logs').

Notice that the direction of the assimilation in the Coeur d'Alene example is the reverse of that in Turkish in two respects. First, the assimilation is regressive. Second, the change is from a front vowel, [i] or [ɛ] to a non-front vowel under the influence of a nonfront vowel, [ɑ]. As in the Turkish example, the assimilation in Coeur d'Alene is a very natural process, given our understanding of the phonetic properties of vowels.

8.2.9 Umlaut

Another natural process closely related to vowel harmony is a form of regressive vowel assimilation called **umlaut**. One umlaut process fronts back vowels which are followed by a nonlow front segment [i, ɩ, y, e, ɛ]. In English, the remnants of an umlaut process which at one time affected all of the Germanic languages except Gothic can be seen in word pairs such as *goose/geese* and *man/men*. The words *geese* and *men* developed from earlier forms which had suffixes beginning with *i*. These suffixes have since been lost. Thus, the phonetic motivation of umlaut in these words has completely disappeared from English.

8.3 NONASSIMILATORY PROCESSES

Although by far the largest number of natural phonological processes are assimilatory, there are some rather common processes which do not seem to be cases of assimilation. The exact causes of some of these processes are not known, but they occur often enough to be considered natural.

8.3.1 Rhotacism

Rhotacism, the change of a strident fricative—usually [z]—to [r], is one such change. Since [z] is often the result of intervocalic voicing of [s], some languages such as Sanskrit and Latin manifest an alternation between [s] and [r]. English shows evidence of this process in word pairs such as *was/were, plus/plural, osculate/oral, adhesion/adhere*.

8.3.2 Breaking

Another common process which does not appear to be assimilatory is the breaking of long vowels. **Breaking**, the process by which long vowels become diphthongs, occurs in many dialects of English. The vowel of *be* has broken to [ïi] in some American dialects. Some American dialects also show breaking of lengthened [æ] before fricatives, as in *bash* [bǽiš], *grass* [grǽis], and *half* [hǽif]. The breaking of a lengthened vowel before the velars [g] and [ŋ] is also common: *bag* [bǽig], *egg* [ɛ̌ig], *hang* [hǽiŋ]. As is the case with rhotacism, the exact cause of breaking is not known. (See Labov, Yaeger, and Steiner, 1972, for experimental evidence from a number of American English dialects. See also Miller, 1972, 1973; and Stampe, 1972.)

8.3.3 Vowel Reduction

One of the most common processes to occur in stress languages is the reduction of contrast among unstressed vowels. In English, most unstressed syllables have the central vowels [ɨ] or [ə]. In Coeur d'Alene, both [i] and [ɑ] are replaced by [ə] in most unstressed syllables. Of the five Russian vowels [a, i, u, e, o] only [a, i, u] occur in unstressed positions (Jones, 1959).

8.3.4 Apocope and Syncope

The outright loss of segments, particularly in unstressed syllables, is also a common process. Different names are given to this process depending on where in the word it occurs.

Apocope is the loss of a segment or segments at the end of a word. The loss of final *r* in British English and American English in parts of the East is an example of apocope: *storing* [stɔriŋ], but *store* [stɔ]. Sometimes an entire syllable or more may be lost. The Eastern Salish languages Coeur d'Alene and Kalispel have pushed this process nearly to its limits in that all of the word after the primary stressed vowel may be dropped. Thus, the Coeur d'Alene word [hənqʷəqʷɔsqʷɔsm'í] 'dog' is from [hənq'ʷəq'ʷɔsq'ʷɔsm'íčən'sən'] (literally, 'he has little pleats in the bottoms of his feet'). The final six segments, being unstressed, may be dropped.

Syncope is the loss of a segment or segments from some part of the word other than the end. English exhibits syncope in *apostle* [əpásl̩]. Compare *apostolic* [æ̀pəstálɪk], and notice that the [tɑ] before the [l] is lost unless stressed. Similarly the [ɛ] of *angelic* [ænjélɪk] is lost when unstressed as in *angel* [éɪnjl̩].

Apocope and syncope often serve to reduce the length of clusters. In most dialects of English, for example, the [sts] cluster created by suffixing the plural to words such as *post*, *test*, etc., is reduced to [ss] in rapid speech. In a number of dialects final *pt* and *ct* [kt] clusters are simplified by dropping the *t*: [slɛp] *slept*, [fæk] *fact*.

8.3.5 Prothesis and Epenthesis

Another way of simplifying clusters is to insert a vowel between adjacent consonants or to add a vowel at the beginning or end of a word so as to create an extra syllable. The process which adds a vowel in initial position is called **prothesis**. That which adds a vowel or consonant in any other position is known as **epenthesis**.

Spanish has a prothesis rule that adds [e] to prevent the occurrence of word initial *sp*, *st*, and *sc* clusters. Thus, we have *español* 'Spanish', *establir* 'establish', and *escuela* 'school'. English has an epenthesis rule that inserts [ə] between a stem final *t* or *d* and the *d* of the past tense or past participle ending: *added* [ædəd] and *rested* [restəd].

Some epenthesis rules insert a consonant rather than a vowel. The [p] of *assumption*, *redemption*, and *warmth* [wɔrmpθ] is such a consonant: compare *assume*, *redeem*, and *warm*. Though the inserted consonant seems to lengthen the cluster, it does not make it less natural. The introduction of the *p* into the cluster allows for a certain kind of simplification. The several articulatory changes necessary in the transition from *p* to the following voiceless fricative—[θ] in *warmth* and [š] in *assumption* and *redemption*—can be spread out over time and accomplished in two steps. The change from *m* to [θ] involves (1) raising the velum, (2) terminating the voicing and (3) changing from a complete closure at the lips to a fricative articulation at the teeth. If *p* intervenes between *m* and θ, changes (1) and (2) occur in going from *m* to *p*; then (3) is accomplished independently in changing from *p* to [θ]. Epenthetic consonants seem always to have this property of facilitating articulatory transitions.

8.3.6 Metathesis

For a variety of reasons, the order of adjacent segments is often reversed. This reversal is known as **metathesis**. In Clallam, actual aspect forms are derived from nonactual forms by metathesis (Thompson and Thompson, 1969). Actual forms are used for present and past events; nonactual forms are used for future or expected events.

Nonactual	Actual	
čkʷút	čúkʷt	'shoot'
x̣,'ít	x̣íč't	'scratch'
q x̣ít	q'íx̣t	'tie up'
qq'ít	qíq't	'restrain'

8.3.7 Dissimilation

Dissimilation is the opposite of assimilation. In assimilation a sound becomes more like its surroundings; in **dissimilation** it becomes less so. In Kalispel, whenever two glottalized consonants come together without a vowel intervening, the first becomes deglottalized. Thus, the word for 'six' is [t'áq'ən] but the word for 'six days' is [tq'ənčstá]. In the latter form, the vowel *a* is lost from the stem when a suffix is added. Since this brings the [t'] next to the [q'], the [t'] deglottalizes.

8.4 NATURAL PHONOLOGY

At present it is not clear just how all the information we have accumulated about natural processes is to be integrated into the grammars of individual languages. Stampe (1969) has suggested that if a process is natural, it will be manifest in a given language unless that language invests something in blocking it, either partially or totally. This claim is tantamount to saying that certain processes are simply what children learning a language will do naturally unless they find evidence in the language that they should not do it. In other words, natural processes cost no effort to learn; only in learning to block these processes must the child expend effort. However, since phonological theory has not yet been able to provide us with a complete and reliable account of natural processes, we are forced to write even the most natural rules as though they were specific rules of the language under consideration rather than universal processes. The rules we present can be interpreted in the spirit of Stampe's work, though, if each rule which reflects a natural process is taken as a description of that part of the natural pattern for languages in general which has not been blocked in the language under discussion.

Eventually it may be possible to write a universal grammar which defines the form language will naturally take, all other things being equal. Given such a grammar, it would be necessary in describing individual languages only to note those areas where the language in question deviated from the most natural pattern. Through markedness theory, steps have been made in this direction, but a great many questions are left to be answered before phonologists can write this sort of natural phonology. (For further discussion see, for example, Chen, 1973; Schane, 1972; and the papers in Bruck *et al.*, 1974.)

8.5 SUMMARY

Not only are some sounds and sound sequences more natural than others, the processes of sound change also vary in degree of naturalness. Among the most natural phonological processes—those which occur most widely in languages of the world—are various types of assimilations, such as: (1) **nasalization,** the process whereby a vowel or consonant becomes nasalized in the environment of a nasal consonant; (2) **nasal assimilation,** the assimilation of a nasal consonant to the position of an adjacent obstruent; (3) **palatalization**, the assimilation of a consonant to the palatal articulation of an adjacent front vowel or glide; (4) **assibilation**, the change of a palatalized stop to a strident affricate; (5) **intervocalic voicing**, the voicing of an obstruent between vocalic segments; (6) **intervocalic weakening**, the change of a stop to a continuant between resonant segments; (7) **obstruent voicing** and **devoicing,** the assimilation of an obstruent to the voicing of adjacent obstruents; (8) **vowel assimilation**, the change of some feature or features of a vowel to make it more like some other segment; and (9) **umlaut**, a regressive assimilation of back vowels to front ones.

Some nonassimilatory processes also seem to be natural to language. Among these are (1) **rhotacism**, the change of [z] to [r]; (2) **breaking**, the change of a long vowel to a diphthong; (3) **vowel reduction**, the reduction of contrasts among unstressed vowels; (4) **apocope**, the loss of a segment or segments in word-final position; (5) **syncope**, the loss of one or more segments within a word; (6) **prothesis**, the addition of a segment in word-initial position; (7) **epentheses**, the addition of a segment elsewhere in the word; (8) **metathesis**, the reversal of adjacent segments; and (9) **dissimilation**, the changing of a sound so that it becomes less like other sounds in its environment.

EXERCISES FOR CHAPTER 8

1. Which of the following rules seem the most natural? What natural processes do they involve?

    1. [f, s, x] become [v, z, γ] between vowels
    2. [p, t, k] become [b, d, g] finally
    3. [p, t, k] become [b, ð, Ø] between vowels
    4. [p, k] become [t] after [n]
    5. [v, γ] become [p, k] before [t]
    6. [f, θ, x] become [p, t, k] before [s]
    7. [sp, st, sk] become [p, t, k] initially
    8. [sp, st, sk] become [səp, sət, sək] initially
    9. [sVp, sVt, sVk] become [sp, st, sk] between vowels
    10. [mr, nr] → [mbr, ndr]

2. In the Turkish examples given below, the final consonant of the items in Column **a** is changed if a suffix is added (as in Column **b**). What natural process accounts for these changes? (acc.=accusative)

	(a)			**(b)**	
1.	[dip]	'bottom'		[dibi]	'bottom' (acc.)
2.	[a:gač]	'tree'		[a:gaǰɯ]	'tree' (acc.)
3.	[šɛrit]	'tape'		[šɛridi]	'tape' (acc.)
4.	[grup]	'group'		[grubu]	'group' (acc.)
5.	[prɛnsip]	'principle'		[prɛnsibi]	'principle' (acc.)
6.	[ɛt-]	'to do'		[ɛdɛr]	'he does'
7.	[git-]	'to go'		[gidɛr]	'he goes'
8.	[güt-]	'to pasture'		[güdɛr]	'he pastures'

3. The Nyangumarda future ending is basically *lapa*. From the following examples, name the process whereby [p] becomes [m] in the future ending. (Ignore the vowel alternations.)

1.	wurra + lapi + yi	They'll tell (someone)
2.	kaku + luma + ŋu	He won't tell you
3.	wirri + lima + ŋu	He'll put (it near) you
4.	wirri + lipa + li	You and I will put (it somewhere)
5.	kalku + lupa + li	You and I will care for (it)
6.	yurpa + lapa + li	You and I will rub (it)
7.	wirri + limi + rni	I'll put (it somewhere)
8.	yurpa + lama + rna	I'll rub (it)
9.	yurpa + lama + n	You will rub (it)
10.	yurpa + lami + nʸi	All of us will rub (it)

(Based on Hoard and O'Grady, 1976)

4. In Nez Perce, a Sahaptian language of the Pacific Northwest, [c] becomes [s] if it occurs after a consonant and before [n] or [w]. Compare yúʔc 'poor, pitiful' / yúʔsne 'poor' (object case), and ʔoylá:qc 'six' / ʔoylá:qswa 'six (of men)'. What kind of process is this? The basic Nez Perce consonant system is as follows:

p	t	c	k	q	ʔ
	ł	s	x	x̣	h
m	n				
w		y			
	l				
p'	t'	c'		k'	q'
m'	n'				
w'		y'			
	l'				

Given this consonant system, can the change of [c] to [s] be stated as one process in distinctive feature notation? (Based on Aoki, 1970)

5. Yawelmani is a dialect of Yokuts, an American Indian language of California. From the examples of Yawelmani aorist and passive aorist verb forms given below, determine the environment(s) where long vowels become short vowels.

Aorist	Passive Aorist	
1. pana:hin	panat	'arrive'
2. ʔile:hin	ʔilet	'fan'
3. ʔa:milhin	ʔamlit	'help'
4. wo:wulhin	wowlut	'stand up'
5. ṣe:niṭ'hin	ṣenṭ'it	'smell'
6. hoyo:hin	hoyot	'name'

(Based on Kuroda, 1967)

6a. Southeast Ambrym (a Malayo–Polynesian language of the New Hebrides) has a rule of apocope. Examine the examples below and state the environment for this rule.

(hili) →) hil	'hair'	hilin	'his hair'
(vaŋe →) vaŋ	'belly'	vaŋen	'his belly'
(luho →) luh	'tooth'	luhon	'his tooth'
asou	'wife'	asoun	'his wife'
he	'hand'	hen	'his hand'

b. The basic vowels of Southeast Ambrym are [i, u, e, o, æ, a]. There is a rule which changes [o] to [e] before [i, e, æ] in noninitial syllables. What type of process is illustrated by this rule? State the rule in distinctive features, ignoring the restriction to noninitial syllables.
(Based on Parker, 1968, 1970)

7. Chamorro is a Malayo–Polynesian language spoken in the Mariana Islands, including Guam. Consider the following Chamorro noun forms.

gúmaʔ	'house'	i gímaʔ	'the house'
fóggon	'stove'	ni féggon	'the stove'
túŋoʔ	'to know'	in tíŋoʔ	'we know'
lágu	'north'	sæn-lægu	'towards north'

a. What natural process do these forms illustrate?
b. Using distinctive features, formulate the rule for this process.
   (Based on Topping, 1973: 52)

8. In native Chamorro words, high and low vowels occur in one environment while mid and low vowels occur in another. The basic Chamorro

vowels are [i, u, e, o, æ, a]. Consider the following examples and determine the distribution of the Chamorro vowels. (Hint: Consider stress and syllable structure.)

1. nífen	'teeth'		7. tómmo	'knee'
2. bǽba	'open'		8. lókkaʔ	'tall'
3. húyoŋ	'outside'		9. títek	'rip'
4. bába	'bad'		10. húlat	'overpower'
5. lémmai	'breadfruit'		11. dílok	'bend'
6. péknoʔ	'killer'		12. búsoʔ	'lump'

(Based on Topping, 1973: 53–55; 1968)

9 morphology and phonology

9.1 INTRODUCTION

In the preceding chapters we saw that spoken language can be broken down into syllables, which can be divided into individual sound segments, which in turn can be broken down into distinctive features. In addition to sounds and units of sound, language can also be divided into units of meaning. Thus, words are composed on the one hand of sound units (syllables and segments) and on the other of meaning units called morphemes.

The **morpheme** is the smallest unit of meaning. Words and phrases can be decomposed into morphemes, but a morpheme cannot be further divided into meaningful units. Some words, such as *storm, banana, hurl,* and *green,* are made up of only a single morpheme. Others such as *stormy, bananas, hurling,* and *greenish* are composed of two morphemes. *Stormy,* for example, contains the morphemes *storm* and *-y,* an adjective marker which occurs also in *rainy, crazy, classy,* and the like. Still other words are composed of several morphemes. *Unreasonable* consists of the three morphemes *un-* (a negative marker) *reason,* and *-able* (an adjective marker). *Un-* is found also in *unpleasant* and *-able* in *likeable.* The word *unsportsmanlike* is made up of five morphemes: *sport, man, like,* the negative marker *un-,* and the plural marker *s* (added here to *sport*). None of these five units or any of those above that we called morphemes is divisible in such a way that the resultant pieces can be associated with meanings which are components of the whole.

If a word can be subdivided into meaningful parts but the parts cannot be associated in any reasonable way with the meaning of the whole, the word is a single morpheme. Consider the word *barn*. We can divide this word into the meaningful pieces *bar* and *-n*. There is an *-n* morpheme which occurs in *shown*, *seen*, and *known*, for instance, as a past participle marker. The word *barn*, however, is not the past participle of *bar*. Hence, we cannot arrive at the meaning of *barn* by combining the meanings of *bar* and *-n*. The other possible divisions of *barn*, *b-arn* and *ba-rn*, are equally unfruitful. We conclude that *barn* is but a single morpheme since no way of dividing it yields components whose meanings add up to the meaning of *barn*.

The divisions between morphemes are typically marked with a #. The # boundary is called the **external juncture**. Thus, we represent *boys* as *boy#s*, *snowy* as *snow#y*, and *higher* as *high#er*.

It is only accidental if a morpheme coincides with one of the phonological units we have discussed in the earlier chapters. Some morphemes are composed of only part of a syllable. This is the case with the *-s* at the end of *boys*. Others are represented by a single syllable, as in *boy*, *high*, and *work*. Still others are represented by two, three, or more syllables, as in the words *orphan*, *venison*, and *Massachusetts*.

9.2 CLASSES OF MORPHEMES

Morphemes fall into two major classes: roots and affixes. A **root** is the basic element in a word. In the words *unkind* and *placid* the roots are *kind* and *plac*. Roots like *kind*, which can occur by themselves as full words, are called **free roots**. The root *plac*, found also in *placate* and *implacable*, does not by itself constitute a whole word; such roots, which occur only in conjunction with one or more other morphemes, are called **bound roots**.

Affixes are morphemes that occur only in conjunction with a root or some combination of roots and other affixes. The part of a word to which an affix is attached is called the **stem**. A root by itself may be a stem. This is the case in the words *unkind*, *showy*, and *placid*. Or a stem may consist of a root plus one or more affixes. In *uncomfortable*, *un-* is affixed to the stem *comfortable* and *-able* to the stem *comfort*. Thus, a stem may contain a stem.

There are three types of affixes: **prefixes**, which are added before the stem; **suffixes**, which are added after the stem, and **infixes**, which are inserted into the stem.

In English, suffixes and prefixes are extremely common. The following list contains but a tiny fraction of the possible examples of English prefixes and suffixes:

PREFIXES	SUFFIXES
un⌢kind	plac⌢*id*
ré⌢gard	rig⌢*or*
dé⌢tract	fuzz⌢*y*
bé⌢friend	scen⌢*ic*
mis⌢fire	bak⌢*er*
in⌢vert	stomp⌢*ed*

Infixes are inserted between the segments of a root. In the Philippine language Bontoc (as reported in Gleason, 1955: 79), for example, mutatives are marked by infixing *um* after the first consonant of the root:

bato	'stone'	bumato	'is becoming stone'
fikas	'strong'	fumikas	'is becoming strong'
fusul	'enemy'	fumusul	'is becoming an enemy'
pusi	'poor'	pumusi	'is becoming poor'

Affixes function in two main ways: as inflectional markers and as derivational markers. **Inflectional affixes** are the morphemes which (1) decline nouns and pronouns for number, gender, and case; (2) conjugate verbs for such things as aspect, mood, voice, number, and tense; and (3) mark adjectives for the comparative and superlative. In English, the *-s* of *cats*, the *-m* of *them*, the *-d* of *baked*, the *-ing* of *going*, and the *-er* of *taller* represent inflectional affixes.

Derivational affixes are morphemes which (1) establish the grammatical classification (part of speech) of a stem, (2) change the grammatical class of a stem (e.g., from noun to verb), or (3) change the subclassification of a stem (e.g., from noun to agent noun). In English, there are many derivational affixes. Among them are the following:

AFFIX	CHANGE	EXAMPLES
-ic	noun to adjective	scene/scenic
-ness	adjective to noun	still/stillness
-ize	noun to verb	item/itemize
-ize	adjective to verb	regular/regularize
-ion	verb to noun	locate/location
-ist	noun to agent noun	guitar/guitarist
-er	verb to agent noun	bake/baker

9.3 MORPHOLOGICAL PROCESSES

The study of how words are constructed from morphemes is called **morphology**. Morphology is concerned with identifying the roots and affixes of a given language and with describing how these morphemes are combined to form words.

There are four major morphological processes which, when applied to stems, produce new words. These are: (1) **affixation**, the addition of prefixes, suffixes, and infixes to a stem; (2) **reduplication**, the repetition of all or some part of a stem; (3) **symbolism**, changes in the structure of the stem itself; and (4) **compounding**, the combination of two or more root morphemes. By far the most common of these processes is affixation, which we have discussed above.

Reduplication is also very common. In Hawaiian, for example, words of more specialized meaning are formed by complete reduplication of the stem (Elbert, 1970).

holo	'run'	holoholo	'go for walk or ride'
lau	'leaf'	laulau	'leaf food package'
muʔu	'cut off'	muʔumuʔu	'gown without a train'
ʔolu	'pleasant'	ʔoluʔolu	'pleasant, cool'

Reduplication may be either total, as in the examples above, or only partial. An example of partial reduplication can be seen in Snohomish (Hess, 1966), where certain augmentatives (forms that mean 'larger than' or 'more than') are formed by reduplicating the first consonant of the root. A [ə] is inserted between the identical consonants.

STEM	AUGMENTATIVE	
cəwát	cəcəwát	'know'
jədís	jəjədís	'tooth'
ɬádəyʔ	ɬəɬádəyʔ	'woman'
yáʔyəʔ	yəyáʔyəʔ	'friend'

The third morphological process, symbolism, produces new words by altering the stem in some way. In English, for example, the past tense of certain verbs is formed by changing a vowel or consonant in the stem, as in *fight/fought, sit/sat, meet/met, build/built,* and *send/sent.*

The process of compounding produces words by combining two or more roots. English has numerous words such as *baseball, washroom, typewriter,* and *schoolbus,* which are the result of compounding. The same is true of many other languages as well. Consider, for example, the following Diegueño compounds (Langdon, 1970: 135):

COMPOUND		COMPONENT ROOTS			
aləmi	'beard'	aˑ	'mouth'	ləmis	'fur'
matsay	'desert'	ʔəmat	'earth'	saˑy	'to be dry'
ʔəčiɬič	'devil'	ʔiˑčix	'heart, chest'	-ɬič	'to be bad'

COMPOUND		COMPONENT ROOTS	
saɫʸə mak 'shoulder blade'	-saɫʸ 'arm, hand'	-mak	'to be behind, in back of'

9.4 ARBITRARINESS

In a given language, sounds and meanings are paired arbitrarily in the morpheme. There is no sequence of sounds that is naturally or predictably associated with a given meaning. The same meaning is associated with the sounds represented by *garçon* in French and by *Knabe* in German. On the other hand, approximately the same sound sequence which in English has the meaning 'to wager' (*bet*), in German means 'bed' (*Bett*) and in French, 'animal' (*bête*). The sound-meaning pairings for these words is clearly arbitrary.

A number of people, from the ancient Greeks forward, have maintained that there must be some natural connection between words and their meanings: that the word *man*, for example, has some manlike quality, or that the word *dog* is inherently doggish. But this certainly does not seem to be true of the vast majority of morphemes in any known language. Even onomatopoetic forms, (those which are intended to imitate nonlinguistic sounds) display a good deal of arbitrariness. For instance, in English, bells supposedly go *ding-dong*, while in German they go *bim-bam*; English dogs say *bow-wow*, *woof*, or *yap*, French dogs say *gnaf-gnaf*, and so forth. It is clear that a rather large range of speech sounds will qualify as imitations, and that no natural connection exists between such words and the sounds they purport to imitate.

Just as there is no direct connection between onomatopoetic sounds and the phenomena they imitate, neither is there any discernable connection between how a sound is articulated and what it means. Words containing the vowels [ɪ] or [i] often have as part of their meaning the notion 'smallness' (e.g. *little, pigmy, bit, teeny, wee*), and many words containing [ɒ] or [ɑ] have something to do with 'largeness' (e.g. *tall, large*). It might therefore seem plausible that there is some basic relationship between 'smallness' and the sounds [i] and [ɪ], and 'largeness' and [ɑ] and [ɒ]—particularly since the vowels of *little* and *teeny* are made with a small jaw opening whereas those of *large* and *tall* are made with a large jaw opening. However, it is clear that some words arbitrarily run counter to this tendency in the most severe way— by reversing it. The word *small*, for example, has the same vowel as *tall* and the word *big* has the same vowel as *little*. Such counterexamples make any symbolic connection between sound and meanings seem unlikely. Then, too, for the vast majority of words with these sounds—words like *in, since, team, sweet, fall,* and *farm*—size is not a part of the meaning at all.

9.5 LEXICAL ENTRIES AND PHONOLOGICAL RULES

Since the pairing of sound and meaning in a morpheme is arbitrary, at least a certain portion of the information about how to pronounce any particular morpheme must be learned by a language user and stored in the mind as unique information about that morpheme. And, of course, the meanings of these morphemes must also be learned and stored. Linguists refer to all the information stored for a particular morpheme as a **lexical entry**. The whole set of lexical entries for a language is called its **lexicon**.

Some linguists feel that the lexicon contains entries for full words instead of for morphemes. It is difficult to know for certain whether the mind stores only full words, both words and morphemes, or only individual morphemes. (For a discussion of this question, see Jackendoff, 1975.)

Each lexical entry includes an **underlying representation** (also called an **underlying form** or **base form**). The underlying representation contains information about the pronunciation of the morpheme (or word). But not all of the information about how to pronounce a given morpheme or word must be stored in the lexicon. Some aspects of pronunciation are determined by processes which apply to many morphemes of the language. Much about the pronunciation of each morpheme is therefore describable by phonological rules. Only the part of the pronunciation not describable by rules need be stored in the lexicon as part of a lexical entry.

The description of how a morpheme is actually pronounced in a given word is called a **surface representation**. The phonological rules act on the underlying representation of a morpheme or word to determine the shape of its surface representation. To illustrate this point, let us consider the pronunciation of the English words *tar*, *top*, *till*, and *team*. These words are representative of a large class of English words which begin with *t*. That each of these words begins with *t* is a fact that must be learned. There are also a large number of words, like *star*, *stop*, *still*, and *steam*, that begin with initial *st*. That each of these words contains a *t* as its second sound must be learned. However, the fact that the *t*'s in *tar*, *till*, and *team* are aspirated, whereas those of *star*, *still*, and *steam* are not, need not be learned for each of these words. The appearance of aspirated *t* at the beginning of a syllable is predictable, as is the appearance of unaspirated *t* after initial *s*. We can state the rule for aspiration informally as: syllable initial *t* is pronounced [tʰ].

Since the presence of aspiration is predictable in English, the difference between [t] and [tʰ] is ignored in underlying forms. In the lexical entries for English words, then, there is only one kind of *t*. Each of the segments represented in an underlying form is called a **phoneme**. We enclose phonemic symbols in diagonals rather than in brackets, for example, /t/. We thus represent the lexical entry for [tʰar] *tar* as /tar/ and that of [star]

star as /star/. An underlying representation may also be called a **phonemic transcription.**

Notice that English orthography, in using only the letter *t* for both [t] and [tʰ], takes advantage of the rule of aspiration, and represents in spelling only one kind of *t*. It is not uncommon for writing systems to be based partially on underlying forms.

We can see then that phonological rules not only allow the language user to store less information about the words he knows, but they also allow him to predict many details of the pronunciation of a word he encounters for the first time. You may never before have come across the words *Tillamook* and *Steilacoom*, but you know that the *t* in the first is pronounced with aspiration, and in the second, without. Another rule of English inserts a [p] between a stem ending in [m] and a suffix beginning with a voiceless consonant. This rule is responsible for the *p*'s in *assumption, consumptive, presumption,* and *redemption.* (Compare *assume, consume, presume,* and *redeem.*) The *p* is added in pronunciation even if it is not indicated in the orthography; notice the [p] between the *m* and *th* of *warmth.* Since the [p] can be introduced by an epenthesis rule (see 8.3.5), it is not part of the underlying representation of any of these words.

The degree to which the underlying forms of a language differ from their corresponding surface representations is determined by the rules of that language. The more an underlying form differs from its surface representation, the more **abstract** it is. In recent years there has been a good deal of debate concerning the abstractness of underlying forms. Phonologists on both sides of the issue have put forth strong arguments, and at present it is hard to know whether those favoring quite abstract representations or those favoring more concrete representations are correct. (See Braine, 1974; Brame, 1973a; Harms, 1973b; Hyman, 1970, 1973; Kiparsky, 1968a; Kisseberth, 1969; Kuroda, 1967; Lightner, 1975; Nessly, 1973; Ohala, 1974; and Schane, 1973.)

We should also note that the terms *phoneme* and *phonemic* have been used in several ways in the phonological literature of the twentieth century. The usage suggested in this chapter is quite different from some earlier uses of the term. The articles in Joos, 1957, and Makkai, 1972, as well as Gleason, 1961; Pike, 1947; Halle, 1959; and Chomsky, 1964, give valuable historical perspective on the evolution of these terms.

9.6 THE ALTERNATION OF ALLOMORPHS

Morphemes often have different surface representations in different contexts. The alternate surface representations of a morpheme are called its

allomorphs. One of the important goals of phonology is to account for allomorphic alternations. To the degree possible, this is accomplished by relating each of the surface representations to the underlying representation by means of phonological rules. For example, the allomorphs of the regular English plural morpheme are [əz], [s], and [z]. The possessive and third-person singular, present-tense morphemes have the same allomorphs:

	Plural	Possessive	Third Person Singular
[əz]	glasses	glass's	(it) sneezes
[s]	cats	cat's	(it) meets
[z]	dogs	dog's	(it) feeds

The forms [əz], [s], and [z] occur in different environments. The conditions under which each of these variants occurs can be stated as follows:

1. [əz] after [s, z, š, ž, č, ǰ]
2. [s] after a voiceless consonant other than [s, š, č]
3. [z] elsewhere

If we choose /z/ as the underlying form of these suffixes, we can account for the [əz] endings with an epenthesis rule. This rule will insert a [ə] between a stem final [+strident, +coronal] sound and the suffixed [z]. The sounds [s, z, š, ž, č, ǰ] comprise the set of [+strident, +coronal] sounds in English. The epenthesis rule apparently facilitates pronunciation by breaking up clusters of similar or identical consonants.

The occurrence of the [s] in forms such as *cats* and *tops* can then be attributed to assimilation of the /z/ to the voicelessness of a preceding consonant. This assimilation yields a syllable coda consistent with the universal devoicing constraint (see 8.2.7) which requires that no voiced consonant follow a voiceless one in the same syllable coda. The forms ending in [z], of course, undergo no change.

Choosing /z/ as the underlying form allows us to account for all the alternate forms of the morphemes in question with two natural rules. Had we chosen /s/, we would then have been forced to posit a rule which was both less natural and less well motivated than the devoicing rule: namely, one that voiced /s/ after a voiced consonant or vowel. Although [z] is a somewhat less natural sound than [s], the choice of /z/ and a very natural devoicing rule seems preferable to choosing /s/ and a far less natural rule.

Taking /əz/ as the underlying form would have committed us to a rule of ə-deletion. The /ə/ of /əz/ would be deleted except when preceded by a [+strident, +coronal] sound. After ə-deletion, a *z* following a voiceless consonant would be devoiced to [s] exactly as for the solution which takes /z/ to be the underlying form. There is very little difference in choosing between the /əz/ and the /z/ solutions. Both require only quite natural rules to derive correct surface forms. For purposes of discussion, we have arbitrarily taken /z/ to be the basic form.

There is another case of morpheme alternation in English similar to that just described. The endings for the regular preterite and past participle are [əd], [t], and [d].

[əd]	padded
[t]	picked
[d]	penned

The environments for these variants may be summed up as follows:

4. [əd] after [t, d]
5. [t] after voiceless consonants other than [t]
6. [d] elsewhere

In order to explain these allomorphic variations, we choose /d/ (again, somewhat arbitrarily) as the underlying form and then posit rules to account for the other forms. For verbs ending in voiced sounds we need no phonological rule to account for the preterite and past participle forms. Verbs such as *bang* and *rob*, for example, become *banged* and *robbed* simply through the addition of /d/.

The preterites and past participles of verbs ending in [t] or [d], such as *pat* and *add*, are subject to an epenthesis rule which inserts a [ə] into contexts such as t____d # and d____d #, again breaking up clusters of similar or identical consonants.

For verbs ending in voiceless consonants other than [t], however, the addition of the /d/ suffix results in an impermissible sequence—a voiceless obstruent followed by a voiced one. The [d] endings of forms such as *work#d* and *zip#d* are therefore changed to [t] by assimilation to the preceding voiceless sound.

9.7 MORPHOLOGICALLY CONDITIONED ALTERNATES

The alternation of the suffixes discussed thus far can be attributed to the phonological nature of the stems to which they are attached. Such alternations, which can be accounted for on purely phonetic grounds without reference to specific morphemes, are said to be **phonologically conditioned** or to exhibit **automatic alternation**. However, the distribution of some allomorphs cannot be accounted for phonologically. Rather, the specific set of morphemes with which each alternate occurs must be listed. When allomorphs are distributed in this manner, they are said to be **morphologically conditioned**.

The plural morpheme in English has several morphologically conditioned allomorphs. Following the stems *ox-* and *child(r)-*, the plural marker takes the form *-en* ([n̩]), *oxen* and *children*; following *medi-* and *criteri-* it is *-a* ([ə]), *media* and *criteria*; and after *radi-* and *fung-* it is *-i* ([ay]), *radii* and *fungi*. Notice that these last two stems, unlike the majority of stems in English, must have an *-us* ([əs]) suffix to mark them as singular, *radius* and *fungus*. The stems *medi-* and *criteri-* also require explicit phonetic singulars, *-um* ([m̩]) and *-on* ([n̩]), *medium* and *criterion*. Furthermore, a number of stems, such as *mouse*, *goose*, and *man*, have plurals expressed by vowel symbolism, *mice*, *geese* and *men*.

Obviously, the addition of an [n̩] or [ay] suffix is not the usual method of pluralizing English nouns. Because the representations of the plural morpheme enumerated in the preceding paragraph are the result of borrowings from other languages or the reflection of processes left over from an earlier period in the history of English, they apply to only a small percentage of the nouns in the language. By far the largest number of English noun stems have as their plurals either [s], [z], or [əz].

It would be satisfying theoretically if all the phonetic representations of the English plural could be shown to be phonologically conditioned variants of the same underlying representation. But this cannot be done. There is nothing in the phonetic structure of *radi-*, for example, that can plausibly be linked to the fact that it takes [ay] as plural. *Lady* has virtually the same phonetic structure and yet takes the /z/ plural; it is impossible to tie the initial [r] of *radi-*, as opposed to the [l] of *lady*, to its plural in any regular way, since many words with initial [r] have the /z/ plural. A similar argument can be made in the case of *man*. The word *pan*, which is very similar in phonetic structure, does not have a symbolic plural; and again, since many words beginning with [m] have the /z/ plural, there is no way to link 'starting with an [m]' to 'having a symbolic plural'. It is, rather, an idiosyncratic fact about the morpheme *man* that it has a symbolic plural. Such facts, which are the result of historical accident, must be learned as characteristics peculiar to specific morphemes. In the lexicon, a root such as *radi-* or *man* must be marked as having a special morphological characteristic. Such roots are called **exceptional** or **irregular**.

However, for some irregular plurals we need not indicate in the lexical entry what their morphologically conditioned plurals will be. In the case of words such as *fungus* and *criterion*, which have singular endings, the plural form is predictable once the singular form is known. But the form of the irregular singular must be specified lexically because there is no phonological conditioning for the *-us* singular of *fung-* and *radi-* as opposed to the singular form *lady*, which has no ending, just as there is none for their different plurals. Similarly, there is no phonological conditioning to explain why the singular forms *medium* and *criterion* have the singular endings *-um* and *-on*. For each of the stems which has a singular ending, the form of that ending must be listed in the lexicon as an idiosyncratic feature of the stem. Nothing need be noted concerning its plural form, however, since the plural is predictable given the singular. Stems which take the nasal singular endings have the plural suffix *-a*; those with the *-us* singular have the plural *-i*. The predictability of the plural *-i*, given the singular *-us*, can be stated by a rule. Rules of this kind, which link certain irregular features of morphemes to others, are called **lexical redundancy rules**. Thus, 'nasal singular implies [ə] plural' is a lexical redundancy rule which allows us to simplify somewhat the lexical entries for such words as *medium* and *criterion*.

The suffixing of /z/ and /d/ is a **productive** process in English; these are the suffixes added to new words coming into the language. The morphologically conditioned processes are **nonproductive**. Thus, if an English speaker is told that the nonsense syllable *yig* is a noun and then asked to put it into the plural, he will produce *yig#z*, not *yig#n* on the analogy of *oxen*. If told that *yig* is a verb and asked to put it in the past tense, he will without hesitation produce the form *yig#d*. It is highly unlikely that he would produce instead a form like *yag* on analogy with the verb *sing* (which has the past form *sang*). *Sing* is marked lexically for the symbolic processes it undergoes in the past and past participle; but regular verbs, like regular nouns, need no such special footnotes in the lexicon.

9.8 SUMMARY

The smallest meaningful unit of speech is the **morpheme**. Some words, such as *man*, consist of a single morpheme; others such as *gentleman*, *gentlemanly*, and *ungentlemanly* consist of more. Morphemes and syllables bear no predictable relationship to one another. Morphemes are units of meaning whereas syllables are units of sound. Some words, such as *untie*, have the same number of morphemes and syllables. But this is merely coincidental. A morpheme may be only part of a syllable (as is the *-s* of *dogs*), or it may encompass several syllables (as does *Massachusetts*).

There are two major types of morphemes: roots and affixes. **Roots** are morphemes that form the basis of words. Roots that can constitute a whole word are called **free roots**; those that cannot are called **bound roots**. **Affixes** are morphemes which are added to a stem. Any root or combination of roots and affixes to which an affix is added is called a **stem**. Affixes are divided into three types depending on where they occur in relation to the stem. Those preceding the stem are called **prefixes**, those inserted into the stem, **infixes**, and those following the stem, **suffixes**. Affixes function in the inflectional and derivational systems of languages.

The study of morphemes, their structure, and how they function to form words is called **morphology**. There are four major processes of word formation: (1) **affixation**, the addition of an affix to a stem; (2) **reduplication**, the repetition of all or part of a stem; (3) **symbolism**, a change in the structure of a stem; and (4) **compounding**, the combination of two or more roots, with or without accompanying affixes.

The pairing of sound and meaning within the morpheme is arbitrary. Therefore, information about how to pronounce a morpheme and about what it means must be learned and stored in the mind of the speaker. All of the information stored for a particular morpheme is called its **lexical entry**. A **lexicon** is the list of all the lexical entries for a particular language.

Each lexical entry includes, along with information about the semantic and syntactic nature of the morpheme, an underlying representation (also called a base form or underlying form). The **underlying representation** contains that information about the pronunciation of a morpheme that is not predictable on the basis of general rules. The segments of an underlying representation are called **phonemes**.

The description of an actual utterance is called a **surface representation**. Phonological rules act upon underlying representations to produce surface representations.

A morpheme may have more than one surface representation, depending on context. The alternate surface representations of a morpheme are called its **allomorphs**. The alternation of some allomorphs such as the regular plural endings of English, can be predicted on purely phonetic grounds. Such allomorphs are said to be **phonologically conditioned**. Other allomorphs, which occur only with specific morphemes, are said to be **morphologically conditioned**.

EXERCISES FOR CHAPTER 9

1. Find the roots and derivational suffixes in the following English words. For set (d), formulate a rule that accounts for the absence of the final consonant of the root.

(a)	(b)	(c)	(d)
arrival	truth	pursuit	explosive
perusal	growth	complaint	defensive
refusal	width	restraint	abrasive
denial	warmth	joint	adhesive
trial	depth	transcript	decisive
referral	tilth		abusive

2. What morphological processes are exemplified in the Hausa words given
   below?

1. [sɛnyi]	'cold'	[sɛnyɪ-sɛnyi]	'somewhat cold'
2. [gɪřma]	'largeness'	[gɪřmɐ-gɪřmɐ]	'moderate large- ness'
3. [yɛwa]	'plenty'	[yɛwɐ-yɛwɐ]	'moderate plenty'
4. [mɐgɐna]	'speech'	[mɐgɐnɐ-mɐgɐnɐ]	'speechlike sounds'
5. [šud'i]	'blue'	[šud'ɪ-šud'ɪ]	'bluish'
6. [řuwa]	'water'	[řuwɐ-řuwɐ]	'watery'
7. [bɐk'i]	'black'	[bɐk'ɪ-bɐk'ɪ]	'blackish'
8. [dabba]	'animal'	[dabbobi]	'animals'
9. [ʔofɪs]	'office'	[ʔofɪsoši]	'offices'
10. [masɪnjɐ]	'messenger'	[masinjoji]	'messengers'
11. [dɐře]	'night'	[dɐřoři]	'nights'
12. [kasʊwa]	'market'	[kasʊwoyi]	'markets'
13. [taba]	'cigarette'	[tabobi]	'cigarettes'
14. [ʔɐsɪbɪti]	'hospital'	[ʔɐsɪbɪtoči]	'hospitals'
15. [kwɐs]	'course'	[kwɐsoši]	'courses'
16. [kafɪntɐ]	'carpenter'	[kafɪntoči]	'carpenters'

   (Based on Hodge and Umaru, 1963; Hausa is spoken in West Africa)

3. In the following Spanish words find the roots and affixes.

el libro	'the book'
el mundo	'the world'
la casa	'the house'
la mesa	'the table'
el toro	'the bull'
la vaca	'the cow'
el niño	'the son'
la niña	'the daughter'
el muchacho	'the boy'
la muchacha	'the girl'
el muchacho alto	'the tall boy'
la muchacha alta	'the tall girl'
el muchacho gordo	'the fat boy'
la muchacha gorda	'the fat girl'

4a. English spelling often gives a constant representation to a morpheme even
    though the pronunciation varies. Which of the following pairs of words
    illustrate this and which do not?

clean / cleanliness	hear / heard
mean / meant	retain / retention

steal / stealth   serene / serenity
keep / kept   sane / sanity
sweep / swept   divine / divinity

b. English orthography often shows vowel differences among related words. Compare *mouse, mice; goose, geese; sing, sang, sung; drive, drove;* and *dig, dug.* Do these orthographic changes suggest that the underlying representations of the members of a given set, say *sing, sang, sung,* are the same or different?

5. Analyze each of the following English words into its component morphemes. Define each morpheme that you isolate. Then look up the etymology of each word in a dictionary. How well do your morphemic analyses and definitions agree with the etymologies?

include   prefix
exclude   suffix
preclude   presume
incite   subsume
excite   assume
infix   adhere
affix   inhere

6. Find the roots and affixes in the following English words. Which of the affixes are derivational and which inflectional?

smaller   spiteful
lovely   elder
his   oxen
warmth   broken
sings   realize
loudest   snowy

7. Swedish has a number of 'strong' verbs for which the past tense, supine, and past participle forms show the application of symbolic morphological processes. (The supine forms are used in perfect tenses.) Determine the number of symbolic processes needed to account for the Swedish strong verb forms given below in phonetic transcription.

	INFINITIVE	PRESENT	PAST	SUPINE	PAST PART.
1. 'bind, tie'	bɪnda	bɪndəř	band	bɵndɪt	bɵndən
2. 'bite'	bi:ta	bi:təř	be:t	bi:tɪt	bi:tən
3. 'offer, invite'	byʉ:da	byʉ:dəř	byö:d	byʉ:dɪt	byʉ:dən
4. 'burn'	břɪnna	břɪnnəř	břan:	břɵnnɪt	břɵnnən
5. 'burst'	břʉsta	břʉstəř	brast	brɵstɪt	brɵstən

	INFINITIVE	PRESENT	PAST	SUPINE	PAST PART.
6. 'break'	břü:ta	brü:təř	brö:t	brʉ:tɪt	brʉ:tən
7. 'drink'	dřɪkka	dřikkəř	dřak:	dřɵkkɪt	dřɵkkən
8. 'drive'	dři:va	dři:vəř	dře:v	dři:vɪt	dři:vən
9. 'fall'	falla	falləř	föl:	fallɪt	fallən
10. 'travel'	fɑ:řa	fɑ:ř	fu:ř	fɑ:řɪt	fɑ:řən
11. 'freeze'	fřü:sa	fřü:səř	fřö:s	fřü:sɪt	frʉ:sən
12. 'rub'	gni:da	gni:dəř	gne:d	gni:dɪt	gni:dən
13. 'seize'	gři:pa	gři:pəř	gře:p	gri:pɪt	gri:pən
14. 'cut, hew'	hɵgga	hɵggəř	hög:	hɵggɪt	hɵggən
15. 'hold'	hɔlla	hɔlləř	höl:	hɔllɪt	hɔllən
16. 'tie'	knü:ta	knü:təř	knö:t	knʉ:tɪt	knʉ:tən
17. 'let, permit'	lo:ta	lo:təř	lɛ:t	lo:tɪt	-lo:tən
18. 'enjoy'	nyʉtta	nyʉ:təř	nyö:t	nyʉ:tɪt	nyʉ:tən
19. 'run, flow'	řɪnna	řɪnnəř	řann	řʉnnɪt	řʉnnən
20. 'tear'	ři:va	ři:vəř	ře:v	ři:vɪt	ři:vən
21. 'sing'	šʉŋŋa	šʉŋŋəř	šöŋ:	šʉŋŋɪt	šʉŋŋən
22. 'write'	skři:va	skři:vəř	skře:v	skři:vɪt	skři:vən
23. 'beat, strike'	slo:	slo:ř	slu:g	slɑ:gɪt	slɑ:gən
24. 'run'	spřiŋŋa	spřɪŋŋəř	spraŋ:	spřʉŋŋɪt	sprʉŋŋən
25. 'fail'	svi:ka	svi:kəř	sve:k	svi:kɪt	svi:kən
26. 'take'	ta:(ga)	ta:(gə)ř	tu:g	ta:gɪt	ta:gən
27. 'howl'	çʉ:ta	çʉ:təř	çö:t	çʉ:tɪt	— — —
28. 'win'	vɪnna	vɪnnəř	van:	vɵnnɪt	vɵnnən
29. 'twist, turn'	vři:da	vři:dəř	vře:d	vři:dɪt	vři:dən
30. 'eat'	ɛ:ta	ɛ:təř	o:t	ɛ:tɪt	ɛ:tən

8. Yawelmani has six cases: subject, possessive, object, indirect object, ablative, and locative. Assume that the subject forms do not have an affix. Which Yawelmani case endings seem to have a single underlying form with phonologically conditioned allomorphs? Do any case endings seem to be morphologically conditioned, i.e., to have more than one basic form? Does the addition of any of the case endings seem to produce phonological changes in the noun stems?

	'husband'	'wood-rat'	'cloud'
Subj.	po:lum	hidsic'	k'iley
Poss.	po:lmun	hidisc'in	k'ile:yin
Obj.	polma	hidisc'i	k'iley
Ind. Obj.	polma:ni	hidisc'e:ni	k'ileymi
Abl.	polma:nit	hidisc'e:nit	k'ileynit
Loc.	polmaw	hidisc'iw	k'ile:yaw

	'a place to stay overnight'	'large basket'	'road'
Subj.	laga:ʔiy	ʔanas	pil
Poss.	laga:ʔe:yin	ʔana:sin	pilin
Obj.	laga:ʔey	ʔanas	pila
Ind. Obj.	laga:ʔeyni	ʔanasni	pilni
Abl.	laga:ʔeynit	ʔanasnit	pilnit
Loc.	laga:ʔe:yaw	ʔana-siw	pilaw

(Based on Kuroda 1967: 30, 38)

10 phonological rules

10.1 INTRODUCTION

Although we have talked a good deal about phonological processes and the rules which govern them, our discussion has been restricted to rather informal descriptions. However, for the sake of clarity and comparability, linguists have devised a more formal way of stating phonological rules. In this system, symbols are used to formalize notions such as 'becomes' and 'in the environment of'. These symbols, together with the distinctive features, comprise a shorthand for discussing phonological processes. Consider, for example, the English rule which changes *v* to *f* before a voiceless sound, as in *twelfth* and *fifth* (compare *twelve* and *five*). Using symbols and distinctive features, this rule can be stated as follows:

(1) DEVOICING

$$\begin{bmatrix} +\,\text{str} \\ -\,\text{cor} \end{bmatrix} \rightarrow [-\,\text{vd}] \,/\,\underline{\hspace{1.5em}}[-\,\text{vd}]$$

In a rule such as this, the set of distinctive features to the left of the arrow, in this case [+str, −cor], identifies the sound or sounds which will undergo the process. This part of the rule is referred to as the **input**. The input to the devoicing rule is the class of sounds [v, f]. Only the features

141

that uniquely specify this group of sounds are mentioned in the rule. For English, the feature [+str] identifies the class of sounds [f, v, s, z, š, ž, č, ǰ]. The [—cor] segments among these are [f, v]. Of these, [v] is [+vd] and will be changed by the rule. The sound [f] will not be changed even though the rule is allowed to apply to it, because it is already [—vd]. Hence, the feature specifications [+str] and [−cor] sort out from all the sounds of English exactly the sound ([v]) which is affected by this rule. Any further specifications would be redundant.

Since the input takes on the characteristics listed to the right of the arrow, the feature specifications on the right represent the result or **output** of a phonological process. In Rule (1), the result of the process is that [v] becomes its voiceless counterpart [f].

Whatever is to the right of the diagonal is the **environment** in which the rule applies. The environment is composed of the **determinant** (the factor influencing the change, in this case a [−vd] segment), and the underscore. The **underscore**,____, indicates where in the environment the segment or segments undergoing the change are located with respect to the determinant. In Rule (1) the underscore shows that the input directly precedes a voiceless sound.

10.2 INFORMAL DEVICES

Several informal devices are employed to simplify rule writing. Among these are the alphabetic phonetic symbols sometimes used instead of distinctive feature specifications. The capital letters V and C are used in a similar manner: V in a rule replaces the feature specifications for the class of vowels, C for the class of nonvowels. Capital letters are also used at times to denote the class of nasals, N, the class of resonants, R, and the class of glides, G. The accent marks ['] for primary stress and [`] for secondary stress also appear in informal presentations.

To ensure that you can easily read and understand the rules, we will often supplement our formal rules with informal descriptions. Thus, we write the specifications for alveolar stops as follows:

$$
\begin{bmatrix}
+\text{cons} \\
-\text{son} \\
+\text{cor} \\
+\text{ant} \\
+\text{int} \\
-\text{str}
\end{bmatrix}
$$
(t, d)

This practice is not in common use, but we believe it to be of help to those learning to read rules and of no harm to anyone else.

10.3 PHONOLOGICAL DOMAINS

Phonological rules always apply within some specifiable unit of language. Some operate only within syllables, others only within morphemes, and still others within larger units such as words, phrases, or sentences. The scope of a particular rule is called the **domain** of that rule. If no junctures are specified in a rule, its domain is the syllable. Domains other than the syllable must be specifically provided for. By a convention that assigns boundaries (Chomsky and Halle, 1968: 12–13), each major part of speech, each phrase, and each sentence is bounded by external junctures. The sentence *The man threw the balls* will therefore have the array of boundaries shown in Figure 10.1. According to the boundary convention, each

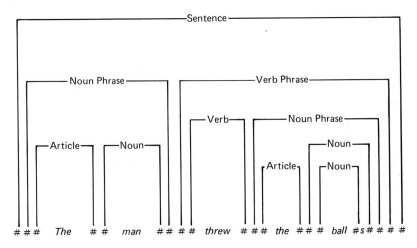

Figure 10.1
Domains

of the words in this sentence (or in any other sentence) is bounded at each end by at least two external junctures [#]. Since affixes are not major parts of speech, only one juncture is inserted between a stem and an affix. As you can see in the diagram, *ball*, being a noun, a major part of speech, has #'s at each end. And *balls*, also being a noun (a plural one), has #'s at each end.

This method of assigning junctures guarantees that a word in a sentence will be bounded by no less than two #'s at each end. Even a single-word sentence such as *Help!* will have at least its own boundaries and the sentence boundaries marked. The word domain is thus defined as # #____# #. Notice that where a stem and affix meet, there is only one juncture but where two words meet there are at least two junctures—one for each word.

As was noted above, if no boundaries are mentioned in a rule, that rule applies only within the domain of a single syllable. Thus, when it is necessary to specify that the domain of a rule crosses a syllable, stem, or word boundary, we must mention the syllable boundary [−] or the appropriate number of external junctures in the rule.

10.4 DELETION AND ADDITION RULES

Perhaps the simplest rules to state are those which delete or add segments. In their formulation, both of these types of rules require the null sign, ∅. In rules which delete segments, the null sign follows the arrow, →∅. This sequence of symbols may be read as either 'becomes null' or 'is deleted'. Thus, a rule that deletes a *t* when it is between two *s*'s would be framed informally as follows:

(2)   t → ∅ / s____s

Here, the position of the underscore clearly represents the notion 'between'. Thus, Rule (2) is read: "The sound segment /t/ is deleted in the environment between an *s* and another *s*." This rule could, of course, be made formal by replacing the phonetic symbols with the appropriate feature specifications.

In rules that add segments, the null sign precedes rather than follows the arrow. The sequence of symbols ∅ → is read as 'add' or 'insert'. A rule which inserts an epenthetic *t* into *ls* clusters, for example, is informally written:

(3)   ∅ → t / l____s

Again, the underscore is positioned so that it represents the notion 'between'. Rule (3) is read: "Insert a *t* in the environment between an *l* and an *s*." The order of elements in the environment requires that the *l* must precede the *s* in the cluster. Rule (3) would not apply to an *sl* cluster.

10.5 ASSIMILATORY RULES

In Chapter 8 we said that the most common type of phonological process is assimilation. A phonological rule describes an assimilation if its output and its environment share one or more features which were not a part of the input. There are two types of assimilatory processes: progressive and regressive assimilation. These are illustrated by the two palatalization rules below.

$$(4) \qquad [+\text{cons}] \rightarrow \begin{bmatrix} -\text{bk} \\ +\text{hi} \end{bmatrix} \Big/ \begin{bmatrix} -\text{cons} \\ -\text{bk} \\ +\text{hi} \end{bmatrix} \underline{}$$
$$(\text{i, y})$$

$$(5) \qquad [+\text{cons}] \rightarrow \begin{bmatrix} -\text{bk} \\ +\text{hi} \end{bmatrix} \Big/ \underline{} \begin{bmatrix} -\text{cons} \\ -\text{bk} \\ +\text{hi} \end{bmatrix}$$
$$(\text{i, y})$$

As you can see, these rules are very similar. They have the same input, the same output, and are made up of the same elements. In fact, they differ only in the arrangement of the elements in their environments. In Rule (4), the segment (either *i* or *y*) which causes palatalization precedes the consonant undergoing the process; in Rule (5) it follows. The assimilation in (4), then, is progressive. Progressive assimilation is indicated in a rule by placing the underscore *after* the determinant. In Rule (5), which describes a regressive assimilation, the underscore is placed *before* the determinant. The features shared by the output and the environment in these rules—[−bk, +hi]—are the features which define palatalization in consonants.

10.6 METATHESIS

There are still other kinds of rules which describe neither additions, deletions, nor assimilations. They merely indicate that certain natural classes of sounds change in predictable ways in certain contexts. Among these are the rules which describe metathesis. Such rules require a somewhat different format than the rules described thus far. Because these rules involve the rearrangement of segments, their inputs must consist of two symbols rather than one. Rule (6) is an example of a metathesis rule.

$$(6) \qquad \text{sk} \rightarrow \text{ks} \: / \underline{} \#$$

This rule metathesizes stem final *sk*.

The output of a metathesis rule, then, consists of the same two symbols as the input, but in reverse order.

10.7 RULE ORDER

In general, simple and revealing phonological rules can be written only if the rules apply sequentially and in a definite order. The application of rules is such that the underlying representation of a word provides the input to the first applicable rule. The output of this rule then becomes the input to the next applicable rule and so forth until all rules have applied. The output of the last rule to apply is the surface representation.

The pair of English rules Sonorant Nasalization and Nasal Deletion illustrates rule ordering. Sonorant Nasalization accounts in particular for the nasalization of vowels occurring directly before a nasal, as in *hand* [hænd], *pen* [pẽn], *string* [strĩŋ] and so forth. However, it also accounts for the nasalization of other sonorants, such as the *r* in *farm* [fãr^{n}m]. This rule is stated as:

(7) Sonorant Nasalization

$$[+\text{son}] \rightarrow [+\text{nas}] \,/\, \underline{\quad}[+\text{nas}]$$

Another rule of English optionally deletes nasals before a voiceless obstruent, as in *damp* [dæp], *can't* [kæt], and *rank* [ræk]. The rule for nasal deletion is written as follows:

(8) Nasal Deletion

$$[+\text{nas}] \rightarrow \emptyset \,/\, \underline{\quad}\begin{bmatrix} -\text{son} \\ -\text{vd} \end{bmatrix}$$

The pronunciation of a word like *bent* [bẽt] shows that the Sonorant Nasalization and Nasal Deletion rules are ordered in relation to each other. The underlying form of *bent* is /bɛnt/. To arrive at the surface representation [bẽt], with its nasalized vowel, Sonorant Nasalization must apply first, yielding [bẽnt]. Then Nasal Deletion applies to yield [bẽt]. If Nasal Deletion applied first, its output [bɛt] could not undergo Sonorant Nasalization. Thus, these two rules are ordered:

(a) Sonorant Nasalization
(b) Nasal Deletion

A display of forms arranged so that they reveal the changes which follow from ordered applications of rules is called a **derivation**. Below is the derivation for *bent*:

Underlying form	/bɛnt/
Sonorant Nasalization	bɛ̃nt
Nasal Deletion	bɛ̃t
Surface representation	[bɛ̃t]

Besides a strictly linear application of rules, as in the derivation of *bent*, other ordering schemes are possible. In Chomsky and Halle (1968) a cyclic application of rules is proposed to assign stress placement for English words. A cyclic application of rules requires that when the last rule of a set of ordered rules has been applied, the rules are then applied all over again from the beginning. The first pass through the rules applies to the innermost element of the words. Successive cycles apply to derived elements. For example, in the derivation of *theatricality* Chomsky and Halle's rules first apply to the noun *théater* and places stress on the first syllable. The next pass through the rules, or cycle, reassigns stress on the second syllable of the adjective *thèátrical* (and the stress on the first syllable is automatically reduced). The next cycle through the rules assigns primary stress to the noun *thèàtricálity* on the fourth syllable (and again the stress on the syllable that had previously received primary stress is reduced). A cyclic view of rule application has also been advanced by Kisseberth, 1972, and by Brame, 1974. The cyclic view of stress assignment in English has been challenged by, for example, Ross, 1973; Hoard and Sloat, 1973; and Sloat, 1974.

10·8 ORDERING RELATIONSHIPS

If the ordering of a pair of rules either increases or decreases the number of forms to which one of the rules applies, we say those two rules **interact**. (See Chafe, 1968.) The two rules in the derivation of *bent* clearly interact, since if they occurred in the opposite order, the forms that underwent Nasal Deletion would not undergo Sonorant Nasalization. Rules may interact in several ways. If a pair of rules, A and B, are ordered so that A creates segments which are either inputs or determinants for B, then it is said that A **feeds** B, or that A and B are in a **feeding order**. For example, suppose a language had the following two rules:

(9)   i → e /____r

(10)   e → a /____Ca

These two rules are ordered so that (9) feeds (10). In other words, Rule (9) supplies new cases of *e* for Rule (10) to apply to. The feeding order of these rules ensures that in this language all underlying sequences /ira/ end up as surface [ara].

If, on the other hand, a pair of rules, *A* and *B*, are ordered so that *A* changes segments which otherwise would be either inputs or determinants for *B*, it is said that *A* **bleeds** *B* or that *A* and *B* are in a **bleeding order**. Consider, for example, Rules (11) and (12).

(11)   u → i /＿＿li

(12)   u → o /＿＿l

Since Rule (11) changes some of the *u*'s which occur before *l* to *i*'s, Rule (12) has fewer cases of *u* to act upon than it would otherwise have. Thus, Rule (11) bleeds (12).

Rules may also interact in ways more subtle than bleeding or feeding. For instance, if a pair of rules, *A* and *B*, are ordered so that *A* would bleed *B* if their order were reversed, they are said to be in a **counterbleeding order**. The Sonorant Nasalization and Nasal Deletion rules discussed above are in a counterbleeding order since if Nasal Deletion applied first it would bleed Sonorant Nasalization.

Conversely, if a pair of rules, *A* and *B*, are ordered so that *A* would feed *B* if their order were reversed, *A* and *B* are in **counterfeeding order**. If the order of Rules (9) and (10) were reversed, they would be in a counterfeeding order.

Notice that counterbleeding, like feeding, increases the number of forms which are subject to one of the interacting rules and that counterfeeding, like bleeding, reduces the number of forms to which one of the rules will apply. It has been suggested (Kiparsky, 1968b) that, in the history of languages, rules tend to shift into orders that allow the maximum utilization of each of them. Therefore, many linguists feel that feeding and counterbleeding are the natural orders, and that bleeding and counterfeeding are marked orders. Since it is very likely that a child learning his language need invest nothing in learning natural orders, relatively few cases of rules in marked orders should be found (see King, 1969).

Some research has recently been done (e.g., Koutsoudas, *et al.*, 1974; Anderson, 1974) to determine if rule order can be predicted on formal grounds alone, i.e., from the way rules interact or fail to interact. However, no proposal yet advanced seems to cover all types of rule interactions satisfactorily. In the absence of an adequate procedure which automatically determines the order of rule application, it is necessary to specify the order of some interacting rules to ensure that correct outputs are derived.

10.9 ITERATIVE RULES

Phonological rules that can apply more than once to the same form are called **iterative rules**. Iterative rules apply first to the relevant segment nearest one end of a form and then work toward the other end reapplying to each relevant segment in turn.

The Sonorant Nasalization rule of English (Rule 7) is an example of an iterative rule. We repeat it here for convenience:

SONORANT NASALIZATION

$$[+son] \rightarrow [+nas] /\underline{\hspace{1cm}}[+nas]$$

This rule accounts for the nasalization of both the *a* and the *r* in *farm*. The first time that Sonorant Nasalization applies, the $[+son]$ segment *r* is the input and the *m* is the determinant.

$$
\begin{array}{cccc}
f & a & r & m \\
 & [+son] & [+nas] &
\end{array}
$$

Since *r* is $[+nas]$ after the first application, it is the determinant for the next application and the $[+son]$ segment *a* becomes the input:

$$
\begin{array}{cccc}
f & a & r^n & m \\
 & [+son] & [+nas] &
\end{array}
$$

The result of the two applications of the rule is the surface representation [fãr^{n}m].

If Sonorant Nasalization had not already applied to nasalize the *r* in *farm*, the *a* could not have undergone the rule. A rule like this whose earlier applications create environments for its later ones is called a **self-feeding rule**.

Our examination of the word *farm* shows that when Sonorant Nasalization iterates, the series of applications begins as far to the right of the word as the environment will permit. It may be possible to discern by inspecting the formal characteristics of a rule (such as if it is self-feeding or not) whether it applies from right to left (as does Sonorant Nasalization) or from left to right. At present it is not certain that this can be done. Therefore, it is necessary to indicate for each iterative rule which end of the form it applies to first.

10.10 VARIABLES

In order to capture certain kinds of generalizations, symbols called variables are used. **Variables** are Greek letters, such as α (alpha), β (beta), γ (gamma), and so forth, which stand for all values of a feature. To illustrate the function of variables in rule writing, we will use an example from Polish. In Polish, word-final voiced obstruents are replaced by their voiceless counterparts if the next word begins with a voiceless consonant (Schenker, 1966). For example, the /b/ in *zrob to* 'do it' is pronounced [p];

the /g/ in *snieg taje* 'snow melts' is pronounced [k]; and the /z/ of *z tyter* 'from behind' is pronounced [s]. The following rule describes this process:

(13) $[-son] \rightarrow [-vd] / \underline{\qquad} \# \# [-vd]$

Notice that the double # in this rule indicates a word boundary (rather than merely a stem boundary) since each word has a boundary at each end: #zrob##to#.

Polish also has a process which replaces word-final voiceless obstruents with their voiced counterparts if the next word begins with a voiced consonant. Thus, the /p/ of *kup zeszyt* 'buy a notebook' is pronounced [b]; the first /t/ in *kot w butach* 'Puss 'n Boots' is pronounced [d]; and the /s/ of *nas widza* 'they see us' is pronounced [z]. This process may be described as follows:

(14) $[-son] \rightarrow [+vd] / \underline{\qquad} \# \# [+vd]$

However, by writing two separate rules, we treat voicing and devoicing as unrelated processes, and thus fail to capture an important generalization. Instead of two rules, what is needed here is a single rule which states that an obstruent at the end of a word has the same value for voicing as the initial consonant of the next word. In order to write such a rule, we use a variable. If only one variable is needed in a rule, it is customary to use alpha. Therefore we can restate Rules (13) and (14) as:

(15) POLISH VOICING ASSIMILATION

        $[-son] \rightarrow [\alpha vd] / \underline{\qquad} \# \# [\alpha vd]$

For each application of a rule, the value assigned to a variable is the same each time it occurs in the rule. Thus, if the specification [αvd] represents $[-vd]$ in the environment, it will represent $[-vd]$ in the output, but if it represents $[+vd]$ in the environment, the output will be $[+vd]$. The same is true of variables attached to two different features. If a rule specifies [αant] for the output, but [αcor] for the environment, the value for [anterior] must be + if [coronal] is + and it must be − if [coronal] is −. The variable performs a matching function, then. Whatever value a certain feature has, same value is given to any other feature marked with the same variable. Variables therefore always appear in sets. A feature specified with an unpaired variable would be vacuous. If a segment may be either + or − for a certain feature, independent of anything else in the rule, that feature is simply not mentioned.

It is sometimes necessary to write a rule stating that the specifications for two features must be opposite, rather than the same. This can be accomplished by placing a negative sign before one of the matching variables. Consider for a moment the following processes:

(16) $[-\text{cons}] \rightarrow [-\text{rnd}] / \underline{\quad}[+\text{lo}]$

(17) $[-\text{cons}] \rightarrow [+\text{rnd}] / \underline{\quad}[-\text{lo}]$

Using variables and the negative sign, these two rules can be made into one:

(18) $[-\text{cons}] \rightarrow [-\alpha\text{rnd}] / \underline{\quad}[\alpha\text{lo}]$

Rule (18) states that whatever value the feature [low] has in the environment, the output will have the opposite value for the feature [rounded].

Some assimilation rules require the use of more than one variable. In English, for example, nasals assimilate in both coronality and anteriority to a following tautosyllabic obstruent. These facts could be expressed by the four rules (a) through (d).

(a) $\text{nasal} \rightarrow \begin{bmatrix} -\text{cor} \\ +\text{ant} \end{bmatrix} / \underline{\quad} \begin{bmatrix} -\text{son} \\ -\text{cor} \\ +\text{ant} \end{bmatrix}$ e.g., *camp, bombard*
        (m)   (labials)

(b) $\text{nasal} \rightarrow \begin{bmatrix} +\text{cor} \\ +\text{ant} \end{bmatrix} / \underline{\quad} \begin{bmatrix} -\text{son} \\ +\text{cor} \\ +\text{ant} \end{bmatrix}$ e.g., *tent, hand*
        (n)   (alveolars)

(c) $\text{nasal} \rightarrow \begin{bmatrix} +\text{cor} \\ -\text{ant} \end{bmatrix} / \underline{\quad} \begin{bmatrix} -\text{son} \\ +\text{cor} \\ -\text{ant} \end{bmatrix}$ e.g., *ranch, flange*
        (ñ)   (palatals)

(d) $\text{nasal} \rightarrow \begin{bmatrix} -\text{cor} \\ -\text{ant} \end{bmatrix} / \underline{\quad} \begin{bmatrix} -\text{son} \\ -\text{cor} \\ -\text{ant} \end{bmatrix}$ e.g., *tank, finger*
        (ŋ)   (velars)

However, since all these changes are the result of the same phenomenon (nasal assimilation), the process should be given as one rule. Two variables are needed to write this rule. It is the usual practice in such a case to use α and β. We therefore write the English rule for nasal assimilation as follows:

(19) ENGLISH NASAL ASSIMILATION

$$[+\text{nas}] \rightarrow \begin{bmatrix} \alpha\text{cor} \\ \beta\text{ant} \end{bmatrix} / \underline{\quad} \begin{bmatrix} -\text{son} \\ \alpha\text{cor} \\ \beta\text{ant} \end{bmatrix}$$

This rule states that a nasal takes on the values for [coronal] and [anterior] of a following obstruent but that those values need not be the same for the two features. If the rule were written with an alpha on both features, the values for [coronal] and [anterior] could not differ. Such a rule could account for [n] (which is [+cor, +ant]) and [ŋ] (which is [−cor, −ant]) but not for [m] (which is [−cor, +ant]) or [ñ] (which is [+cor, −ant]).

10.11 MIRROR IMAGE RULES

Certain phonological processes require a type of rule called a mirror image rule. As the name implies, **mirror image rules** are rules whose environments are pertinent if read either from left to right or from right to left. In English, for example, /k/ is fronted to [ḳ] after front vowels, as in *peak* [piḳ], *lick* [lɪḳ], *pack* [pæḳ], and *peck* [pɛḳ]. (Compare *poke* [pok] *look* [lʊk], *pock* [pɑk].) This process, which also applies to the other velars /g/ and /ŋ/ could be stated as:

$$(20) \qquad \begin{bmatrix} +\text{cons} \\ -\text{ant} \\ -\text{cor} \\ +\text{bk} \end{bmatrix} \rightarrow [-\text{bk}] \Big/ \begin{bmatrix} -\text{cons} \\ -\text{bk} \end{bmatrix} \underline{\qquad}$$
$$(\text{k, g, ŋ})$$

But if we look further, we see that velars are also fronted *before* a front vowel. Thus, we have forms like *keep* [ḳip], *kill* [ḳɪl], and *cap* [ḳæp], as compared to *cope* [kop], *cool* [kul], and *cup* [kʌp]. This process could also be stated by a rule:

$$(21) \qquad \begin{bmatrix} +\text{cons} \\ -\text{ant} \\ -\text{cor} \\ +\text{bk} \end{bmatrix} \rightarrow [-\text{bk}] \Big/ \underline{\qquad} \begin{bmatrix} -\text{cons} \\ -\text{bk} \end{bmatrix}$$

Writing two separate rules such as (20) and (21) is misleading, however, since only one process is involved. To capture the fact that velar consonants are fronted either before or after a front vowel, we write a mirror image rule:

(22) Velar Fronting

$$\begin{bmatrix} +\text{cons} \\ -\text{ant} \\ -\text{cor} \\ +\text{bk} \end{bmatrix} \rightarrow [-\text{bk}] \;\ast\Big/ \underline{\qquad} \begin{bmatrix} -\text{cons} \\ -\text{bk} \end{bmatrix}$$

The asterisk directly before the diagonal means that the environment can be read either from left to right, as stated, or from right to left. In writing mirror image rules like (22), where the determinant is on only one side of the underscore, the asterisk and the underscore are sometimes omitted and the environment simply stated as:

$$/\begin{bmatrix} -\text{cons} \\ -\text{bk} \end{bmatrix}$$

Rules written without an underscore are called **neighborhood rules**. In a neighborhood rule, the diagonal is read 'next to'.

Not all processes with mirror image properties can be represented as neighborhood rules, however. In Mainland Comox (a Salish language of British Columbia) /ə/ becomes [u] between two high consonants if either is rounded (Davis, 1971). To state this fact, we can write the following mirror image rule:

(23) COMOX ROUNDING

$$\text{ə} \rightarrow \text{u} \ \ */\begin{bmatrix} +\text{hi} \end{bmatrix}\underline{\quad}\begin{bmatrix} +\text{hi} \\ +\text{rd} \end{bmatrix}$$

Reading the environment of Rule (23) from right to left, the consonant preceding /ə/ is rounded; from left to right, the consonant following /ə/ is rounded. Comox Rounding cannot be written as a neighborhood rule because it has a part of the determinant on each side of the underscore and the parts are different.

10.12 PARENTHESIS NOTATION

We have seen thus far how two notational devices—variables and mirror image rules—can be used to combine the description of related processes into a single rule. Parenthesis notation is another device that makes it possible to describe general processes properly. **Parenthesis notation** allows for the inclusion of optional elements in the statement of a rule. Suppose a language has a rule that fronts /a/ to [æ] if it precedes /y/. The surface representation of the form /aye/ would therefore be [æye]. The rule could be written informally as follows:

(24) $\text{a} \rightarrow \text{æ} / \underline{\quad}\text{y}$

Suppose further that in this language, /a/ is fronted to [æ] if the next syllable starts with a /y/ even if a consonant intervenes. Thus, the surface form of /atye/ would be [ætye]. This process could be described as:

(25) $\text{a} \rightarrow \text{æ} / \underline{\quad}\text{Cy}$

Parenthesis notation can be used to combine Rules (24) and (25) into a single rule:

(26) $a \rightarrow æ$ / ____(C)y

The parentheses indicate an optional element. Thus, Rule (26) will apply to a form whether or not it has a consonant before the /y/.

Rule (26) can alternatively be framed as:

(27) $a \rightarrow æ$ / ____$C_0^1 y$

This rule is read: "a becomes æ before zero to one consonants followed by a y." By convention, a subscript indicates the minimum number of segments or junctures involved and a superscript indicates the maximum. Thus, $[+\text{cons}]_1^3$ means 'from one to three consonantal segments'. Informally, this would be represented as C_1^3. If only a subscript appears, the lack of superscript indicates that the maximum is unbounded. Thus $[+\text{son}]_0$ means 'from zero to n sonorant segments'. The numerical specification $_1^1$ is generally omitted, so that $[+\text{son}]$ is read as 'one and only one sonorant segment'.

If a set of statements such as (24) and (25) can be combined by parenthesis or superscript–subscript notation into a single rule, they are said to be cases or **expansions** of that rule. The expansions of a rule have a special relationship to one another. For one thing, they have a definite order of application, the longest expansion applying first. Consider, for example, the following rule (where S = syllable):

(28) $S \rightarrow [+\text{stress}]$ / ____S_0^2

This rule incorporates three expansions:

(a) $S \rightarrow [+\text{stress}]$ /____SS
(b) $S \rightarrow [+\text{stress}]$ /____S
(c) $S \rightarrow [+\text{stress}]$ /____

If these expansions were not ordered, there would be no way of predicting which one would apply to certain forms. For example, consider a word with the structure SSS. If expansion (a) applied to this form, the stress would fall on the third syllable from the end, called the **antepenult**: S̉SS; if (b) applied, however, the stress would fall on the second syllable from the end, the **penult**: SS̉S; and if (c) applied, the stress would fall on the final syllable: SSS̉. But since these expansions are ordered, expansion (a) takes precedence, so forms with three or more syllables are stressed on the antepenult. Expansion (a) takes precedence because the relationship between the expansions of a parenthesized rule is such that once the longest expansion of a rule has applied, no shorter expansion can apply to the elements that figured in applying the longer expansion. Such a relationship is called a **disjunction**; and the expansions are said to be **disjunctively ordered**. Consider what would happen if the expansions of Rule (28) were not disjunctive. After case (a) had applied, the form discussed above would be left with two unstressed syllables. Case (b) could therefore apply to stress the penult. This would leave one unstressed syllable which would then become the input of (c). Thus, this word, and indeed every word of sufficient length in the language, would be stressed on the last three syllables. The principle of disjunctive ordering prevents this unhappy outcome. Because of this principle words of three or more syllables are stressed on the antepenult [by case (a)], disyllabic words on the penult [by case (b)], and monosyllables on their only syllable [by case (c)]. The last case of a set of disjunctively ordered expansions or rules is called the **elsewhere** case (see Kiparsky 1973).

In Chapter 9 we mentioned that morphemes are typically separated by the external juncture ($\#$). However, many phonologists recognize another juncture: $+$. The $+$ is called the **internal juncture**. According to Chomsky and Halle (1968) the internal juncture has a special relationship to parenthesis notation. In a rule, any sequence of elements AB is to be read as containing an optional internal juncture: $A(+)B$. This means that any rule which applies to a sequence of segments, [l s] for instance, will also apply to those segments when they are separated by an internal juncture: [l+s]. No rule can be written which will apply to a sequence of adjacent segments but not to the same sequence separated by a $+$. The converse is not true, however. A rule which explicitly specifies $A+B$ is not to be interpreted $A(+)B$, but only as $A+B$. Thus, if a $+$ is written into a rule, an internal juncture must be present in a form for the rule to apply to it. Neither the syllable boundary nor the external boundary has the special status that $[+]$ has. If a rule is to apply across a syllable or external boundary, it must mention that boundary.

Some phonologists use the distinction between the external and internal junctures to mark two classes of affixes, those which have a strong phonological effect on (or are strongly affected by) morphemes to which they are attached and those which have little or no effect. For example, in English the noun suffixes *-th* and *-ness* might be distinguished in this way. When *-th* is added to *wide* the stem vowel changes: *width*. But when *-ness* is added to *wide* there is no change in the stem vowel. If the underlying form of *width* were taken to be *wide+th* and that of *wideness* to be *wide$\#$ness*, a rule could be written to change the vowel of *width* without changing the vowel of *wideness*. The rule would simply not mention $\#$ in its environment.

10.13 ANGLE BRACKETS AND CONDITIONS ON RULES

Besides variables, mirror image rules, and parenthesis notation, linguists have still another notational device for capturing generalizations about phonological processes: angle brackets. Like variables, angle brackets serve a matching function. As an example, suppose that in a certain language /t/ is palatalized before front vowels at all heights, and in this same language /d/ is palatalized before [i] and [e] but not before [æ]. If generality were not a consideration, we could state these facts as two rules:

(29)

$$\begin{bmatrix} +\text{ant} \\ +\text{cor} \\ +\text{int} \\ -\text{vd} \end{bmatrix} \rightarrow \begin{bmatrix} +\text{hi} \\ -\text{bk} \end{bmatrix} / \underline{\hspace{1cm}} \begin{bmatrix} +\text{syl} \\ -\text{bk} \end{bmatrix}$$

(t)   (t^y)   (i,e,æ)

(30)

$$\begin{bmatrix} +\text{ant} \\ +\text{cor} \\ +\text{int} \\ +\text{vd} \end{bmatrix} \rightarrow \begin{bmatrix} +\text{hi} \\ -\text{bk} \end{bmatrix} / \underline{\hspace{1cm}} \begin{bmatrix} +\text{syl} \\ -\text{bk} \\ -\text{lo} \end{bmatrix}$$

(d)   (d^y)   (i, e)

However, because these processes are clearly related, it is preferable to write them as a single rule. Since the inputs of (29) and (30) together form a natural class (alveolar stops) and since the determinant of (30) is a subset of the determinant of (29), these rules can be collapsed in the following way:

(31)

$$\begin{bmatrix} +\text{ant} \\ +\text{cor} \\ +\text{int} \\ \langle +\text{vd} \rangle \end{bmatrix} \rightarrow \begin{bmatrix} +\text{hi} \\ -\text{bk} \end{bmatrix} / \underline{\hspace{1cm}} \begin{bmatrix} +\text{syl} \\ -\text{bk} \\ \langle -\text{lo} \rangle \end{bmatrix}$$

This rule states that alveolar stops are palatalized before front vowels, but if the stop is voiced, then the front vowel must not be low. In a given rule, all of the material in angle brackets must be considered part of a given expansion.

An alternative way of representing the generalization captured in (31) is by writing the general case, followed by a condition:

(32)

$$\begin{bmatrix} +\text{ant} \\ +\text{cor} \\ +\text{int} \end{bmatrix} \rightarrow \begin{bmatrix} -\text{bk} \\ +\text{hi} \end{bmatrix} / \underline{\hspace{1cm}} \begin{bmatrix} +\text{syl} \\ -\text{bk} \end{bmatrix}$$

Condition: if input = [+vd], then determinant ≠ [+lo]

The symbol ≠ is read 'does not equal' or 'cannot be'. Rule (32) therefore reads: "Alveolar stops become palatalized before front vowels. But if the input is voiced the determinant cannot be low." In this case, then, precisely the same results can be obtained by placing a condition on the rule as by using angle brackets. These two devices are not totally interchangeable, however. Some processes which call for conditions cannot be represented easily with angle brackets. For example, if a language had a rule which changed [ə] to [u] before *p, b, f,* and *m,* but not before *v,* we could write a general rule followed by this condition:

$$\text{Condition:} \quad \text{Input} \neq \begin{bmatrix} -\text{int} \\ -\text{nas} \\ +\text{vd} \end{bmatrix}$$
$$(v)$$

Angle brackets would be of little use in this case. The sound *v* does not represent an easily definable subset of the labial consonants. No single feature or combination of features has values that will separate *v* from the whole set without separating out some other sound or sounds as well. Limiting the class to [+int] would exclude not only *v,* but also *f* and *m.* Similarly, limiting the determinant to [−vd] would separate out both *b* and *m* along with *v.* We use conditions, then, when we must exclude some subset of a group of sounds whose complement is not a natural class.

Some rules have conditions which cannot be stated positively. Suppose, for example, that in some language [ɑ] became [æ] in every environment except before *k* and *g.* Given the features of Chapter 6, the set of 'all segments except *k* and *g*' is not a natural class. Therefore, the environment for this rule cannot be specified positively as a coherent class. However, the set of environments in which the rule does *not* apply is an easily stated natural class, since both *k* and *g* are velar stops. This fact can be stated as a **negative constraint**, a condition that specifies the environment in which a rule does not apply. Thus, using such a constraint, the rule that shifts [ɑ] to [æ] can be written as follows:

$$(33) \quad \quad \text{ɑ} \rightarrow \text{æ} / \underline{\quad\quad} \sim \begin{bmatrix} +\text{int} \\ -\text{ant} \\ -\text{cor} \end{bmatrix}$$
$$(k, g)$$

The symbol $\sim$ is here to be read 'not' or 'except'. Negative constraints are used whenever the set of items which fails to undergo a rule is a natural class but its complement is not.

10.14 BRACES NOTATION AND NATURAL CLASSES

The phonological rules we have discussed thus far have been written in terms of natural classes; or, in the case of negative constraints, in terms of the complements of natural classes. Sometimes, however, linguists wish to collapse rules even in the absence of a natural class. Consider the following rules:

(34)   æ → a / ____ #

(35)   æ → a / ____ r

The determinants of these rules (a word boundary and an *r*) do not comprise a natural class. These rules may nevertheless be collapsed if we use another formal device, braces:

(36)   æ → a / ____ $\left\{ \begin{matrix} \# \\ r \end{matrix} \right\}$

Braces are read 'either . . . or', and Rule (36) states that [æ] will become [a] either at the end of a word or before an *r*.

By and large, phonological rules involve elements which can be represented as natural classes. Therefore, in the description of a given language, the number of rules using braces notation should be small. In fact, some phonologists (e.g., McCawley, 1974) say that the number should be zero. It is maintained that any rule which requires braces *ipso facto* states an invalid generalization. This is tantamount to saying that phonological rules involve only natural classes. This strong claim may in fact be correct, but at present the case for it does not seem conclusive. In any event, most contemporary phonological descriptions make some use of braces notation.

10.15 EXCEPTIONS

In any language, some forms will fail to undergo one or more of the rules that their phonological shape indicates they should undergo. Perhaps the most common reason for this is that languages often incorporate foreign words into their lexicon without completely naturalizing them. Coeur d'Alene provides us with an example. In regular cases, when the nominalizer *s-* is prefixed to a stem beginning with a glottal stop, the two sounds merge to yield a laryngealized *y*. This rule can be stated informally as:

(37)   Fricative Laryngealization
              s + ʔ → y'

Fricative Laryngealization applies regularly to the form / s + ʔiɬən / to yield [y'iɬən] '(the act of) eating'. Compare [ʔiɬən] 'he eats'. But the initial glottal stop of the borrowed root [ʔapls] 'apples' does not merge with *s-*, as in the form [sʔáplsalqʷ] 'apple tree'. (The suffix [ʔalqʷ] means 'tree'. We leave it to the reader to deduce the source of the root.) The root [ʔapls] must be marked in the lexicon as not undergoing Fricative Laryngealization. A note on a lexical entry indicating that a form does not undergo a certain rule is called a **rule feature**. Rule features are enclosed in square brackets. They consist of the name of the rule preceded by a minus sign. Thus, the rule feature in the lexical entry for Coeur d'Alene [ʔapls] is [−Fricative Laryngealization].

In the preceding discussion, we have described certain phonological regularities (by means of rules). It is currently a matter of controversy whether or not such regularities reflect rules actually used by speakers to produce linguistic forms. Since the number of words in any speaker's lexicon is finite, it is not logically necessary to assume that rules are used to produce derived or inflected forms. It could be that speakers simply learn all the words in a language by rote. However, there is no doubt that regularities can be extracted from language data, and at the present time the majority of scholars in the field of phonology would take at least some of these regularities to be evidence of rules in the minds of speakers.

10.16 SUMMARY

The following symbols and devices are commonly employed in writing phonological rules:

1. **Square brackets** [ ] are used to enclose feature specifications such as [+lo], phonetic symbols such as [b], and surface representations such as [kʰæt'].
2. The **arrow** → is placed between the input and the output of a rule. It is read 'becomes'.
3. The **diagonal** or **slash mark** / is placed after the output of a rule. It is read 'in the environment of', 'before', 'after', or 'next to', depending on what follows.
4. The **underscore** _____ is used to indicate the location of the input in relation to the determinant.
5. The **external boundary** # separates morphemes, words, phrases, and sentences.
6. The **internal boundary** + separates morphemes that are more closely bound than those separated by #.
7. The **null sign** ∅ is used to denote deletion or addition. The configuration →∅ is to be read 'is deleted', whereas ∅→ is read 'add' or 'insert'.
8. The **variable signs** α, β, γ, and so forth are used to link features in one part of a rule with features of the same value in another.
9. The **asterisk** *, when placed next to the diagonal in a rule, means

that the environment of that rule may be read either from right to left or from left to right.

10. **Parentheses** ( ) are used to mark optional elements in a rule.
11. **Angle brackets** ⟨ ⟩ are used to link elements of a rule which must be taken together as a condition on the application of a rule.
12. The symbol ∼ is used to specify a negative environment, one in which a rule does not apply.
13. **Braces** { } are used to collapse rules in the absence of natural classes. They are read 'either . . . or'.

Informal devices are often used in place of distinctive feature specifications in rule writing. These devices include phonetic symbols and a number of capital letters such as V (meaning 'any vowel'), C ('any consonant'), N ('any nasal'), R ('any resonant'), and G ('any glide').

Phonological rules always apply within some specifiable unit of language. The scope of a particular rule is the **domain** of that rule. If no boundary markers are given in a rule, the domain of that rule is the syllable. By convention, each major part of speech, each phrase, and each sentence are bounded by external junctures. Since affixes are not major parts of speech, only one juncture is inserted between a stem and an affix. The domain of the word is defined as # #____# #.

If the ordering of a pair of rules either increases or decreases the number of forms to which one of the rules applies, we say those two rules **interact**. If a pair of rules, A and B, are ordered so that A creates segments which are either inputs or determinants for B, then we say that A **feeds** B, or that A and B are in a **feeding order**. If, on the other hand, a pair of rules, A and B, are ordered so that A changes segments which otherwise would be either inputs or determinants for B, we say that A **bleeds** B or that A and B are in a **bleeding order**. Rules may interact in ways more subtle than bleeding or feeding. If a pair of rules, A and B, are ordered so that A would bleed B if their order were reversed, we say they are in a **counterbleeding order**. If a pair of rules, A and B, are ordered so that A would feed B if their order were reversed, A and B are in **counterfeeding order**.

Iterative rules are phonological rules which can apply more than once to the same form. They apply first to the relevant segment nearest one end of a form and then work toward the other end reapplying to each relevant segment in turn. A rule whose earlier applications create environments for its later ones is called a **self-feeding rule**.

Some forms in any language fail to undergo one or more of the rules that their phonological shape indicates they should undergo. This is indicated by a note in the lexical entry called a **rule feature**, which is enclosed in square brackets and consists of the name of the rule preceded by a minus sign.

EXERCISES FOR CHAPTER 10

1. Some phonologists have proposed that certain English suffixes are added
   to a stem with an external juncture ($\#$), some with an internal juncture
   ($+$), and that some suffixes have variable juncture depending on the
   stem. Assuming this position, decide whether the suffix of each of the
   following examples is added with $\#$ or $+$. Certain phonological processes apply to the examples with $+$. What are the effects of these
   processes?

PAST TENSE	ADJECTIVIZER (*-ic*)	NOMINALIZER (*-t*)
1. left	16. Homeric	26. content (cf. contain)
2. heard	17. scenic	27. past (cf. pass)
3. said	18. moronic	28. pursuit
4. spent	19. titanic	29. complaint
5. built	20. static	30. detent [dítènt]
6. wept	21. pacific	(cf. detain)
7. logged	22. satiric	
8. lost	23. sophomoric	
9. hoped	24. terrific	
10. swept	25. demonic	
11. painted		
12. paddled		
13. bent		
14. feared		
15. tried		

2. Luiseño (a Uto-Aztecan language spoken in California) has a rule of
   vowel syncope. A vowel is deleted if it is preceded by a short stressed
   vowel and a single consonant and is followed by a single consonant and
   a vowel. Examples are (ignore the change from [č] to [š]):

páči	'to wash'	pášku	'to leach acorn flour'
čáqʷi-	'to seize'	čáqʷla-	'to wrestle'

Another rule deletes the second of two vowels before a vowel and a
following consonant, as shown by the following examples:

tównav-	'to make baskets'	tównavuk	'used to make baskets'
hédi-	'to open'	hédik	'used to open'
sámsa-	'to buy'	sámsak	'used to buy'
ʔélku-	'to beg'	ʔélkuk	'used to beg'

State these rules in the formal notation of this chapter. (Based on Munro
and Benson, 1973.)

3. In Eskimo (Kuskokwim dialect) the fricatives have a number of variants. Determine the rules which account for the variants of *f*, *s*, *x*, and *x̧* found in examples 1–23.

1.	[ɸ:atʰ:ɔ́]	/ffattúu/	'right now'
2.	[náu̯ɸ:a]	/náuffa/	'where are'
3.	[qau̯βi̯áq]	/qaufíaq/	'sand'
4.	[nəˇqó:βutəˇq]	/naqúufutaq/	'belt'
5.	[kuskukfák]	/kuskukfák/	'Kuskokwim'
6.	[áqfəˇqóq]	/aqfaqúq/	'run'
7.	[tunúvni]	/tunúfni/	'behind you'
8.	[uŋú:vəˇn]	/uŋúfan/	'heart'
9.	[ávɣɪlnuq]	/afxilnuq/	'six'
10.	[látšatšskiiaɣaq]	/látsatsskiiaxáq/	'blue (mud) swallow'
11.	[tšmái̯]	/tsmái/	'hello'
12.	[nazáɣluq]	/nasáxluq/	'sweetheart'
13.	[tái̯zɣu]	/táisxu/	'give it to me'
14.	[natstuq]	/nátstuq/	'to go up the hills'
15.	[ats:áq]	/atssáq/	'berry'
16.	[naɣístuq]	/naxístuq/	'louse'
17.	[íxtuq]	/íxtuq/	'den'
18.	[ámɣəˇq]	/ámxaq/	'sleeve'
19.	[aɣá:i̯ún]	/axáaiún/	'god'
20.	[qátɣəˇq]	/qátxaq/	'chest'
21.	[ávɣɪlnuq]	/áfxilnuq/	'six'
22.	[ɬóx̧tuq]	/ɬúx̧tuq/	'to fix'
23.	[px̧:í̯q]	/px̧x̧íq/	'to wipe'

(Based on Mattina, 1970)

4. Tangale (a Chado-Hamitic language spoken in Nigeria) has a rule of vowel harmony. Formulate this rule on the basis of the data below. The function of the affixes is given with each set of examples.

IMPERATIVE (+u/ʊ)
1. seb+u 'look!'
2. kɛn+ʊ 'enter'

CONTINUOUS (+i/ɪ)
3. naŋ sol+i 'I am pulling'
4. naŋ wɔl+ɪ 'I am dyeing'

PERFECT (+go/gɔ/ko/kɔ)
5. 'n wee+go 'I have seen'
6. 'n kas+kɔ 'I have cut'

VERBAL NOUNS (+o/ɔ, +a)
7. tug+o 'pounding'
8. wʊd+ɔ 'farming'
9. top+a 'start'
10. tɔp+a 'answer'
11. wʊl+a 'wedding'
12. lɔp+a 'will'

VERBALIZER (+e/ɛ, +i, ɪ)
13. riy+e 'to multiply'
14. rɪy+ɛ 'to satisfy'

15. ɓel+i	'to be ashamed'	21. wob+i	'to embrace'
16. ɓel+ɩ	'to cross'	22. wɔb+ɩ	'to grab hold'
17. pod+i	'to take out'	23. suk+e	'to make a shallow hole'
18. pɔd+ɩ	'to go out'	24. sʊk+ɛ	'to winnow'
19. tob+i	'to start'		
20. tɔb+ɩ	'to answer'	(Based on Jungraithmayr, 1971)	

5. Formulate rules to account for the alternations of long and short vowels in the following data from Bravanese Swahili. Wherever V: alternates with V, assume that V: is basic. Treat examples 13, 14, 19, 21, 26, 27, and 28 as if they were single words.

1. wona '(to) see'
2. we:ne 'saw'
3. xa:dira '(to) be able'
4. xabari 'news'
5. so:ma '(to) read'
6. ibu:ku 'book'
7. ma:limu 'teacher'
8. malimuwe 'his teacher'
9. malimuwo 'your teacher'
10. mta:na 'room'
11. mta:nawe 'his room'
12. mtana:mi 'in (the) room'
13. malimu wa: saba '(the) seventh teacher'
14. malimu wa pi:li '(the) second teacher'
15. nu:mba 'house'
16. nu:mbaye 'his house'
17. numba:ni 'in the house'
18. nu:mbaya ⎫
19. numba ya:ka⎭ 'my house'
20. cilice ⎫
21. cili ca:ke⎭ 'his bed'
22. nikono 'arms'
23. niko:ni 'in the kitchen'
24. nkuku 'chicken'
25. soma:ni 'read (pl.)'
26. malimu wi:tu 'our teacher'
27. numba ya ma:limu 'the house of the teacher'
28. cili ca mu:ntu 'the bed of the man'

(Based on Goodman, 1967)

6. Sre (a Mon-Khmer language of Vietnam) has a causative prefix *tən-*.

What is the rule which accounts for the deletion of the *n* of *tən-* before certain consonants? ['] indicates a long vowel with falling pitch.

1a.	dùh	'to fall'		1b.	tənduh	'to cause to fall'
2a.	lik	'to come out'		2b.	təlik	'to cause to come out'
3a.	po	'to feed at the breast'		3b.	tənpo	'to suckle'
4a.	mù?	'to descend'		4b.	təmù?	'to cause to descend'
5a.	čʰet	'to die'		5b.	tənčʰet	'to kill'
6a.	duh	'to be hot'		6b.	tənduh	'to heat up'
7a.	ŋač	'goodbye (greeting)'		7b.	təŋač	'to bid farewell'
8a.	guh	'to wake up'		8b.	tənguh	'to wake someone up'
9a.	hòr	'to flow'		9b.	tənhòr	'to pour'
10a.	kah	'to remember'		10b.	tənkah	'to remind'
11a.	riŋ	'to be flat, level'		11b.	tənriŋ	'to make flat, level'

(Based on Manley, 1972)

7a. The first three examples below show the basic Nyangumarda vowels of the future (F), actual (A), unrealized (U), and the first- and third-person singular suffixes. The basic process of vowel assimilation is shown in such examples as 4–9. Vowel assimilation does not apply to the second vowel of a root; e.g., *yurpa* does not become *yurpu*. Examples 10–30 show that vowel assimilation is blocked by the high vowels in the suffixes *li* 'you and I', *ŋu* 'to you', *ku* (dative), and *lu* (ergative). Based on examples 1–30, formulate an iterative rule for Nyangumarda vowel assimilation.

1. yurpa + lama + rna
   rub-F-I
   'I will rub (it)'

2. yurpa + rna + rra
   rub-A-he
   'He rubbed (it)'

3. yurpa + rna + ma + rna
   rub-A-U-I
   'I was about to rub (it)'

4. wirri + limi + rni
   put-F-I
   'I will put (it somewhere)'

5. wirri + rni + rri
   put-A-he
   'He put (it somewhere)'

6. wirri + rni + mi + rni
   put-A-U-I
   'I was about to put (it somewhere)'

7. kalku + lumu + rnu
   care for-F-I
   'I will care for (it)'

8. kalku + rnu + rru
   care for-A-he
   'He cared for (it)'

9. kalku + rnu + mu + rnu
   care for-A-U-I
   'I was about to care for (it)'

10. yurpa + lapa + li	'You and I will rub (it)'
11. yurpa + rna + li	'You and I rubbed (it)'
12. yurpa + rna + ma + li	'You and I were about to rub (it)'
13. wirri + lipa + li	'You and I will put (it somewhere)'
14. wirri + rna + li	'You and I put (it somewhere)'
15. wirri + rni + ma + li	'You and I were about to put (it somewhere)'
16. kalku + lupa + li	'You and I will care for (it)'
17. kalku + rna + li	'You and I cared for (it)'
18. kalku + rnu + ma + li	'You and I were about to care for (it)'
19. wurra + lama + ŋu	'(He) will tell you'
20. wurra + rna + ŋu	'(He) told you'
21. wurra + rna + ma + ŋu	'(He) was about to tell you'
22. wirri + lima + ŋu	'(He) will put (it near) you'
23. wirri + rna + ŋu	'(He) put (it near) you'
24. wirri + rni + ma + ŋu	'(He) was about to put (it near) you'
25. kaku + luma + ŋu	'(He) won't tell you'
26. kaku + rna + ŋu	'(He) didn't tell you'
27. kaku + rnu + ma + ŋu	'(He) was about not to tell you'
28. walʸpili	'white man' (from 'white fellow')
29. walʸpila + ku	'white man (dative case)'
30. walʸpila + lu	'white man (ergative case)'

b. The Nyangumarda sounds that cause *a* to assimilate to *i* or *u* are: *i*, *u*, *y*, *t*ʸ, *l*ʸ, *n*ʸ, and *w*. In part (a) of this exercise the effect of *i* or *u* on following vowels can be seen. Modify the vowel assimilation rule formulated on the basis of examples 1–30 to handle also the assimilations in examples 31–37. Ignore the effect of palatal consonants on a preceding vowel. The basic vowel of the suffixes not previously encountered is *a*, as in: *ŋarra* 'if', *ya* 'they', and *n*ʸ*a* 'all of us'.

31. yurpa + rna + ma + rra + ŋarra	'If he were about to rub (it) . . . .'
32. yurpa + rna + mi + nʸi + ŋirri	'If all of us were about to rub (it) . . .'
33. wurra + lapi + ya + ŋu	'They will tell you'
34. wurra + lapi + yi	'They will tell'
35. kalku + rni + yi	'They cared for (it)'
36. kalku + rni + ya + ŋu	'They cared for you'
37 yurpa + rna + mi + nʸa + ŋu	'All of us were about to rub you'

c. Examples 32–37 above show the effect of a palatal consonant on a preceding vowel. Formulate a rule of regressive vowel fronting on the basis of examples 32–37 and examples 38–41, below. On the basis of examples 38–41 determine the order in which regressive vowel fronting and progressive vowel assimilation apply.

38. kalku + rnu + mi + n^{y}i   'All of us were about to care for (it)'
39. kalku + rnu + mi + yirni   'We were about to care for (it)'
40. kalku + rnu + mi + n^{y}urru   'All of you were about to care for (it)'
41. kalku + rnu + mi + yi   'They were about to care for (it)'

d. Nyangumarda also has a rule which changes basic *l^y* to *lay* when a morpheme boundary precedes. Consider examples 42–43 and determine the order in which this rule and regressive vowel fronting apply.

42. yurpa + rna + mi + layi   'We two were about to rub (it)'
43. kalku + rni + layi   'We two cared for (it)'

(Based on Hoard and O'Grady, 1976)

11 phonological method

11.1 INTRODUCTION

One of the goals of phonological analysis is to describe the phonological processes which relate alternate forms of morphemes. To achieve this goal phonologists try to use the most economical sound inventory and the fewest rules possible. However, the degree to which we can reduce the sound inventory or the number of rules is limited by the necessity of maintaining the proper balance between the two. In many cases, it would be possible to posit a very small sound inventory at the expense of having a large number of very specific rules. Or, on the other hand, we might be able to posit only one or two rules if we had an extremely large number of underlying sounds. Possible solutions, however, are constrained by considerations of naturalness. Clearly, we cannot posit sound inventories that are in conflict with implicational laws; nor do we posit rules which cannot be explained as manifestations of some natural process. Linguists call rules which describe highly unlikely or seemingly unnatural processes **crazy rules** (Bach and Harms, 1972). We try very hard to avoid writing crazy rules.

11.2 THE METHODS OF PHONOLOGICAL ANALYSIS

Phonological analysis, like other scientific endeavors, involves the formation and testing of hypotheses. Suppose, for example, that we wish to describe the relationship between the German words *Tag* [tɑk] 'day', which ends in the voiceless consonant [k], and *Tage* [tɑgə] 'days', which ends in the corresponding voiced consonant [g] followed by [ə]. Because they do not have identical meanings and they have only partially similar phonetic shapes, we might hypothesize that the two words are distinct morphemes. This is tantamount to saying that their partial similarity in meaning and form is accidental. We would probably dismiss this hypothesis quickly, because upon further examination we find that there are other pairs of German words which differ in parallel ways. In the following data each word in the first column ends in a voiceless consonant and each correspond-ing word of the second column ends with the voiced counterpart of that consonant followed by [ə].

Sieg	[zik]	'victory'	*Siege*	[zigə]	'victories'
Weg	[vek]	'path'	*Wege*	[vegə]	'paths'
Dieb	[dip]	'thief'	*Diebe*	[dibə]	'thieves'
Urlaub	[ʊrlawp]	'vacation'	*Urlaube*	[ʊrlawbə]	'vacations'
Tod	[tot]	'death'	*Tode*	[todə]	'deaths'
Ried	[rit]	'marsh'	*Riede*	[ridə]	'marshes'

If we were to follow out the hypothesis that the singular and plural forms are distinct but accidentally similar morphemes, we would end up with fourteen different morphemes (and an uncomfortable number of 'accidental' similarities).

However, we know from studying other languages that the meaning component 'plural' which differentiates *Tag* and *Tage* is often represented by an affixed morpheme. This leads us to hypothesize that the [ə] on the ends of the plural forms is a suffixed morpheme marking plurality. This second hypothesis leaves two forms, [tɑk] and [tɑg] meaning 'day', which not only have the same meaning, but occur in different environments: [tɑk] does not occur with the suffix; [tɑg] does not occur without it. We are therefore led to conclude that [tɑk] and [tɑg] are variants of the same morpheme. Such a conclusion cannot be dismissed easily. If we posit a plural suffix [ə], we will have only eight morphemes, the seven stems meaning 'victory', 'path', 'thief', 'vacation', 'death', and 'marsh', and, of course, the suffix meaning 'plural'. Since there are many other similar word pairs in German, the number of distinct morphemes we save is actually much greater than our sample indicates.

In the second hypothesis a rule is needed to explain the alternation of voiced and voiceless segments in the stems. At this point, we are confronted by a typical problem. There are two very natural rules, intervocalic voicing and final obstruent devoicing, either of which might describe the alternation. We must decide which rule best accounts for the data. It might be that an intervocalic voicing rule voices obstruents when the vowel marking the plural is added. However, in other German words, such as *Hüte* [hütə] 'hats', *Lacke* [lakə] 'varnishes', and *Kreppe* [krɛpə] 'crepes', the plural suffix is preceded by a voiceless stop. This provides convincing evidence that the rule involved is not intervocalic voicing.

We therefore reject the intervocalic voicing hypothesis and turn to a second possible rule, final obstruent devoicing. Such a rule accounts nicely for the alternation of [tɑk] and [tɑg], since only in the form [tɑk] does an obstruent appear at the end of the word. Final devoicing also accounts for the other forms we have considered; and since there are, in fact, no German words which end in a voiced obstruent, it explains a great deal more as well. Thus, the devoicing rule has the advantage of being both plausible and general.

In discovering the process involved, we also determine the underlying forms of the morphemes. For example, if we take the underlying forms of [tɑk] and [tɑg + ə] to be /tɑg/ and /tɑg + ə/, the surface form [tɑk] is explainable as a result of final devoicing. But if we assume that /tɑk/ is underlying, we have no generalizable explanation for [tɑg + ə]. If we assumed an underlying form /tɑk + ə/ and a rule of intervocalic voicing, we could account for *Tage*, but we would have to find some ad hoc way to keep the rule from applying to *Lacke* /lak + ə/. Through a process of elimination, therefore, we have arrived at the solution which involves the smallest number of underlying morphemes and the most general, plausible, and natural rule possible.

The German problem we have just considered is, of course, a very simple one since it involves only one phonological rule. Any reasonably large body of linguistic data will contain forms which require a number of rules. In essence, though, the procedure for analyzing such data is the same one of forming and testing hypotheses. When more than one rule is involved, however, it sometimes becomes necessary to account for their interaction. Usually, this is a matter of discovering the order in which the rules apply by testing various possible orders against the surface forms. The order that accounts for the surface forms is assumed to be the correct one. Below, we will illustrate this method by working out the solution to a problem with several interrelated rules.

11.3 FORMING PARADIGMS AND DETERMINING THE MORPHEMES

In solving the problem above, we grouped together a number of German words which were related in a certain way: namely, nouns containing a stop which was voiceless in the singular form but voiced in the plural. A set of related forms such as this is called a **paradigm**. Frequently, paradigms are composed of root morphemes combined in various ways with derivational and inflectional affixes. In phonological analysis, paradigms are extremely useful because they facilitate the comparison of allomorphs in different phonological environments. Most analyses begin with the collection of paradigms.

Let us assume that we have already arrived at the paradigm in Table I and wish to analyze the phonological structure of the language of which they are a part.

In describing these forms, the first task is to separate the words into their component morphemes. To do this, we begin by comparing the various columns in the paradigms. Comparing the column of perfect forms with that of simple present forms, we find that all the perfect forms end in *t*, whereas the present forms end in various consonants. We hypothesize, therefore, that the perfect is marked by simply suffixing a *t* to the end of the stem.

Since the causative forms have no apparent affix, we set aside for the moment the causatives and look at the noun forms. By comparing the columns containing the singular, plural, and genitive forms, we find that all plurals end in *er* and all genitives in *id*. We take these endings to be the plural and genitive suffixes.

The ablative forms are somewhat more difficult. All except one of these, the form [čʰækt], glossed 'from the rock', end in *t* preceded by a vowel. However, since three different vowels appear before *t* in the ablative forms, it is difficult to know which, if any, is the basic one. We tentatively conclude that the ablative suffix is either -*t* or -*Vt*. We now have two possible morphemes with the same shape: -*t*. This is not disturbing, however, because the morphemes involved are in different syntactic and semantic spheres: one is affixed only to verbs and the other only to nouns. (A similar situation occurs in English where the -*s* suffix is used to denote both plural nouns and third-person singular verbs.)

We regard the possible vowel in the ablative morpheme simply as *V* because at this point there is no way to determine which of the vowels, [a], [u], or [o], is underlying and which are derived by rule. In fact, there seems to be nothing in the environment of these vowels which can be pointed to as systematic. The preceding vowels do not seem to be relevant, since in the form [lo:pat], [a] is preceded by an [o:]; in [pʰodut], [u] is preceded by an [o]; in [batut], [u] is preceded by an [a]; and in [čʰedat], [a] is preceded by [e]. Neither is there any discernible pattern to the preceding consonants. Our inability to state a cause for the vowel change suggests that these vowels may be a part of the underlying form of the stem. The form [čʰækt], in which no vowel at all appears, supports the hypothesis that the *t* alone is

Table I DUBUN (A HYPOTHETICAL LANGUAGE)

	PRESENT		PERFECT		CAUSATIVE	
1.	[maːs]	'reach'	[mast]	'have reached'	[mæːs]	'cause to reach'
2.	[kʰot]	'exceed'	[kʰett]	'have exceeded'	[kʰet]	'cause to exceed'
3.	[dub]	'abound'	[dipt]	'have abounded'	[dib]	'cause to abound'
4.	[jær]	'be green'	[jært]	'have been green'	[jer]	'make green'
5.	[lin]	'be yellow'	[lint]	'have been yellow'	[lin]	'make yellow'
6.	[reːg]	'be blue'	[rekt]	'have been blue'	[reːg]	'make blue'

	SINGULAR		PLURAL		GENITIVE (*sing.*)		ABLATIVE (*sing.*)	
7.	[loːp]	'fruit'	[loːper]	'fruits'	[leːpid]	'of the fruit'	[loːpat]	'from the fruit'
8.	[bat]	'house'	[bačer]	'houses'	[bæčid]	'of the house'	[batut]	'from the house'
9.	[guːl]	'stack'	[guːler]	'stacks'	[giːlid]	'of the stack'	[guːlot]	'from the stack'
10.	[čʰæːg]	'rock'	[čʰæːjer]	'rocks'	[čʰeːjid]	'of the rock'	[čʰækt]	'from the rock'
11.	[čʰed]	'hole'	[čʰejer]	'holes'	[čʰejid]	'of the hole'	[čʰedat]	'from the hole'
12.	[pʰod]	'bird'	[pʰojer]	'birds'	[pʰejid]	'of the bird'	[pʰodut]	'from the bird'

the ablative morpheme. But we will leave this as an undecided issue for now and turn our attention to determining the base forms of the stems.

In attempting to find the most basic forms of the root morphemes, we first examine the sets in which the stems seem to change the least. Often these are the most transparent cases. Of the verbs, the set [lin]/[lint]/[lin] displays the fewest changes from form to form. We therefore hypothesize that /lin/ is the base form of the stem meaning 'be yellow'. If the perfect marker $+t$ is added to this base form, we get [lint], the precise surface form that is given for 'have been yellow'. The causative form [lin] is identical with our base form. This suggests that there is no causative morpheme. However, the following vowel alternations make us reject this hypothesis:

PRESENT	CAUSATIVE
[ma:s]	[mæ:s]
[kʰot]	[kʰet]
[dub]	[dib]
[jær]	[jer]

Possibly, the alternations here could be accounted for with rules of vowel symbolism. The forms [mæ:s], [kʰet], and [dib] could be derived from [ma:s], [kʰot], and [dub] by replacing a back vowel with the corresponding front one. The form [jer] would require a separate rule replacing the [æ] of [jær] with [e]. However, since vowel fronting and replacement of [æ] with [e] seem to be part of the formation of the perfect and the genitive also, we will not write rules for the causative forms until we have investigated further.

Among the nouns, the following sets of forms change the least:

SINGULAR	PLURAL	GENITIVE	ABLATIVE
[lo:p]	[lo:per]	[le:pid]	[lo:pat]
[gu:l]	[gu:ler]	[gi:lid]	[gu:lot]

In these forms, the stem vowel changes only in the genitive. Otherwise, they follow the pattern of adding $+er$ to the stem in the plural, $+id$ in the genitive, and $+(V)t$ in the ablative.

11.4 POSITING BASE FORMS AND RULES

We can now postulate a set of tentative base forms for the nouns. By comparing the singular and ablative paradigms, it seems reasonable to suggest that the base forms for the nouns are:

7. /lo:pa/	10. /čʰæ:g/
8. /batu/	11. /čʰeda/
9. /gu:lo/	12. /pʰodu/

Each of these forms except /čʰæ:g/ ends in a vowel. In each case this vowel is the one which appears in the ablative form preceding the *-t*. We take the several different vowels of the ablative forms to be part of the stem rather than of the suffix. The ablative suffix, then, is just *-t*, not *-(V)t*. We pointed out above that the quality of the second vowel in the ablative forms was not phonetically predictable and differed from noun to noun. If we took the vowel to be part of the ablative ending, we would have several morphologically conditioned allomorphs of the suffix and would have to list the noun with which each allomorph occurs. However, making the vowel a part of the underlying form of the noun recognizes both the unpredictability of its quality and its dependence on the noun. This treatment requires us to posit rules of apocope and syncope; but the conditioning for these rules is phonological. The final vowel of the underlying form must be deleted in the singular, where it would be word final, and in the plural and genitive, where it would precede another vowel. The fact that there are no word-final vowels in the data and no cases of one vowel preceding another supports our hypothesis that the following rules apply:

(1)   APOCOPE

$$V \rightarrow \emptyset \; / \; \underline{\hspace{1cm}} \# \#$$

(2)   SYNCOPE

$$V \rightarrow \emptyset \; / \; \underline{\hspace{1cm}} V$$

The ablative form [čʰækt], which lacks a vowel, is also accounted for by the underlying forms we have posited. This form has no vowel before the ablative suffix because there is no second vowel in the noun stem.

Notice that some of the noun stems posited here have long vowels. There seems to be no plausible way to derive long vowels from underlying short ones. The ablative form [čʰækt] has a short vowel while its posited underlying stem has a long vowel. The conditioning here seems clear enough, though. The short vowel precedes a cluster of consonants and long vowels do not. We therefore consider the long vowels to be underlying and posit a rule which shortens a long vowel before a consonant cluster.

(3)   CLUSTER SHORTENING

$$V: \rightarrow V \; / \; \underline{\hspace{1cm}} CC$$

The perfect forms of the verbs confirm our rule. Only short vowels occur before consonant clusters.

Thus far, we have posited base forms for the noun stems and five inflectional suffixes. We have also posited three phonological rules: one deleting final vowels, one deleting the first of two consecutive vowels, and one shortening long vowels before clusters.

Having posited tentative underlying noun stems, we must now decide on base forms for the verb stems. Finding no real evidence to the contrary, we begin by positing underlying forms which are the same as the least complicated surface form: the present. We must now relate these underlying forms to the perfect forms. We can start by considering the perfect forms of [dub] and [re:g]. If the final segments of these forms are underlyingly voiced, why do they become voiceless in the perfect? Or conversely, if the final segments are underlyingly voiceless, why do they become voiced in the present and causative forms? Since we have already posited a rule that deletes word-final vowels, it could be hypothesized that the present, as well as the causative form, has a vowel suffix which conditions intervocalic voicing and is subsequently deleted. However, since the present and causative forms of the first two verbs do not end in voiced segments, we reject this possibility in favor of a rule which devoices the final segments of [dub] and [re:g] when followed by the perfect suffix -*t*. In both forms, a voiced stop— [b] or [g]—is devoiced before [t]. And if we look further, we find that in the ablative of the noun [čʰæ:g], [g] also devoices before [t]. This seems to be a rather clear case of regressive voicing assimilation, and we write a rule to reflect this:

(4)   VOICING ASSIMILATION
$$\begin{bmatrix} -\text{son} \\ +\text{vd} \end{bmatrix} \rightarrow [-\text{vd}] \, / \underline{\hspace{1cm}} [-\text{vd}]$$

This rule is actually more general than the data necessitates. Because the only fricative in our data is [s], we have no direct evidence that fricatives devoice in the environment of a following [t]. We also lack evidence that voiceless sounds other than [t] condition devoicing. On the other hand, we have no evidence that they do not. Since rules should predict beyond the data, they are written in the most general possible terms. If further evidence showed that only stops devoiced before [t], we could simply alter the features of the environment so that the rule read:

(5) $\begin{bmatrix} +\text{int} \\ +\text{vd} \end{bmatrix} \rightarrow [-\text{vd}] \, / \underline{\hspace{1cm}} [-\text{vd}]$

If we found that only [t] conditioned devoicing, we could rewrite our rule as:

(6) $\begin{bmatrix} -\text{son} \\ +\text{vd} \end{bmatrix} \rightarrow [-\text{vd}] \, / \underline{\hspace{1cm}} \begin{bmatrix} +\text{int} \\ -\text{vd} \\ +\text{ant} \\ +\text{cor} \\ -\text{str} \end{bmatrix}$

However, unless such evidence makes revision necessary, we leave the rule in its most general form, as shown in Rule (4).

At this point in our analysis, two very obvious problems remain unsolved: first, why do some of the stem vowels change in certain forms; and second, why do some of the stops at the ends of singular nouns become affricates in the plural and genitive singular forms?

To consider the second problem first, we can observe that in all the data, affricates occur only before the front vowels [æ], [e], and [i]. Nowhere do we find an affricate followed by [u], [o], or [a]. This leads us to posit another rule:

$$(7) \qquad [+\text{int}] \rightarrow \begin{bmatrix} +\text{cor} \\ +\text{str} \end{bmatrix} / \underline{\qquad} \begin{bmatrix} V \\ -\text{bk} \end{bmatrix}$$

A rule which changes stops directly to affricates does not reflect a natural and expected process. But it does reflect a set of linked processes, each of which is quite natural. If we examine the input and output of Rule 7, we see that they are the beginning and end points of palatalization and assibilation. (See 8.2.)

However, as written, our palatalization rule is more general than the data permit. Since in the plural form [lo:per] and in the genitive forms [le:pid] and [pʰejid], [p] does not become a coronal affricate before front vowels, we must alter the input of this rule to exclude labial stops:

$$(8a) \qquad \begin{bmatrix} +\text{int} \\ -\text{lab} \end{bmatrix} \rightarrow \begin{bmatrix} +\text{cor} \\ +\text{str} \end{bmatrix} / \underline{\qquad} \begin{bmatrix} V \\ -\text{bk} \end{bmatrix}$$

The verb forms [kʰett], [kʰet], [dipt], [dib] and the noun form [gi:lid] indicate that we must restrict the application of the palatalization rule even further. It applies only to stops preceded by a vowel. The environment for palatalization must be changed to:

$$(8b) \qquad V \underline{\qquad} \begin{bmatrix} V \\ -\text{bk} \end{bmatrix}$$

This restriction on palatalization is not totally unexpected. Phonological processes of even the most natural kinds are often restricted to specific environments.

The one major problem left to be solved, then, is explaining the changes which occur in some of the stem vowels. If we examine the forms that change, we see that in each case where there is a nonfront vowel in the present or singular forms, the front vowel corresponding to it in height appears in one of the other forms. Thus, [a] alternates with [æ], [o] with [e], and [u] with [i]. We therefore hypothesize that the process taking place is the fronting of back vowels, (that is, umlaut). But since we have not as yet determined what is conditioning the change, we cannot formulate a rule.

Although umlaut would account for most of the vowel changes, there are still two alternating pairs—[jær] ∼ [jer] and [čʰæ:g] ∼ [čʰe:jid]—left unaccounted for. In both pairs, an underlying front vowel, [æ] or [æ:], is raised to become a mid vowel, [e] or [e:]. We cannot easily incorporate this change into an umlaut rule, but will need a separate rule of raising.

The rules for umlaut and raising cannot be stated until we determine the environments in which these processes occur. If we look again at the plural forms, we see that umlaut and raising do not apply to them.

PLURAL
[lo:per]	'fruits'
[bačer]	'houses'
[gu:ler]	'stacks'
[čʰæ:jer]	'rocks'
[čʰejer]	'holes'
[pʰojer]	'birds'

Therefore, we can eliminate the [e] of the plural suffix as a possible determinant for the umlaut and raising rules. In the genitive forms, however, both processes apply, which leads us to conclude that something in the genitive morpheme is conditioning umlauting and raising of stem vowels.

GENITIVE (*sing.*)
[le:pid]	'of the fruit'
[bæčid]	'of the house'
[gi:lid]	'of the stack'
[čʰe:jid]	'of the rock'
[čʰejid]	'of the hole'
[pʰejid]	'of the bird'

The likely candidate, of course, is the [i], since it is both front and high. We therefore hypothesize that the environment for both rules is:

$$(9) \qquad / \underline{\quad} C \begin{bmatrix} V \\ +hi \\ -bk \end{bmatrix}$$

The umlaut and raising rules can be tentatively formulated as:

$$(10) \qquad V \rightarrow [-bk] / \underline{\quad} C \begin{bmatrix} V \\ +hi \\ -bk \end{bmatrix}$$

$$(11) \qquad \begin{bmatrix} -bk \\ +lo \end{bmatrix} \rightarrow [-lo] / \underline{\quad} C \begin{bmatrix} V \\ +hi \\ -bk \end{bmatrix}$$

We noted earlier that for some reason the underlying stem vowels /i/ and /e/ did not change in the perfect or the genitive. We can now see why.

These vowels are already [−bk] and [−lo] and thus would not be affected by the rules we have just written.

Rules (10) and (11) now lead us to reevaluate the base forms we have posited for the perfect and causative suffixes. These rules state that a form will have an altered stem vowel if it precedes a [+hi, −bk] vowel. The stem vowels of several perfect and causative forms show an alternation very similar to that found in the genitives. This suggests that an [i] is present in the underlying form of the perfect and causative suffixes. The perfect suffix, then, could be either /+ti/ or /+it/.

Since we have no rule available which could account for the loss of a vowel between the stem and the t of the perfect suffix, but we do have a rule of apocope, we assume that the i follows the t. If this is the case, we must amend the environment for the fronting and raising rules to allow more than one consonant to intervene between the vowels.

$$(12) \qquad / \text{——} \ C_0 \begin{bmatrix} V \\ -bk \\ +fr \end{bmatrix}$$

This environment is more general than is necessary to account for the available data, in which no more than two consonants ever intervene between vowels.

For the perfect suffix we now posit /+ti/ and for the causative, /+i/. The Apocope rule explains why the underlying i of these forms is not present in the surface forms. Being word final, it is deleted.

Looking again at the forms with underlying /æ/, we find that wherever the vowel is followed by two consonants, as in the perfect form [jært] and the ablative [čhækt], raising does not occur. Thus, the raising rule is limited to the following environment.

$$(13) \qquad / \text{——} \ C_0^1 + \begin{bmatrix} V \\ -bk \\ +hi \end{bmatrix}$$

The way the rule is now written, not more than one consonant may intervene between the /æ/ and the /+i/ suffix.

To recapitulate, we have posited the following base forms for the noun and verb stems:

1. /maːs/	7. /loːpa/
2. /kʰot/	8. /batu/
3. /dub/	9. /guːlo/
4. /jær/	10. /čʰæːg/
5. /lin/	11. /čʰeda/
6. /reːg/	12. /pʰodu/

Further, we have the following inflectional morphemes:

1. /+er/   plural
2. /+id/   genitive singular
3. /+t/   ablative singular
4. /+ti/   perfect
5. /+i/   causative

And finally, to account for the differences between the underlying forms and the surface forms, we have seven phonological rules:

1. Apocope: $V \rightarrow \emptyset \ / \ \underline{\quad} \# \#$

2. Syncope: $V \rightarrow \emptyset \ / \ \underline{\quad} V$

3. Cluster Shortening: $V: \rightarrow V \ / \ \underline{\quad} CC$

4. Voicing Assimilation: $\begin{bmatrix} -\text{son} \\ +\text{vd} \end{bmatrix} \rightarrow [-\text{vd}] \ / \ \underline{\quad} [-\text{vd}]$

5. Palatalization: $\begin{bmatrix} +\text{int} \\ -\text{lab} \end{bmatrix} \rightarrow \begin{bmatrix} +\text{str} \\ +\text{cor} \end{bmatrix} / \ V \ \underline{\quad} [-\text{bk}]$

6. Umlaut: $V \rightarrow [-\text{bk}] \ / \ \underline{\quad} C_0 \begin{bmatrix} V \\ +\text{hi} \\ -\text{bk} \end{bmatrix}$

7. Raising: $\begin{bmatrix} V \\ -\text{bk} \\ +\text{lo} \end{bmatrix} \rightarrow [-\text{lo}] \ / \ \underline{\quad} C_0^1 \begin{bmatrix} V \\ +\text{hi} \\ -\text{bk} \end{bmatrix}$

11.5 ORDERING THE RULES

It is not enough simply to give the base forms and the rules which apply to them. For a complete statement of the phonology of a language, we must also determine the order in which the rules apply. Rule order becomes particularly important where there are several processes involved because a change in the placement of even one rule can seriously affect the surface forms.

Determining rule order is to some degree a matter of trial and error. But it is not entirely so. Probably the best way to begin is by looking for pairs or sets of rules that interact. Among the rules at hand, Apocope interacts with Palatalization, Umlaut, and Raising, since front vowels could be deleted by Apocope and because front vowels (all of them, in the case of Palatalization, and /i/ in the case of Umlaut and Raising) comprise the environments of the other three rules. If Apocope applied before the other three rules, it would bleed all of them. Unless we find data proving otherwise, we will assume that Palatalization, Umlaut, and Raising precede Apocope, since counterbleeding order is unmarked whereas bleeding order is marked.

Syncope would feed Palatalization, Umlaut, and Raising if it were ordered before them. By deleting some back vowels in back-vowel plus front-vowel sequences, new instances of front vowels in the correct environment for Palatalization, Umlaut, and Raising are produced. Syncope would counterfeed the other three rules if it followed them, since the back vowels that block application of Palatalization, Umlaut, and Raising would still be present in forms when these rules apply. We must look to the data to see what the correct order is. For the time being we put Syncope before the other three rules, so that it is in the more natural feeding order.

Umlaut produces front vowels, and front vowels are the environments of Palatalization and Raising. So if Umlaut applies before Palatalization and Raising, these rules would be in an unmarked feeding order.

Palatalization and Raising seem not to interact. Further, Cluster Shortening and Voicing Assimilation seem not to interact with each other or with any other of the rules.

If we arbitrarily order Cluster Shortening and Voicing Assimilation at the end of the list, we have the following natural order.

1. Syncope
2. Umlaut
3. Palatalization
4. Raising
5. Apocope
6. Cluster Shortening
7. Voicing Assimilation

We would expect a language not to depart too much from this natural order. We can now check the rules against the forms to see if the natural ordering is maintained. If applying the rules in the natural order derives incorrect forms, we know that it is not maintained. We must then apply the rules in various orders to the base forms until we hit upon an order which produces all (or nearly all) the occurring surface forms. This we can assume to be the correct order for the language under consideration.

It sometimes takes a good deal of rule shuffling and not a little inventive imagination to arrive at an order which works for every form. To determine the correct order of the rules we posited for Dubun, we begin by writing out the base forms with their various endings:

	PRESENT	PERFECT	CAUSATIVE
1.	/ma:s/	/ma:s + ti/	/ma:s + i/
2.	/kʰot/	/kʰot + ti/	/kʰot + i/

	3. /dub/	/dub + ti/	/dub + i/
	4. /jær/	/jær + ti/	/jær + i/
	5. /lin/	/lin + ti/	/lin + i/
	6. /re:g/	/re:g + ti/	/re:g + i/

	SINGULAR	PLURAL	GENITIVE	ABLATIVE
7.	/lo:pa/	/lo:pa + er/	/lo:pa + id/	/lo:pa + t/
8.	/batu/	/batu + er/	/batu + id/	/batu + t/
9.	/gu:lo/	/gu:lo + er/	/gu:lo + id/	/gu:lo + t/
10.	/čʰæ:g/	/čʰæ:g + er/	/čʰæ:g + id/	/čʰæ:g + t/
11.	/čʰeda/	/čʰeda + er/	/čʰeda + id/	/čʰeda + t/
12.	/pʰodu/	/pʰodu + er/	/pʰodu + id/	/pʰodu + t/

We then apply the rules to the underlying forms and check the results against the surface forms for exact matches. Among the verbs, all the underlying forms of the present are the same as their surface forms. Since none of the rules apply, we eliminate these forms from further consideration. Further, none of the rules apply to the ablative forms [lo:pat], [batut], [gu:lot], [čʰedat], and [pʰodut] or the singular noun [čʰæ:g]. All the other forms undergo some rule (or rules) which cause them to differ from their base forms.

We next look to surface forms which can be explained by a single rule. The perfect and causative forms [lint] and [lin] and the causative form [re:g] can be explained as having undergone Apocope, which deletes their final vowels. The same is true of the noun forms [lo:p], [bat], [gu:l], and [pʰod]. Only one rule, Syncope, is needed to account for the plural forms [lo:per] and [gu:ler]. The form [čʰæ:ǰer] can also be accounted for by a single rule: Palatalization. Obviously, forms derived by a single rule are of little help in determining rule order. Those requiring two rules, on the other hand, can be helpful. Consider, for example, the forms [kʰett], [kʰet], and [dib]. Comparing these words to their underlying forms, we see that Umlaut and Apocope have applied. Since for a vowel to undergo Umlaut it must be followed by an [i], and Apocope would remove the [i], we now can state the order of these two rules in Dubun:

Umlaut

Apocope

This agrees with the natural ordering for these rules.

The genitive forms [gi:lid] and [le:pid] also undergo two rules: Syncope and Umlaut. Since the Umlaut rule does not allow for an intervening vowel, the stem final vowel of the underlying forms /gu:lo + id/ and /lopa + id/ must be deleted before Umlaut applies. We conclude, therefore, that the Syncope rule feeds Umlaut. We now have three rules placed in a tentative order:

Syncope
Umlaut
Apocope

This ordering still follows the natural order, in which Umlaut follows Syncope but precedes Apocope.

Some other forms which undergo two rules are [čʰeĭer] and [pʰoĭer]. Here the rules that apply are Syncope and Palatalization, and since Palatalization occurs only directly before a front vowel, Syncope must have applied first to delete the intervening back vowels.

So far we apparently have the natural rule order:

Syncope
Umlaut
Palatalization
Apocope

But, this ordering is incorrect. If we look again at the form [kʰet] we see that palatalization must follow the deletion of the /+i/ suffix or this form would be [kʰeč] instead, since the /i/ would have caused the /t/ to palatalize to [č]. We therefore must reorder our rules as follows:

Syncope
Umlaut
Apocope
Palatalization

At this point the rule order of Dubun departs from the natural order. In the most natural order Apocope would follow Palatalization to form a counterbleeding relationship. Instead it precedes, thus forming a less natural bleeding relationship.

The form [ĭer] also undergoes two rules: Raising and Apocope. Since Raising cannot occur unless an *i* is present in the environment, we must order it before Apocope deletes the final *i*'s. Our rule order therefore becomes:

Syncope
Umlaut
Raising
Apocope
Palatalization

We still have no clear-cut evidence as to the order of Umlaut and Raising. If we consider the genitive form [bæčid], however, we see that Umlaut cannot precede Raising. If it did, a feeding order would result so that /a/ followed by a single consonant which was fronted to [æ] would automatically be raised to [e]. Since the surface form is [bæčid] and not *[bečid], we know the ordering of these two rules must be Raising and then Umlaut, an unnatural counterfeeding order.

The rules are now ordered in the following way:

1. Syncope
2. Raising
3. Umlaut
4. Apocope
5. Palatalization
6. Cluster Shortening
7. Voicing Assimilation

If we look again at the base forms that we have posited, we find that they still contain some predictable information. The voiceless aspirated sounds [pʰ, tʰ, čʰ, kʰ] are found only in initial position; their unaspirated counterparts occur elsewhere. The underlying forms can thus be simplified by replacing [pʰ, tʰ, čʰ, kʰ] with the more natural [p, t, č, k]. A rule of initial aspiration like that for English will account for the surface forms.

(14) INITIAL ASPIRATION

$$\begin{bmatrix} +\text{int} \\ -\text{vd} \end{bmatrix} \rightarrow [+\text{HSP}] \, / \, \#\underline{\quad}$$

This rule does not interact with any of the others. So we place it at the end of the order along with Cluster Shortening and Voicing Assimilation:

8. Initial Aspiration

The order of these eight rules is not totally natural since it contains a bleeding relationship (between Palatalization and Apocope) and a counterfeeding relationship (between Umlaut and Raising). However, we can be fairly certain that it is the correct one for Dubun because it results in all the correct surface representations, as is illustrated by the sample derivations given below (DNA means 'does not apply').

	/maːs + ti/	/dub + ti/	/batu + id/	/čæːg + t/	/jær + i/
1. Syncope:	DNA	DNA	batid	DNA	DNA
2. Raising:	DNA	DNA	DNA	DNA	jeri
3. Umlaut:	mæːsti	dibti	bætid	DNA	DNA
4. Apocope:	mæːst	dibt	DNA	DNA	jer
5. Palatalization:	DNA	DNA	bæčid	DNA	DNA
6. Cluster Shortening:	mæst	DNA	DNA	čʰægt	DNA
7. Voicing Assim.:	DNA	dipt	DNA	čʰækt	DNA
8. Initial Asp.:	DNA	DNA	DNA	čʰækt	DNA
9. Surface form:	[mæst]	[dipt]	[bæčid]	[čʰækt]	[jer]

11.6 SUMMARY

The analysis of the hypothetical language Dubun given above is intended to demonstrate some of the methods phonologists commonly employ. Of course, many of the steps so painstakingly outlined here can be eliminated (or at least abbreviated) by those experienced in phonological analysis. Nevertheless, most contemporary linguists go about solving phonological problems in much the same way as we did in our analysis of Dubun. By positing and testing hypotheses about the shape of underlying forms and about the nature and order of the rules which change these base forms to the correct surface representations, linguists work out coherent explanations for the morpheme alternations found in a language. The attempt to formulate a more or less complete phonological analysis for a large amount of data is challenging. See, for example, Halle, 1959; Chomsky and Halle, 1968; McCawley, 1968; Schane, 1968; Harris, 1969; and Hoard and O'Grady, 1976.

EXERCISES FOR CHAPTER 11

1. For the hypothetical language Dubun discussed in this chapter, suppose that [bu:d] 'rise' and [lo:v] 'walk' are the present tense forms of two additional verbs. What do you predict as the perfect and causative forms? Suppose also that [ma:k] 'tree' (sing.), [makt] 'tree' (abl. sing.), [næ:s] 'goat' (sing.), and [næst] 'goat' (abl. sing.), are Dubun noun forms. What do you predict for the plural and genitive singular forms?

2a. In Nez Perce, k becomes x before k, q, n, l, or word finally; and q becomes $\underset{.}{x}$ before k, n, l, or word finally. Consider the examples below and determine whether the environments where $k \rightarrow x$ and $q \rightarrow \underset{.}{x}$ can be stated as a single process.

tamitk'áyn	'for huckleberry' (from: tamitk + ʔáyn)
temi:cx	'huckleberry'
temicéxki	'with huckleberry'
temicxnu:c	'without huckleberry'
tú:qise	'I smoke tobacco'
tú:x̣	'tobacco'
t'i:x̣lu	'talking squirrel' (t'i:q 'talk')

Do these changes seem to be natural, or are they crazy rules? Why? (Based on Aoki, 1970)

2b. Abau (spoken in New Guinea) is reported to have the following basic inventory:

p		k	i			u
m	n		e			o
					ə	
	s	h		ɛ		ɔ
w	r	y			a	

The stops *p* and *k* are voiced following nasals. The *r* is [d] after *n*, [l] initially, [r] intervocalically, and [t] or [řə] word-finally. Does a distinctive feature analysis of these changes suggest that /r/ should be reanalyzed as /t/? Keep in mind that, everything being equal, a phonological description seeks both the most natural inventory and the most general rules possible, given the data. (Based on Laycock, 1965)

3. For the Chamorro examples given below, determine the underlying form of the plural subject prefix and the rules which derive the plural subject forms. Do these rules need to be ordered?

	VERB STEM		PLURAL SUBJECT FORMS
1.	poʔlo	'put'	mamoʔlo
2.	bende	'sell'	mambende
3.	tañaʔ	'taste'	manañaʔ
4.	daggao	'throw'	mandaggao
5.	kati	'cry out'	maŋati
6.	godde	'tie'	maŋgodde
7.	faʔom	'clobber'	mamaʔom
8.	hanao	'go'	mananao
9.	naʔi	'give'	mannaʔi
10.	ŋaŋas	'chew'	maŋŋaŋas
11.	ǰuteʔ	'throw'	manǰuteʔ
12.	čægi	'try'	mañægi

(Based on Topping, 1973: 49–50)

4. Determine the underlying forms and rules that account for the Diegueño verb forms given below. Diegueño is a Yuman language spoken in California.

1.	ʔa:	'I go'
2.	ma:	'you go'
3.	kaʔ	'go! (sing.)'
4.	wa:	'he goes'
5.	ʔənak	'I sit'
6.	mənak	'you sit'

   7. kənak   'sit! (sing.)'
   8. wənak   'he sits'
   9. ʔəto: 'I hit (him)'
 10. kətoʔ   'hit (him)! (sing.)'
 11. wəto: 'he hit (him)'
 12. taʔa: 'I am going'
 13. təwa: 'he is going'
 14. taʔyiw   'I am coming'
 15. tu:yiw   'he is coming'
 16. taʔyu:w   'I was standing there'
 17. təməyu:w   'you are standing there'
 18. tu:yu:w   'he is standing there'

(Based on Langdon, 1970: 140–148)

5. Nez Perce has morphological processes of partial and total reduplication.
Use the examples below to formulate rules for Nez Perce reduplication.
What additional rules are necessary to account for the phonological
alternations?

   1. caʔt   'good'
   2. cicáʔt   'good (distributive)'
   3. x̣áʔwit   'sharp (of points)'
   4. x̣ix̣áʔwit   'sharp (distributive)'
   5. weptú:x   'intelligent'
   6. wiwé:ptux   'intelligent (distributive)'
   7. ʔískic   'trail'
   8. heʔískic   'trails'
   9. ʔéhew   'wounded'
 10. heʔéhew   'wounded (distributive)'
 11. há:twal   'son'
 12. hahátwal   'sons'
 13. máqs   'gall'
 14. maqsmáqs   'yellow'
 15. ʔílp   'reddish skin eruption'
 16. ʔilp'ílp   'red'
 17. cé:mul   'hail'
 18. cemulcé:mul 'sleet'
 19. qíʔyax   'squawfish'
 20. qíʔyaxqiʔyax 'little squawfish'

(Based on Aoki, 1970: 42, 57)

6a. Determine the underlying forms and phonological rules that account
for the Nez Perce nominal forms given below.

1. wex̣éqc   'frog'
2. wex̣weqéne   'frog (object)'
3. wex̣weqécpe   'at the frog'
4. wex̣weqeníme   'frog-place'
5. wex̣weqt'áyn   'for a frog'
6. wex̣weqecpípem   'among frogs'
7. calácac   'cedar'
8. calcána   'cedar (object)'
9. calcácpa   'at the cedar'
10. calcaníma   'cedar-place'
11. calcacpípam   'among cedars'
12. té:qet   'raspberry'
13. teqé:ne   'raspberry (object)'
14. teqé:cpe   'at raspberry'
15. teqecníme   'Raspberry-Place'
16. teqecpípem   'among raspberries'
17. cá:mas   'wild rose'
18. camsá:spa   'at the wild rose'
19. qá:msic   'kows (edible root)'
20. qá:msicna   'kows (object)'
21. qamsicpípam   'among kows'
22. qeqíc   'qeqí:c' (edible root somewhat like kows)
23. qeqí:cne   'qeqí:c (object)'
24. qeqí:cpe   'at qeqí:c'
25. qeqi:tpípem   'among qeqí:c'
26. pá:ps   'red fir tree'
27. papspípam   'among red fir trees'
28. łic'á:n   'bitterroot'
29. łic'á:nna   'bitterroot (object)'
30. łic'a:npípam   'among bitterroot'

b. Given the form [yá:ka^{ʔ}] 'brown bear', what is the form meaning 'among brown bears'? What is the form meaning 'Brown Bear-place'?

(Based on Aoki, 1970: 46–48)

7. For the Nzema examples of singular and plural nouns given below, determine the basic plural allomorph(s) and the phonological rules necessary to derive the plural forms.

Singular	Plural		
tʊba	adʊba	'bottle'	
tabʊa	ndabʊa	'board'	
tĩʔ	edĩleʔ	'pinch'	
kila	ŋgila	'mouse'	(Continued on p. 188)

Table II

	hand	bone	belly	hair	tooth	wife	edible thing
Uninflected	he	si	vaŋ	hil	luh	asou	a
1st sing.	heok	siuk	vaŋok	hiluk	luhok	asouk	avak
2nd sing.	hem	sim	vaŋom	hilum	luhom	asoum	am
3rd sing.	hen	sin	vaŋen	hilin	luhon	asoun	an
1st dual incl.	heralu	siralu	vaŋeiralu	hiriralu	luheiralu	asuoralu	aralu
1st paucal incl.	heretel	siratel	vaŋeiratel	hiriratel	luheiratel	asuoratel	aratel
1st plural incl.	her	sir	vaŋer	hilir	luhor	asuor	ar
1st dual excl.	hemæl	simæl	vaneimæl	hilimæl	luheimæl	asuomæl	amæl
1st paucal excl.	hemætel	simætel	vaŋeimætel	hilimætel	luheimætel	asoumætel	amætel
1st plural excl.	hemæm	simæm	vaŋeimæm	hilimæm	luheimæm	asoumæm	amæm
2nd dual	hemil	simil	vaŋeimil	hilimil	luheimil	asoumil	amil
2nd paucal	hemitel	simitel	vaŋeimitel	hilimitel	luheimitel	asoumitel	amitel
2nd plural incl.	hemi	simi	vaŋeimi	hilimi	luheimi	asoumi	ami
2nd plural excl.	hemim	simim	vaŋeimim	hilimim	luheimim	asoumim	amim
3rd dual	healu	sialu	vaŋealu	hilialu	luhealu	asoualu	aalu
3rd paucal	heatel	siatel	vaŋeatel	hiliatel	luheatel	asouatel	aatel
3rd plural	he	si	vaŋe	hili	luhe	asoue	ae

(Based on Parker, 1970)

187

SINGULAR	PLURAL	
akɔlɛ	ŋgɔkɔlɛ	'fowl'
kwasia	ŋqwasia	'fool'
ᵏpɔba	mᵍbɔba	'good nugget'
ɛᵏpa	mᵍba	'bed'
fũtĭ	ævũtĭ	'corpse'
sua	æzua	'house'
k̂wia	ñk̂wia	'dog'
ešɛlɛʔ	ňšɛlɛʔ	'a kind of bird'
ɛhan(ĭ)	ŋgan(ĭ)	'trap'

(Based on Chinebuah, 1970; Nzema is spoken in Ghana)

8. For the Southeast Ambrym personal possessor noun paradigms given in Table II (p. 187), determine the base forms and the phonological rules which account for the surface forms. The term **paucal** means 'three or four'. For example, the form *heratel* means 'our hands' where 'our' refers to three or four individuals.

selected bibliography

ABERCROMBIE, David. 1967. *Elements of General Phonetics*. Chicago: Aldine.
ANDERSON, Stephen R. 1974. *The Organization of Phonology*. New York: Academic Press.
———. 1976. "Nasal consonants and the internal structure of segments." *Language* 52, 326–44.
——— and Paul KIPARSKY, eds. 1973. *A Festschrift for Morris Halle*. New York: Holt, Rinehart and Winston.
AOKI, Haruo. *Nez Perce Grammar*. University of California Publications in Linguistics, Volume 62. Berkeley and Los Angeles: University of California Press.
ARMSTRONG, Lilias E. 1967. *The Phonetic and Tonal Structure of Kikuyu*. London: Dawsons of Pall Mall.
BACH, Emmon, and Robert T. HARMS. 1972. "How do languages get crazy rules?" In Robert P. STOCKWELL and Ronald K. S. MACAULAY, eds., *Linguistic Change and Generative Theory*, 1–21. Bloomington: Indiana University Press.
BAILEY, Charles-James N., and Roger W. SHUY, eds. 1973. *New Ways of Analyzing Variation in English*. Washington, D.C.: Georgetown University Press.
BRAINE, Martin D. S. 1974. "On what might constitute learnable phonology." *Language* 50, 270–99.
BRAME, Michael K. 1973a. "On the abstractness of phonology: Maltese ʃ." In BRAME, 1973b, 22–61.
———, ed. 1973b. *Contributions to Generative Phonology*. Austin: University of Texas Press.
———. 1974. "The cycle in phonology: Stress in Palestinian, Maltese, and Spanish." *Linguistic Inquiry* 5, 39–60.

BROSNAHAN, L. F., and Bertil MALMBERG. 1970. *Introduction to Phonetics.* Cambridge: Cambridge University Press.

BRUCK, Anthony, Robert A. Fox, and Michael W. LAGALY, eds. 1974. *Papers from the Parasession on Natural Phonology.* Chicago: Chicago Linguistic Society.

CAIRNS, Charles E. 1969. "Markedness, neutralization, and universal redundancy rules." *Language* **45**, 863–85.

CAMPBELL, LYLE. 1974. "Phonological features: Problems and proposals." *Language* **50**, 52–65.

CHAFE, Wallace L. 1968. "The ordering of phonological rules." *International Journal of American Linguistics* **34**, 115–36.

CHANG, Kun, and Betty SHEFTS. 1964. *A Manual of Spoken Tibetan (Lhasa Dialect).* Seattle: University of Washington Press.

CHEN, Matthew. 1973. "On the formal expression of natural rules in phonology." *Journal of Linguistics* **9**, 223–49.

CHINEBUAH, I. K. 1970. "Consonant mutation in Nzema." *Journal of West African Languages* **7**, 69–84.

CHOMSKY, Noam. 1964. "Current issues in linguistics." In FODOR and KATZ, 1964, 50–118.

——— and Morris HALLE. 1965. "Some controversial questions in phonological theory." *Journal of Linguistics* **1**, 97–138. Reprinted in Makkai, 1972, 457–85.

——— and ———. 1968. *The Sound Pattern of English.* New York: Harper and Row.

COWAN, William. 1965. "A note on the phonemes of /Mɔ̀rɔ́/." *Journal of African Languages* **4**, 114–17.

CRAWFORD, James M. 1973. "Yuchi phonology." *International Journal of American Linguistics* **39**, 173–79.

DAVIS, John H. 1971. "Notes on Mainland Comox phonology." In HOARD and HESS, eds., 1971, 12–31.

DAY, Christopher. 1973. *The Jacaltec Language.* Indiana University Publications: Language Science Monographs, Volume 12. The Hague: Mouton.

ELBERT, Samuel H. 1970. *Spoken Hawaiian.* Honolulu: University of Hawaii Press.

ELERT, Claes-Christian. 1964. *Phonologic Studies of Quantity in Swedish.* Uppsala: Almqvist and Wiksell.

FERGUSON, Charles Z. 1966. "Assumptions about nasals: A sample study in phonological universals." In Joseph H. GREENBERG, ed., *Universals of Language*, 53–60. Cambridge, Mass.: M.I.T. Press.

FODOR, Jerry A., and Jerrold J. KATZ, eds. 1964. *The Structure of Language.* Englewood Cliffs, N.J.: Prentice-Hall.

FROMKIN, Victoria A. 1972. "Tone features and tone rules." *Studies in African Linguistics* **3**, 47–76.

FRY, Dennis. 1955. "Duration and intensity as physical correlates of linguistic stress." *Journal of the Acoustical Society of America* **27**, 765–68.

———. 1958. "Experiments in the perception of stress." *Language and Speech* **1**, 126–52.

GLEASON, H. A., Jr. 1955. *Workbook in Descriptive Linguistics.* New York: Holt, Rinehart and Winston.

———. 1961. *An Introduction to Descriptive Linguistics*, rev. ed. New York: Holt, Rinehart and Winston.

GOODMAN, Morris. 1967. "Prosodic features of Bravanese, a Swahili dialect." *Journal of African Languages* **6**, 278–84.

GREENBERG, Joseph H. 1966a. "Synchronic and diachronic universals in phonology." *Language* **42**, 508–17.

———. 1966b. *Language Universals.* The Hague: Mouton.

GREENBERG, Joseph H. 1970. "Some generalizations concerning glottalic consonants, especially implosives." *International Journal of American Linguistics* **36,** 123–46.

HALLE, Morris. 1959. *The sound Pattern of Russian.* The Hague: Mouton.

———. 1962. "Phonology in generative grammar." *Word* **18,** 54–72. In FODOR and KATZ, 1964, 334–52, and in MAKKAI, 1972, 380–92.

HARMS, Robert T. 1968. *Introduction to Phonological Theory.* Englewood Cliffs, N.J.: Prentice-Hall.

———. 1973a. "Some non-rules of English." Distributed by the Indiana University Linguistics Club.

———. 1973b. "How abstract is Nupe?" *Language* **49,** 439–46.

HARRIS, James W. 1969. *Spanish Phonology.* Cambridge, Mass.: M.I.T. Press.

HESS, Thomas M. 1966. "Snohomish chameleon morphology." *International Journal of American Linguistics* **32,** 350–56.

HOARD, James E. 1971. "Aspiration, tenseness, and syllabication in English." *Language* **47,** 133–40.

———. 1977. "Obstruent voicing in Gitksan: Some implications for distinctive feature theory." To appear in Jonathan KAYE and E.-D. COOK, eds., *Linguistic Studies of Native Canada.* Lisse, The Netherlands: Peter De Ridder Press.

——— and Thomas M. HESS, eds. 1971. *Studies in Northwest Indian Languages.* Paper 11, Sacramento Anthropological Society. Sacramento, Calif.

——— and Geoffrey N. O'GRADY. 1976. "Nyangumarda phonology: A preliminary report." In R. M. W. DIXON, ed., *Grammatical Categories in Australian Languages,* 51–77. Canberra: Australian Institute of Aboriginal Studies.

——— and Clarence SLOAT. 1973. "Variation in English stress placement." In BAILEY and SHUY, 1973, 265–75.

HOCKETT, Charles F. 1955. *A Manual of Phonology. International Journal of American Linguistics,* Memoir 11. Baltimore: Waverly Press.

HODGE, Carleton T., and Ibrahim UMARU. 1963. *Hausa Basic Course.* Washington, D.C.: U.S. Government Printing Office.

HOHEPA, Patrick W. 1967. *A Profile Generative Grammar of Maori. International Journal of American Linguistics,* Volume 33, no. 2, part III. Baltimore: Waverly Press.

HOOPER, Joan B. 1972. "The syllable in phonological theory." *Language* **48,** 525–40.

HYMAN, Larry M. 1970. "How concrete is phonology?" *Language* **46,** 58–76.

———. 1973. "Nupe three years later." *Language* **49,** 447–52.

———. 1975. *Phonology: Theory and Analysis.* New York: Holt, Rinehart and Winston.

——— and Russell G. SCHUH. 1974. "Universals of tone rules: Evidence from West Africa." *Linguistic Inquiry* **5,** 81–115.

JACKENDOFF, Ray. 1975. "Morphological and semantic regularities in the lexicon." *Language* **51,** 639–71.

JAKOBSON, Roman. 1968. *Child Language, Aphasia, and Phonological Universals.* Trans. Allan R. Keiler. The Hague: Mouton.

———. C. G. M. FANT, and M. HALLE. 1952. *Preliminaries to Speech Analysis.* 5th printing, 1963. Cambridge, Mass.: M.I.T. Press.

JONES, Lawrence G. 1959. "The contextual variants of the Russian vowels." In HALLE, 1959, 157–167.

JOOS, Martin, ed. 1957. *Readings in Linguistics, I.* Chicago: University of Chicago Press.

JUNGRAITHMAYR, H. 1971. "The Tangale vowel harmony system reconsidered." *Journal of African Languages* **10,** 1, 28–33.

KING, ROBERT D. 1969. _Historical Linguistics and Generative Grammar_. Englewood Cliffs, N.J.: Prentice-Hall.

KIPARSKY, Paul. 1968a. 'How abstract is phonology?" Unpublished.

———. 1968b. "Linguistic universals and linguistic change." In Emmon BACH and Robert T. HARMS, eds., _Universals in Linguistic Theory_, 171–202. New York: Holt, Rinehart and Winston.

———. 1973. " 'Elsewhere' in phonology." In ANDERSON and KIPARSKY, 1973, 93–106.

KISSEBERTH, Charles W. 1969. "On the abstractness of phonology: The evidence from Yawelmani." _Papers in Linguistics_ **1**, 248–82.

———. 1972. "Cyclical rules in Klamath phonology." _Linguistic Inquiry_ **3**, 3–33.

KOUTSOUDAS, Andreas, Gerald SANDERS, and Craig NOLL. 1974. "The application of phonological rules." _Language_ **50**, 1–28.

KUIPERS, Aert H. 1960. _Phoneme and Morpheme in Kabardian_. The Hague: Mouton.

KURODA, S.-Y. 1967. _Yawelmani Phonology_. Research Monograph No. 43. Cambridge, Mass.: M.I.T. Press.

LABOV, William, Malka YAEGER, and Richard STEINER. 1972. _A Quantitative Study of Sound Change in Progress_. Philadelphia: U.S. Regional Survey.

LADEFOGED, Peter. 1970. "The phonetic framework of generative phonology." _Working Papers in Phonetics, UCLA_, **14**, 25–33.

LANGDON, Margaret. 1970. _A Grammar of Diegueño: The Mesa Grande Dialect_. University of California Publications in Linguistics, no. 66. Berkeley and Los Angeles: University of California Press.

LAPID, Virginia A. 1969. _The Tagalog Verb System and Its Inflectional Morphology_. M.A. thesis. The University of Kansas.

LAYCOCK, D. C. 1965. "Three Upper Sepik phonologies." _Oceanic Linguistics_ **4**, 113–18.

LEBEN, William R. 1971. "Suprasegmentals and segmental representation of tone." _Studies in African Linguistics_, Supplement 2, 183–200.

LEHISTE, Ilse. 1970. _Suprasegmentals_. Cambridge, Mass.: M.I.T. Press.

LIGHTNER, Theodore M. 1971. "Generative phonology." In William Orr DINGWALL, ed., _A Survey of Linguistic Science_, 498–574. Linguistics Program, University of Maryland.

———. 1975. "The role of derivational morphology in generative grammar." _Language_ **51**, 617–38.

MAKKAI, Valerie Becker, ed. 1972. _Phonological Theory: Evolution and Current Practice_. New York: Holt, Rinehart and Winston.

MALMBERG, Bertil, ed. 1968. _Manual of Phonetics_. Amsterdam: North-Holland.

MANLEY, Timothy M. 1972. _Outline of Sre Structure. Oceanic Linguistics_, special publication no. 12.

MATTINA, Anthony. 1970. "Phonology of Alaskan Eskimo, Kuskokwim dialect." _International Journal of American Linguistics_ **36**, 38–45.

McCAWLEY, James D. 1968. _The Phonological Component of a Grammar of Japanese_. The Hague: Mouton.

———. 1974. Review of Chomsky and Halle, 1968. _International Journal of American Linguistics_ **40**, 50–88.

MILLER, Patricia. 1972. "Some context-free processes affecting vowels." _Ohio State Working Papers in Linguistics_ **11**, 136–67.

———. 1973. "Bleaching and coloring." In Claudia CORUM et al., eds., _Papers from the Ninth Regional Meeting of the Chicago Linguistic Society_, 386–97.

MOULTON, William G. 1962. _The Sounds of English and German_. Chicago: University of Chicago Press.

MUNRO, Pamela, and Peter John BENSON. 1973. "Reduplication and rule ordering in Luiseño." *International Journal of American Linguistics* **39**, 15–21.

NESSLY, Larry. 1973. "Nativization and variation in English phonology." In BAILEY and SHUY, 1973, 253–64.

NEWMAN, Paul. 1972. "Syllable weight as a phonological variable." *Studies in African Linguistics* **3**, 301–23.

OHALA, Mahjari. 1974. "The abstractness controversy: Experimental input from Hindi." *Language* **50**, 225–35.

ORR, Carolyn, and Robert E. LONGACRE. 1968. "Proto-Quechumaran", *Language* **44**, 528–55.

PARKER, Gary J. 1968. "Southeast Ambrym phonology." *Oceanic Linguistics* **7**, 81–91.

———. 1970. "Morphophonemics of the inalienable nouns in Southeast Ambrym." *Oceanic Linguistics* **9**, 1–10.

PIKE, Kenneth L. 1943. *Phonetics.* Ann Arbor: University of Michigan Press.

———. 1947. *Phonemics: A Technique for Reducing Languages to Writing.* University of Michigan Publications in Linguistics 3. Ann Arbor.

———. 1948. *Tone Languages: A Technique for Determining the Number and Type of Pitch Contrasts in a Language.* University of Michigan Publications in Linguistics 4. Ann Arbor.

——— and Eunice PIKE. 1947. "Immediate constituents of Mazateco syllables." *International Journal of American Linguistics* **13**, 78–91.

POSTAL, Paul M. 1968. *Aspects of Phonological Theory.* New York: Harper and Row.

Principles of the International Phonetic Association. 1949. London: University College.

PULGRAM, Ernst. 1970. *Syllable, Word, Nexus, Cursus.* The Hague: Mouton.

REDDEN, J. E., N. OWUSU, and associates. 1963. *Twi Basic Course.* Washington, D.C.: U.S. Government Printing Office.

ROSS, John Robert. 1973. "A reanalysis of English word stress (part 1)." In BRAME, 1973b, 229–323.

SAPIR, Edward. 1930. *Southern Paiute, a Shoshonean Language. Proceedings of the American Academy of Arts and Sciences,* vol. 65, nos. 1–3.

SCHANE, Sanford A. 1968. *French Phonology and Morphology.* Cambridge, Mass.: M.I.T. Press.

———. 1972. "Natural rules in phonology." In Robert P. STOCKWELL and Ronald K. S. MACAULAY, eds., *Linguistic Change and Generative Theory,* 199–229. Bloomington: Indiana University Press.

———. 1973. *Generative Phonology.* Englewood Cliffs, N.J.: Prentice-Hall.

SCHENKER, Alexander M. 1966. *Beginning Polish.* New Haven: Yale University Press.

SCHRAMM, Gene M. 1962. "An outline of classical Arabic verb structure." *Language* **38**, 360–75.

SHEFTS, Betty, and Kun CHANG. 1967. "Spoken Tibetan morphophonemics." *Language* **43**, 512–25.

SLOAT, Clarence. 1966. *Phonological Redundancy Rules in Coeur d'Alene.* University of Washington dissertation.

———. 1971. "The phonetics and phonology of Coeur d'Alene *r*." In HOARD and HESS, 124–37.

———. 1972. "Vowel harmony in Coeur d'Alene." *International Journal of American Linguistics* **38**, 234–9.

———. 1974. "Stress in English." *Glossa* **8**, 121–139.

SMITH, L. R. 1975. "Labrador Inuttut surface phonology." *International Journal of American Linguistics* **41**, 97–105.

STAMPE, David. 1969. "The acquisition of phonetic representation." In Robert I. BINNICK *et al.*, eds., *Papers from the Fifth Regional Meeting of the Chicago Linguistic Society*, 443–54. Chicago: Chicago Linguistic Society.

——. 1972. "On the natural history of diphthongs." In Paul M. PERANTEAU *et al.*, eds., *Papers from the Eighth Regional Meeting of the Chicago Linguistic Society*, 578–90. Chicago: Chicago Linguistic Society.

STETSON, R. H. 1951. *Motor Phonetics*. Amsterdam: North-Holland.

STEVICK, Earl W., and Olaleye AREMU. 1963. *Yoruba: Basic Course*. Washington, D.C.: Foreign Service Institute.

SUBBARAO, Karumuri V. 1971. "Vowel harmony in Telugu and parentheses and infinite rule schemata notations." In *Papers from the Seventh Regional Meeting of the Chicago Linguistic Society*, 543–52. Chicago: Chicago Linguistic Society.

THOMPSON, Laurence C., and M. Terry THOMPSON. 1969. "Metathesis as a grammatical device." *International Journal of American Linguistics* **35**, 213–19.

——, ——, and Barbara S. EFRAT. 1974. "Some phonological developments in Straits Salish." *International Journal of American Linguistics* **40**, 182–96.

TOPPING, Donald M. 1968. "Chamorro vowel harmony." *Oceanic Linguistics* **7**, 67–79.

——. 1973. *Chamorro Reference Grammar*. Honolulu: University of Hawaii Press.

TRUBETZKOY, N. S. 1969. *Principles of Phonology*. Trans. A. M. Baltaxe. Berkeley and Los Angeles: University of California Press.

VENNEMANN, Theo. 1972. "On the theory of syllabic phonology." *Linguistische Berichte* **10**, 1–18.

VOGT, Hans. 1940. *The Kalispel Language*. Oslo: Det Norske Videnskaps-Akademi i Oslo.

WANG, William S.-Y. 1967. "Phonological features of tone." *International Journal of American Linguistics* **33**, 93–105.

——. 1968. "Vowel features, paired variables, and the English vowel shift." *Language* **44**, 695–708.

WILKINSON, Robert W. 1974. "A phonetic constraint on a syncope rule in Telugu." *Language* **50**, 478–97.

WOO, Nancy. 1969. *Prosodic Phonology*. M.I.T. doctoral dissertation. Distributed by the Indiana University Linguistics Club.

ZWICKY, Arnold. 1974. "Taking a false step." *Language* **50**, 215–24.

indexes

author index

subject index